OUT OF THE CAGE

Gail Braybon was born and educated in Southampton. She graduated from the University of Sussex and then took an M.Phil. in history at Sussex. She has since been variously unemployed, working as a painter and decorator, and a stall holder and doing clerical jobs. She became a computer programmer in 1981 and is currently Computer Officer for the Faculty of Art and Design at Brighton Polytechnic. Her first book, *Women Workers in the First World War*, was published in 1981.

Penny Summerfield studied history at the University of Sussex, gaining her D.Phil. in 1982. She tutored in economic history at Durham University for two years and is currently lecturer in the social history of education at the University of Lancaster. She is the author of *Women Workers in the Second World War: Production and Patriarchy in Conflict* (1984) and of numerous articles on women's roles in the Second World War. She is married and has two children.

'. . . it was like being let out of a cage . . . .'
Lilian Miles, First World War

'I thoroughly enjoy my four hours working in the afternoon.
I'm all agog to get here. After all, for a housewife who's been a
cabbage for fifteen years – you feel you've got out of the cage
and you're free . . . .'
Part-time war worker, Second World War

OUT OF THE CAGE

WOMEN'S EXPERIENCES IN TWO WORLD WARS

Gail Braybon and Penny Summerfield

PANDORA

London and New York

First published in 1987 by Pandora Press
(Routledge & Kegan Paul Ltd)
11 New Fetter Lane, London EC4P 4EE

Published in the USA by
Routledge & Kegan Paul Inc.
in association with Methuen Inc.
29 West 35th Street, New York, NY 10001

Set in 10 on 11 pt Sabon
by Columns of Reading
and printed in Great Britain
by Cox and Wyman Ltd
Reading, Berks

Library of Congress Cataloging in Publication Data
Braybon, Gail.
   Out of the cage.
   (Pandora history)
   Bibliography: p.
   Includes index.
   1. Women—Great Britain—History—20th century.
2. Women—Employment—Great Britain—History—20th
century.   3. Women—Great Britain—Social conditions.
4. World War, 1914-1918—Women—Great Britain.   5. World
War, 1939-1945—Women—Great Britain.   I. Summerfield,
Penny.   II. Title.   III. Series.
HQ1593.B69   1987   305.4'0941   87-13510

British Library CIP Data also available

ISBN 0-86358-046-7 (c)
      0-86358-228-1 (p)

TO ALINE AND MARJORIE,
AND IN MEMORY OF PADDY

CONTENTS

ILLUSTRATIONS

PREFACE AND ACKNOWLEDGMENTS

We first thought of writing a book about women workers in the First and Second World Wars ten years ago. At that time, Gail had just finished her thesis on men's attitudes to women war workers during the years 1914 to 1920, while Penny was halfway through research into various aspects of the Second World War. Stephen Yeo, tutor to both of us while we were undergraduates at Sussex, happened to be the Internal Examiner for Gail's postgraduate work, and the supervisor of Penny's continuing research. Noticing the similarity in our approach to the problems women encountered as war workers (Penny had just published a paper in *Capital and Class* I, 1977) he suggested we might get in touch with each other, and talk about a book.

This we duly did, as we had remained friends anyway, and we got to the stage of producing a fairly detailed outline, and finding a publisher. There our plans went awry. We were living in very different circumstances, as Gail was unemployed in Sussex, and had plenty of time to get into the project, while Penny was teaching at Durham. What looked just about manageable in the first few months after we signed the contract became rapidly impossible for Penny, as she changed jobs, moved to Lancaster, and had her first baby. We agreed that Gail should see if she could get her work published on its own, while Penny took longer, writing first her thesis, and then a separate book. So, one book on women in the First World War was published in 1981, while the other, on the Second World War, came out in 1984.

That might have been that, particularly as Penny then had numerous teaching and writing commitments, and another baby, while Gail had gone into the world of computing, having been unable to find any work in history. But, we were both disappointed by the fact that our respective books had come out as expensive hardbacks. How many people could afford to buy such things? We still wanted to reach a wider audience, and Gail approached Philippa Brewster, at Pandora, to see if there was any chance of paperbacking her original book. There were doubts about this, and just in passing she mentioned the possibility of writing a new book, with Penny, about women in the two wars – this idea was greeted with enthusiasm. All that remained was to let Penny know about the idea! Fortunately, she too was keen, and suddenly the project was live again.

We wrote our plan, and then gradually started writing, amidst the numerous demands of home and work. We already knew that this would have to be rather different from our earlier books, and that we wanted more people to read it than had ever seen our original work. It soon became obvious, as we became immersed in it, that we should use the words and opinions of the women themselves as much as possible. This turned it into a different book altogether: we were not re-working our old material, we were producing something fresh. As a result, this is a companion to our earlier books, not a replacement. We also realised that we were probably producing something far more interesting than our original joint work would have been. We each had greater confidence in our ideas, and knew that we had already put our opinions on the line, in our individual books. We now had more to say, and more sources than had been available 10 years before. We needed all the help we could get, as we were writing 200 miles apart, and squeezing the work in around all the other projects taking up our time! But in the end we really enjoyed producing this book because we felt that women's wartime experiences would be as important to readers as they were to us.

Many people have helped us in this project. Gail would like to thank the librarians at the Departments of Sound Records, Printed Books and Documents, at the Imperial War Museum, for all their help; Sian Jones, of the Southampton City Museums Education Service, and those who organised the Oral History Project on women's war work, namely Jean Berry, Dr Jan Stovold and Jenny Wing, for allowing access to a valuable collection of interviews and photographs; Antonia Ineson, for allowing her to borrow (and quote from) her thesis on women munition workers, and many conversations in the past about women and war; Alan Scott, for telling her when she had done enough work for the day; and Brighton Polytechnic Computer Centre, for allowing her to borrow on numerous occasions, the wonderful Apple Macintosh, which made this book so much easier to write.

Penny would like to thank Dorothy Sheridan, of the Mass-Observation Archive, and Liz Neeson, Joyce Jeal and Alex Sumner of Thames TV for introducing her to some wonderful sources and beautiful photographs recording women's experiences; Pam Schweitzer of Age Exchange Theatre Trust for granting permission to quote some of the women who appear in Age Exchange's book, *What Did You Do in the War, Mum?*, and for making available personal photographs from their collection (Age Exchange have produced nine books from the oral history archive they are currently building up, and welcome inquiries at 15 Camden Row, Blackheath, London SE3 0QA); Aline Torday, Marjorie Easterby-Smith and Celia Bannister for permission to use their photographs; friends and colleagues for their interest and support, especially Celia Briar and Jane Mark-Lawson; David Smith of Castle Computers, Lancaster, for help in unscrambling word processing problems; Mark for interviewing Marjorie and many other things besides, and Sam and Sarah, who were always ready to create a cheerful diversion.

We would also both like to say thank you to all those women who have talked or written about their lives during the wars, and have allowed their experiences to be used.

CHAPTER 1

INTRODUCTION

This book is about women's experiences in the First and Second World Wars.[1] In it we are aiming to do two things. The first is to make the voices of working women, of whatever class, heard. Women have had much to say about their lives when asked, and the rise of oral history has led to a growing number of fascinating collections of wartime memories in the past few years. As we wrote, we allowed the concerns of the women themselves to influence the form of the book. So we have written about the experience of call up, personal reactions to war, feelings about the pay and the company at work, and the effects of war on women's health and home lives. Women's pride in their work comes through very strongly in their testimony and so too does the sense of freedom many felt when comparing their war work with the confines of home or a typical 'woman's' job. In both wars there were women who felt that they had been 'let out of the cage' even when they were critical of the pay and conditions they had to put up with, and the way that men reacted to them.

The second thing we aim to do is to lay bare the prejudices surrounding women, and show the way in which attitudes towards their roles at home and at work remained remarkably consistent over nearly fifty years. Both wars put conventional views about sex roles under strain. Women were after all working long hours next to men, learning new jobs, and earning better wages than they had before. They were, particularly in the 1939–45 conflict, partners with men in the war effort. Commentators during the First World War feared that women would not want to settle down to being the nation's wives and mothers after the war and expected changes in the relations between the sexes to result from their new work. But the surprise and hostility with which women were greeted when they were once again moved on to new jobs in 1939–45 do not suggest that the First World War had led to permanent changes. And although a larger number of older and married women went out to work during and after the Second World War they were not considered to be as important and valuable as male workers. Nor was there any suggestion that they should stop being primarily responsible for home life. The belief that men and women naturally occupy separate spheres within which they pursue quite different tasks was not shaken during either war: men were not expected to take an equal share of domestic responsibilities; nor was it considered proper that women, like men, should die for their country.

The book is divided into two sections on the respective wars. Although we cover similar themes in each, the two halves of the book are not perfect mirror-images of each other. As individual authors (Gail writing about the First World War and Penny about the Second), we each have our own style, and our own ways of putting things. Had we tried to obliterate these differences we would have made life harder for ourselves, and would probably have produced a less interesting book for the reader! However, other things also affected the way we wrote the two halves of the book, and we need to make these clear.

The wars themselves were quite dissimilar. The fact that they are known as the First and Second World Wars encourages people to see them as alike. But apart from the fact that in each case the main enemy was Germany and the allies were France, the USA and Russia, there were really very few similarities between them. The casualty figures for each war are revealing. In 1914 the population of England, Scotland and Wales was around 37 million. In the following four years 744,000 men in the armed forces and 14,661 men in the Merchant Navy were killed, and 1,117 civilians died in air raids. (Influenza accounted for another astonishing 150,000 deaths in 1918–19.) In 1939 the population was around 40 million. Between 1939 and 1945 closer to one quarter rather than three quarters of a million were slaughtered (264,443), but in addition this time 624 servicewomen were killed. Twice as many merchant seamen met their deaths in the vicious submarine warfare of the Atlantic and British coastal waters (30,248). Far more civilians were killed in air raids (60,595) and almost as many women as men died as a result of bombing.[2]

In the First World War British action was concentrated in Flanders on the 'Western Front' and civilians were relatively safe. The Second World War was more truly a 'world' war. Between 1939 and 1945 there were 'theatres of war' in Europe, the Atlantic, the Mediterranean, North Africa, the Middle East. After Japan entered the war as an 'Axis' ally of Germany and Italy at the end of 1941, there were fronts in the Far East, the Pacific and Burma as well. But though war service took many servicemen and women far from home, successive waves of bombing also brought the danger, fear and tragedy of war to the heart of the civilian population.

In military terms the wars were quite different. The stagnation of trench warfare characterised the First War, whereas the mobility of fighter and bomber planes, fast-moving tanks, warships and submarines was a key feature of the Second. This mobility gave rise to the situation, quite unknown before, where men were fighting for their lives in aeroplanes over the channel by day and then drinking in the village pub near the air base in the evening. Camps and barracks all over Britain were bursting with servicemen and women, especially once American GIs started to arrive in 1942. The presence of so many people in uniform in British towns and villages during the Second World War, compared with their 'invisibility' in Flanders in the First, affected the ways civilians and troops reacted during the two conflicts. Even though some members of the armed forces were posted abroad or captured and held as prisoners of war and did not return home for as long as six years in the Second World War, the division between the home front and the war front was nothing like as stark as it had been in the First.

In spite of the build-up of the British Fleet, and talk of hostilities with Germany, the war in 1914 came as a complete surprise to most people in Britain. When war was actually declared, many were gripped by patriotic fervour. They assumed that this would be a minor skirmish in Europe in which the British would sort out the Germans, after which life would rapidly return to normal. As the months of fighting stretched to years, and the death toll reached appalling heights, enthusiasm waned considerably, even though there always remained a gulf between the fighting men, who experienced the grim conditions of trench warfare and the people at home who carried on with lives that were almost normal. Eventually people simply longed for the war to be over. It became increasingly difficult to hold on to what it was supposed to be about, and discontent was fuelled by the government's industrial policy and its failure to act effectively on such matters as inadequate housing, high rents and food shortages. The experiences of 1914–18 left many with a lasting horror of the whole idea of war, and a determination that there should never again be such a dreadful conflict.

In contrast with the jingoism of 1914 most people were not enthusiastic about going to war in 1939. The fight was seen as something which had to be undertaken, in spite of the strong peace movement of the 1930s. Even though anti-German feeling was whipped up in the press and by politicians, the enemy this time was not such much a nation as a political system headed by a man who would clearly stop at nothing in his pursuit of establishing a 'Greater Germany' and might very well invade Britain. When they went to war this time, the British people knew that they were defending themselves against Hitler and Nazism. The confusion shown by one new recruit in 1914 who told his companions, 'I'm a-goin' ter fight the bloody Belgiums, that's where I'm a-goin',[3] was unimaginable in 1939. The disillusionment which grew during 1917–18 was not repeated in 1944–5. The mounting number of civilian deaths made people all the more desperate not to lose the war, and politicians' promises of rewards for wartime sacrifices increased determination to create in the aftermath of war a more equitable Britain, in which there really would be homes for heroes, with in addition full employment, free health care and a system of state welfare 'from the cradle to the grave'.

As far as women were concerned, the wars were also different in a number of ways. In both, Britain was beleaguered by the submarine blockade which led to shortages of all sorts of essentials from food to soap and clothing. But the interruption to trade was far more serious in the Second War, and the pressure on women to apply their domestic skills to compensating was greater.

When women entered 'men's trades' and the armed forces in the Second World War they knew it had been done before, but like the previous generation they still experienced the amazing feeling of breaking new ground. It was exhilarating for women to take up 'men's work', although it provoked fear in men because it disturbed the status they were used to. The government and trade unions during the Second War learned from their mistakes and successes in the First when it came to organising women's employment, and took careful steps to ensure that women's 'incursion' into men's jobs was not permanent and would not lead to a drastic shaking up of family and economic life after the war. But no one could foresee exactly where the wartime development of industrial and military organisation would lead, and women's role in the forces in particular developed differently. In the First World War servicewomen had been largely confined to very mundane work like cleaning, cooking, clerical work, waitressing and some driving, to release men for active service. But in 1939–45 in addition to these jobs women handled anti-aircraft guns, ran the communications network, mended aeroplanes and even flew them from base to base. By 1943 12,000 servicewomen had been posted abroad. Although they did not in general fire weapons, women did jobs far more like men's than they had twenty-five years earlier. But the question was, would the experiences of participating in the armed services during the emergency and of doing men's work in industry lead to any lasting changes for women?

The distinctive features of the two wars necessarily led us to cover rather different ground in the two halves of the book. But another factor has also coloured the approach taken by each of us. The sources available to us are different. Many books were written about women's work during the First World War, though most of these, interesting as they are, were more concerned with looking at men's reactions to the women and the problems which might emerge than with describing women's own experiences. Only a few like Mrs Peel's *How We Lived Then* and Gilbert Stone's *Women War Workers* really gave women a voice. However, the Women's Collection at the Imperial War Museum gives an amazingly detailed picture of the jobs women did and includes descriptions written by the workers themselves. In addition, the War Work Collection at the Imperial War Museum's Department of Sound Records and the Oral History Project on Women's War Work at Southampton Museum give a much fuller picture of women's own views of work. But although these collections are immensely valuable, they are rather different from the material about women's experiences in the Second World War which is now available.

To begin with there are fewer survivors today from the First World War, so interviews done recently cover a narrower cross-section of women. Most of those interviewed by the Imperial War Museum and the Southampton Museum Oral History Project were very young during the First War, so the experiences recorded are those of girls in their teens and some young married women, but not those of older women upon whom the war must have made a different impact. Those interviewed about the Second World War, in contrast, include many older and married women. There are even some who worked in both wars. Most of the diaries and books written by women in the First World War came from the pens of young upper-middle-class women, like Monica Cosens and Vera Brittain, whereas there is a growing volume of memoirs and diaries about the Second War written by more 'ordinary' women from lower-middle or working-class backgrounds, like Doris White, Celia Bannister and Nella Last.

Also there was no equivalent of Mass-Observation during the First World War. Mass-Observation (M-O) was an organisation set up in 1937 with the aim of increasing knowledge about people's everyday lives and opinions at all levels of society, particularly amongst the great mass of ordinary people, especially women, of whom policy makers, employers and broadcasters typically took very little notice. M-O encouraged volunteers to write freely about their lives in diaries which they sent in regularly, and in other documents like letters and answers to the organisers' specific questions (known as 'directives'). The task appealed particularly to women, and several of the full-time 'observers' were women. The organisers used some of the material in their own reports and books published at the time, but the diaries, letters, directive replies and observations were stored in what became an immense archive where they are now available for researchers to consult. The M-O Archive provides a huge variety of frank accounts of what was going on during the war, from many viewpoints.

M-O operated in this way from 1937 to 1948 and it is no exaggeration to say that it was unique. Another more recent development has been the interest of television companies in making programmes about the Second World War. Penny had the good fortune to be asked to advise the team from Thames TV who made the programme *Women* as part of their series entitled 'A People's War', and was richly rewarded by being given access to the transcripts of interviews they had conducted with a number of women from all over the country who had a wide variety of war experiences. Age Exchange, a theatre company, has also interviewed a large number of London women about their lives and has published a lovely collection of extracts illustrated with wartime photographs, under the title *What Did You Do in the War, Mum?*. This material revealed a lot about what can be done with oral history. Women interviewed only about war work tend, naturally enough, to supply information only about their jobs, rather than their boyfriends, even though all sides of life are needed to give a full picture of a phase of women's history. It is to be hoped that oral history projects will follow the lead given by Thames and Age Exchange, and tap more of women's memories of all aspects of their lives in both world wars as an urgent priority. There are sadly but inevitably shrinking numbers of women around to be interviewed about the First World War.

Although there are differences in the types of material we have used, we have both learnt a great deal from women's own accounts of their experiences in the two World Wars. That testimony goes a long way towards exploding myths which other historians have cherished about the part women played in the wars. The liveliness of the personal histories we have read and listened to, as well as the interest that women have shown in the fact that we have been writing this book, impressed upon us how important the wars, in all their complexity, have been for women in this century. We hope that this book itself will be part of the process by which these experiences will not be forgotten.

Part One
THE FIRST
WORLD WAR

1   May English, a Southampton tram conductor during the First World War

CHAPTER 2

WOMEN BEFORE 1914

This chapter is about the kind of lives women led at home and work in the years immediately before the First World War, and we hope that the words of some of the women themselves, and their contemporary observers, will give life to this description. Women were to be found in diverse trades before 1914, and they certainly had problems which are still with us today — problems arising from the so-called 'double burden' of work and home, and from the belief held by many of their male co-workers, employers or observers that their work and their wages were not really 'important'.

By the end of the nineteenth century the factory system was well-established but it would be a mistake to assume that all working men and women were factory workers. Unmechanised trades remained, like carpentry, metalwork, millinery and dressmaking to name but a few, and so too did agricultural work and domestic service. Britain was by no means fully industrialised by 1914 and the range of jobs available to women varied according to the areas they lived in. By 1911, about 29 per cent of the officially recorded labour force was female, and this figure remained about the same until as late as 1961.[1]

WOMEN'S JOBS

The textile industry was the largest employer of women factory workers. At the beginning of the twentieth century, there were 656,000 women working in textiles, most of whom were weavers or piecers, young women who acted as the male spinners' assistants.[2] To put these figures in perspective, there were a mere 15 women boilermakers at this time compared with 48,804 men. The cotton industry lay at the heart of the industrial revolution, and it remained the largest employer of women outside domestic service. Women were known as quick, neat workers, who did not expect such high wages as men, and although there were male weavers, they were outnumbered by women. In contrast, spinning was largely a man's job, and the men's unions intended to keep it that way. They used the excuse that the work of a mulespinner was too heavy for women, and that it was undesirable for them to strip down to cope with the heat and humidity as men did. Young women acted as assistants, however, and were increasingly employed on ringspinning, a lighter, less skilled trade, by the end of the nineteenth century, but there were few women spinners compared with the numbers in weaving.

Cotton weaving was important because it was one of the very few trades where men and women worked side by side for equal piece-rates. Men often operated additional looms (4 to 6 at once, as opposed to women's 2 to 4) and could make more money this way, but the rate for the job was the same, giving 22s–32s average earnings a week, for a 4-loom weaver, depending upon the quality of the cloth produced. This meant much to the women themselves, who often took pride in their financial independence. In addition, cotton remained one of the few factory industries where married women worked as a matter of course. Many other factory jobs were done almost entirely by young single women, who left work – voluntarily or otherwise – when they married or had children. In the cotton towns of Lancashire, it was acceptable for married women to go on working, and their wages were acknowledged to be important to the family income.

However, women weavers were concentrated in the north of England, and there was no similar tradition of relatively well-paid factory work in London or the south of the country. A number of Victorian MPs, journalists and social commentators disagreed strongly with the idea of women weavers working outside the home after marriage, and a succession of factory acts during the nineteenth century limited women's hours of labour, but by the end of the century wives still worked. No one dared ban women's work in textiles altogether, as their labour was essential, and in the end they managed to benefit from public concern, by getting some improvement in hours, without losing their jobs – unlike the women pit workers, who found themselves without work after a parliamentary campaign against their 'degrading' occupation in the mid-nineteenth century. Such was the horror roused by the idea of women miners living lives of 'sensual indulgence, domestic thriftlessness, dirt, dissipation and quarrels' because of the hot and heavy work they did, stripped half-naked, that they were banned from underground work. Boys over 10, however, were allowed to go on mining.[3]

Women also worked in the woollen and linen industries, but in smaller numbers, and for lower wages. They had jobs in the metal industry, papermilling, boot and shoe, leather, food, clothing, bookbinding, boxmaking, lacemaking and many other factory trades, but their jobs were usually very distinct from men's, and they were always paid less. A number of these trades employed women both in factories or workshops, and as 'outworkers' or 'homeworkers', who did industrial work in their own homes. In the Midlands, for example, women worked in factories making bicycles and jewellery, or shell-filling in munitions (even before the war), or could work as chainmakers in Cradley Heath, where homes contained small forges – much to the horror of those who thought that mothers should not also be blacksmiths. All large towns had their outworkers, including London, which had clothing factories or workrooms for those who went out to work and earned some kind of weekly wage, however small, and was also host to thousands of homeworkers, most of whom were women, who made clothes at horrifyingly low wages, in the same rooms where they lived, ate and slept.

Mrs Froud was just such a worker in the East End. Widowed in her 20s, with children to support, she worked in a clothing factory by day, and took home shirts to sew in her 'free' time.[4] She, and many like her, accepted low wages because she was desperate for money; homeworkers knew that if they did not accept the rates offered, others would. Employers, meanwhile, benefited not only from the use of cheap labour, but from the fact that they did not have to provide factory accommodation, lighting, heating, machines, or even thread.

Tailoring and dressmaking were perhaps the least unpleasant

of the so-called 'sweated trades'. Worse were those which called for their workers to use feathers, fur, glue and other noxious substances, which filled the house with dust, fumes and unpleasant smells, affecting both workers and families. The Victorian Parliament 'discovered' sweating in the 1880s, encouraged by such writers as Andrew Mearnes, with his crusading book *The Bitter Cry of Outcast London*, which pointed out the connection between poor housing, poverty and the sweated trades. As he wrote:

> In many cases matters are made worse by the unhealthy occupations followed by those who dwell in these habitations. Here you are choked as you enter by the air laden with particles of the superfluous fur pulled from the skins of rabbits, rats, dogs and other animals in their preparation for the furrier. Here the smell of paste and of drying match-boxes, mingled with other sickly odours, overpowers you . . . .[5]

A select committee sat to look at the evidence. But in spite of the horrific picture of exploitation which emerged, nothing was done about it, and the problem surfaced again just a few years before the First World War, with a massive exhibition organised by the *Daily News*. The Trade Boards Act led to minimum wages being set in some of these industries from 1909 onwards, but many women in such trades were still unprotected.

Homework was unpleasant, but the fact was that all women's work was hard and low paid, whether it was done at home or in the workshop or factory. The Royal Commission on Labour reports of the 1890s revealed the poor health and stress of women in many jobs. Dressmakers started at 8 in the morning, and did regular overtime in the evening – at rates lower than the normal day rate. Shop assistants, meanwhile, commonly worked from 50 to 70 hours a week, with half-hour breaks for breakfast, dinner and tea: anaemia and indigestion were said to be common. One woman in Lancashire remembered that:

> My sister Florrie would arrive home at nearly midnight, having walked the mile from the tram to our house and after having been on her feet all the long day [. . .] exhausted to

breaking point. She could weep with weariness and though hungry be too tired to eat her supper.[6]

Laundry workers, who experienced continuous hot, damp conditions (70 to 80° F), worked 60, 70 or more hours a week. As Clara Collet reported to the Royal Commission, these hours were not popular, but women had no choice in the matter:

> Witness 146, laundress, single woman, said she would rather have shorter hours with less money. When I pointed out that in her present situation she did not work any longer than was allowed by the Factory Act, the laundresses present were much excited, and declared they wanted no Factory Act but an 8 hours bill. They saw no reason why they should work at the laundry and slave at home, while their husbands only did 8 hours a day.[7]

In the industrial areas of the north there was less homework, and women were more likely to work in factories and workshops before marriage. But from everywhere, including the well-unionised Lancashire cotton workers, and Yorkshire woollen workers, the carpet weavers, the pottery workers, and the metal workers, came complaints about hours, lack of sanitary arrangements, and lack of anywhere to eat food during the day. These conditions were not confined to women of course, for men experienced similar problems, but women received lower wages, and had little chance of escaping from the drudgery of the standard women's trades.

Although so many women worked in industry, the largest employer of women workers on the eve of the First World War was still domestic service. This had been an expanding field of employment throughout the nineteenth century: the growing middle class wanted servants to care for their houses, gardens and children. Numbers were dropping by the end of the nineteenth century, but there were still 1,400,000 women and girls in domestic service in 1911, 214,270 of them in London alone.[8] Most girls went into service in their teens or earlier (the school leaving age was 11 in 1893, 12 in 1896, and only rose to 14 in 1918) and expected to leave on marriage. Many were recruited from the countryside, and came from families who needed to get rid of non-wage-earning daughters as soon as possible. Service was still seen by many parents as a 'safe' occupation for their children in towns, and was also the only job available for many girls, as the old labouring and dairying jobs on farms passed to men. Middle-class employers often persisted in saying that service was an excellent training for such young women; as one wrote in 1914:

> A well-trained domestic servant is of real value to the nation, she makes the best possible wife and mother, as she had acquired a good knowledge of housewifery and habits of cleanliness, puncuality and to some extent, of hygiene.[9]

Today's picture of pre-war domestic service, encouraged by novels and television series, is one of neat uniformed young women in large houses. But many girls worked alone or in pairs for much smaller households. Middle-class families wanted servants to improve their status, and if they could ill-afford them, they simply paid them less money and employed as few as possible. Whatever the prosperity of the employer, servants were at their beck and call all day and everyday, often rising before 6 and finishing late at night, working a 15- or 16-hour day. Half-days off were few, and all links with the outside world were usually discouraged. Servants were supposed to devote their lives to their employer's household, and they left work when married, as 'living in' was the norm.

Some young women liked the 'ladylike' nature of the job, with its neat uniforms, and board and lodgings with the middle classes, although workdresses were likely to be provided by the servants themselves, and many employers were only too happy to economise by feeding them poor-quality food, and housing them in kitchens, sculleries or attics. As one such servant wrote:

> When a girl goes into service at a gentleman's house she is more aliable (sic) to get into better company than factory girls. To be a servant is much more healthier and comfortable. Girls who are in service are generally much more quieter and ladylike than those which are in a factory.[10]

But much more common were the views of a factory girl asked about her work a few years before the First World War:

> When I was about 14 years of age I went into service for about 18 months and I did not like it at all because you are

on from morning till night and you never did get your meals in peace for you are up and down all the time.[11]

In contrast, the life of a factory girl meant that:

. . . you have only got one to serve and you can go to as many classes in a week you have got Saturday and Sunday to yourself and you can see a bit of life and are not shut up all day.[12]

The work was hard and dirty, as Mrs Wilkinson, a day servant in 1914 remembered:

I was only fourteen and six days and I took the job and it was only three-and-six a week but I only worked mornings . . . I used to do vegetables, and the rough cleaning. There was no hoover . . . I'd to brush the carpets, and I'd take the stair carpet on the lawn and drag it up and down the lawn. It was hard work for a girl of fourteen and I didn't like it.[13]

But the lack of freedom, and lack of respect shown by their employers, annoyed women most, and by the years immediately before the war the number of servants was falling. Not surprisingly, women were least likely to take up such work in areas where there were alternative jobs available, and many, like the woman quoted earlier, preferred factory life.

In contrast, the late nineteenth century saw a steady increase in clerical work for women. Earlier secretaries and clerks had been male, but as industry and finance continued to expand, the nature of the office changed, and the way was opened to women 'typewriters' and clerks. They were few in number compared with industrial workers, and it is easy enough, now that clerical work has become a female ghetto, to dismiss this move into mundane office work as being an unfortunate step for women. But for young unmarried middle-class women, white-collar work offered a chance to earn money of their own, and for working-class girls with some education it was a way to escape from the dirt and hard labour of factory work or domestic service.

At the same time, the number of women teaching in schools rose steadily. The 1870 Education Act led to an expansion in public elementary schools for working-class children, and more teachers were required. This career was something an ambitious working-class girl could aim at, although it too proved to be something of a 'dead end' job, for it was unlikely at that time that a working-class woman would become a headmistress and virtually no women became administrators. Numbers of high schools for girls increased as well. Initially these were private schools, many of which were established by the Girls' Public Day School Company, but after 1902 local authorities began to set them up too. These offered more jobs for middle-class women, a growing number of whom were considering careers as well – not least because of the problem of 'surplus' women during the late nineteenth century. Emigration had led to an unbalanced sex ratio in some age groups, and a number of women realised that they could not depend on marriage as a career. Such schools produced a generation of educated young women.

Not all women worked in towns, of course, but by the end of the century, country women had been eased out of farm labouring, and were mostly confined to jobs in the home. They could still find jobs as servants, or as casual workers on the land, but in most areas, unless there was outwork such as knitting, straw-hat, lace or glovemaking for them to do, they found themselves with little chance of a paid job. Farmers were increasingly reluctant to employ them as labourers, and the skilled work in dairying, ploughing or handling horses and stock went to men. Even the old 'gang system', under which teams of young women and children worked on the land in East Anglia, was dying out, and few regretted its passing. As Mrs Burrows said, writing her life story for the Women's Cooperative Guild in 1931, after four years (aged 8 to 12) of working 14 hours a day in the fields, it seemed like heaven to go into a factory in Leeds.[14]

By this time, many farmers' wives too had retreated from physical labour, for different reasons. Wealthier farmers aspired to middle-class status, and the women of the farm no longer mixed with farm servants as they had once done – although small farms still needed their work. By 1914, the countryside was very much worked by men – just how dependent on male labourers farms were was revealed once their men enlisted or were conscripted.

It is important to notice that many women workers *as counted by the Census* were young and single. In many areas, they gave up work to have children. This was hardly surprising. Even if they had been allowed to stay in their jobs, there was nowhere for small children to stay while their parents worked. Crêches were unknown, and childminders cost money. In addition, it was exhausting for women who had already worked such long hours to then feed and bed small children, and do housework. But the cotton workers were a notable exception, usually employing childminders or relatives to make their work possible. And, although less well-known, there were substantial numbers of other women who worked at some time after marriage. They worked because they needed to, as husbands were often sick, unemployed or on low wages themselves, or even because they wanted to – contrary to the belief of many observers at the time, some married women did actually take pride in the fact that they could earn their own wages. Those most desperate for money made up the bulk of homeworkers and charwomen; they took in laundry, ran small shops on a shoe-string from homes, or did the roughest factory work. Others worked for the extras which made the difference between subsistence and moderate comfort. As Clementina Black's book on married women workers showed, working wives were common in many Midland and northern areas, and were not ashamed of working: 'on the contrary, they are proud of their work and unwilling to relinquish it'.[15] Many of these women did not show up in Census figures because they did not declare their work, or were employed by relations.

All women suffered from the assumption that they would *not* work after marriage, however. Employers were reluctant to train young women whom they assumed would only work for a few years; a temporary, unambitious workforce was in any case highly desirable, as wages could be kept low. Married women, in the meantime, often found it hard to get work because of their age and employers' prejudices about employing wives; they were therefore cheap workers also, as they took what employment they could get. In spite of unions' fears that employers would always use cheap women in preference to men, this was often not the case. Employers had a low opinion of women's ability to learn, and assumed that they would or should, leave work after marriage; they preferred to keep them on 'women's work', while men alone had the opportunity of going into 'skilled work'.

Skilled unions themselves would not accept that women *could* do 'men's work', and their prejudices were not just rooted in fear of women's cheapness. Skilled men clung on to their craft status, which established their place at the top of the labour hierarchy. They were reluctant to accept that women might be capable of anything but monotonous drudgery, and believed that woman's place was in the home.

Any young girl leaving school therefore knew that there were precious few options open to her. Even the cotton weavers were not classed as 'skilled', and their wage rates, while good for women, were lower than many men received in other jobs. Of course, the whole queston of what is 'skilled' or 'unskilled' work leads to complex debates. We may look at nineteenth-century examples of bonnets, dresses or lace, and say that this appears to be skilled work – it certainly required much effort and fine workmanship from the milliner or dressmaker. But it was not called skilled work, and it did not pay good rates. It is tempting to say that this was simply because it was done by women, who were in no position to organise apprenticeship, or exclusive unions, as some men were. The attitude was that any woman could pick up a needle and learn to sew or knit; she did not require expensive machinery or training, unlike, say, an engineer.

Another thing to remember is that most women workers were working class. Although there were a few jobs available for single middle-class women before the war, it was still rare for a married middle-class woman to have a job. Her role was to manage the home and the servants. Professional jobs in banking, the civil service, medicine, the law, etc. were completely dominated by men. If anything, the division of labour in middle-class society was even more noticeable than it was amongst the working classes. At least most working-class women had once been out to work, knew about the wage-earning world, physical fatigue, arguments with the foreman or travelling to work. Middle-class women were almost entirely cut off from the 'useful' world of money and industry, and did not expect to work. As one wealthy young woman replied, when asked many years later what she thought she would do, when she was in her teens –

I didn't really think about it much until I was a bit older [after the war]. You see, girls didn't. I didn't suppose I'd need to earn my living.[16]

But it is true to say that there was a strong division of labour throughout society, and this was a burden on both sexes. The man who could not support his family was seen as a failure, and a working-class man whose wife worked was often bitter about his own inability to support her. In the meantime, middle-class wives in financial difficulties had to suffer genteel poverty if their husbands' earnings dropped, for there were few opportunities for them to earn extra money.

WORKING AND LIVING CONDITIONS

Many aspects of life actually improved for working people in towns during the late nineteenth century. Proper roads and lighting made travel easier and safer; workman's trains and buses provided cheaper transport. Supplies of clean piped water meant the end of cholera and other waterborne illnesses which had plagued the early towns. However, conditions at home and work were often deplorable, even for those earning tolerable wages.

By and large, factories and workshops were built to house equipment, not to cater for the needs of workpeople. This meant sheds and rooms which were poorly ventilated, hot in summer and cold in winter. It meant no toilets or cloakrooms, and nowhere to eat. Canteens were virtually unheard of, and most people either went home for lunch, or ate amidst the tools and products of their work, no matter how unhealthy this might be. Some trades, like lead or matchmaking, were known to have poisonous effects on their workers; others were also harmful, although less directly so. Work people were often aware of the dangers, and complained about them, but little was done. It was rare to find a factory like Cadbury's at Bournville, where cloakrooms, playgrounds, toilets, canteens and electric lights were all part of the facilities.

After long hours in poor working conditions, men and women returned to badly built homes. In some of the industrial towns of the north and Midlands, like Manchester or Birmingham, new houses meant better ventilated rooms, running water, and a toilet (in an outhouse). But many people still lived in older houses, which were often subdivided, and depended on a single tap for drinking and washing.

The contrast between middle-class and working-class women's lives becomes even more acute when you look at their domestic lives. Mrs Pember Reeves, in a striking book written in 1913, considered how people lived in one area of London on approximately £1 a week.[17] This was the kind of money a working-class man in full employment might give his wife for housekeeping expenses. These families were not in dire poverty: they were the 'respectable' working class, who managed to get by on what they earned, and did not resort to begging or the workhouse. Her book really showed that for those who were poor, life was quite simply more expensive. Thus a well-to-do middle-class man, on £2,000 a year, might spent £250 a year on rent, rates and taxes, which was an eighth of his income. A poor man, on 24s a week (£62 8s a year), might pay 8s a week in rent, rates and taxes, which was a third of his income. The former would have a large roomy house, running water, and plenty of air and light for his money, while the latter had a couple of rooms in a cramped house shared with others.

In these circumstances, the middle-class woman would have leisure to organise her day in the way she chose, leaving cooking, cleaning, shopping, and much of childcare to servants. The working-class woman spent her life trying to organise money, find time for shopping, work out what was cheapest to buy, and how to cook what little she could afford in one or two saucepans over the fire, while attending to the needs of several children. She also had to clean a home which was almost impossible to keep clean – this was done with washing soda. It was impossible to get rid of the bugs in older houses – they were papered over every now and then – and floors, tables and steps had to be scrubbed at regular intervals. Washday meant filling up the coppers by hand (often carrying the water up flights of stairs), scrubbing clothes, mangling them, and frequently hanging them indoors to dry – then ironing them with a flat iron. The dirty water had to be carried out again, jug by jug.

Everything was more difficult for the low-paid woman.

Weekly or daily earnings meant that expenses had to be spread out accordingly, and food and fuel alike were far more expensive when bought in small quantities. Buying clothes was a constant problem. It was unlikely that anyone in the family had more than one pair of boots for example; when these were beyond repair, money for new ones had to be squeezed out of the food budget. Mrs Pember Reeves reported how one young woman she spoke to only went out at night, when no one could see that she was wearing slippers.

Shopping itself was done at small cornershops at almost any hour of the day, and tiny quantities of each food were bought. Apart from the small amount of money available for this, there was little space to store food in many houses, and anything perishable quickly went off in warm weather. Diet itself was often monotonous, bread, marge and tea being the staples, not least because of cooking problems, and women did their best to feed husbands and children rather than themselves. As for childcare, help came from friends and relations, but children were the mother's responsibility. The fact that they (and their fathers) usually went home for lunch led to more cooking for their mothers. Families were of course larger then, 4.6 being the average number of children per household; 71 per cent of women had 4 or more children, and 41 per cent had 7 or more.[18]

Not surprisingly, women also suffered from many health problems, caused by frequent pregnancy, childbirth, and sheer overwork. These were revealed by a book which came out just before the war – *Maternity* – which was made up of letters from working-class women about their experiences of pregnancy and motherhood.[19] Ill-health was the norm – varicose veins, bronchitis, miscarriages and anaemia were all common, and it seemed that no one ever really expected to feel well. Many women writing in this book deplored the lack of contraceptive advice available, as they were well aware of the cost to themselves of bearing too many children, and by the outbreak of war it was still not really acceptable to admit to limiting your family. Although sheaths and caps were available, many people found these embarrassing or difficult to use, and the withdrawal method, itself unreliable, depended on the readiness of the man to co-operate. (Miscarriage, self-induced by potions, or performed by an illegal abortionist, was still a common and dangerous means of contraception.)

Needless to say, the domestic burden rested almost entirely upon the women, helped (often reluctantly) by ther daughters. Husbands and sons would rarely do more than watch the younger children while the women went out shopping, though there were occasional exceptions in the cotton areas, where wives' paid work was common. Women might well have resented this, but they accepted it. Indeed, it sometimes seems that the mark of a good husband was merely to hand over as much housekeeping money as possible, to be sober, and to be moderate in requirements for sex, since abstinence was still the safest means of contraception.

In view of all the domestic tasks, it seems quite astonishing that women also managed to fit in a day's paid work as well, but a number of them did so. Middle-class observers noted that most homes in the Lancashire cotton towns were neat and clean, in spite of the number of working wives. Such tidiness was bought at a cost, since women had to work until far into the evening to achieve it. This is a description from one Lancashire woman, in 1904:

> On Monday I clear up all the rooms after Sunday, brush and put away all Sunday clothes, and then separate and put to soak all soiled clothes for washing. On Tuesday, the washing is done, the clothes folded and mangled. After the washing, the scullery receives a thorough cleaning for the week. Wednesday is the day for starching and ironing, and stocking darning, as well as the usual week's mending. On Thursday I bake the bread and clean the bedrooms. On Friday I clean the parlour, lobby and staircase, as well as the living room. Saturday morning is left for all outside cleaning – windows and stonework – besides putting all the clean linen on the beds. I finish work on Saturday about 2pm, the rest of the day being free.[20]

Weavers had one big advantage over the women of London that Mrs Pember Reeves described – the ability to earn money themselves. They could afford to buy better clothes and food, pay for some form of childminding, and even afford better accommodation. Nor was the housing crisis so acute outside London. But the fear of falling into debt was universal. Sickness, unemployment, or low wages could drag any family down, and as it was invariably the woman who budgeted, it was the woman who worried most about this, and sacrificed herself to make ends meet. The worry and the scrimping had their effect on the health of both women and children.

These are the words of a wor..an writing in 1914 about her own particular struggle:

> I am a mother of eleven children – six girls and five boys. I was only nineteen years old when my first baby was born. My husband was one of the best, and a good father. His earnings was £1 a week; every penny was given to me, and after paying house rent, firing and light, and clubs [*probably sickness or burial societies*], that left me 11s to keep the house going on; and as my little ones began to come, they wanted providing for and saving up to pay a nurse, and instead of getting nourishment for myself which we need at those times, I was obliged to go without. So I had no strength to stand against it, and instead of being able to rest in bed afterwards, I was glad to get up and get about again before I was able, because I could not afford a woman to look after me.[21]

Another woman said bluntly – '. . . I can say truthfully my children have died from my worrying about how to make two ends meet and also insufficient food', then added, 'A woman with little wage has to go without a great deal at those times, as we must give our husbands sufficient food or we should have them at home and not able to work; therefore we have to go without to make ends meet.'[22]

WAGES AND PROSPECTS

This leads us to wages. Seebohm Rowntree, considering the amount needed for a single person to survive on in 1914, decided that wages of £1 a week were the minimum necessary. Most of the men mentioned in Mrs Pember Reeves' survey (*Round About a Pound a Week*) were earning rather more than this, and passed £1 to their wives for food, lodgings and clothes. This was not a good wage for the time – a skilled worker could earn several pounds a week, while a middle-class professional man would earn £10 a week or more. For example, a bank manager earned somewhere in the region of £600 a year, although a humble cashier had to be content with a mere £150, or around £3 a week – although he could expect his wages to rise as his status in the bank rose. The lower middle classes earned little more than skilled men, but had status and job security, as well as the possibility of a career structure. How did women's wages compare? The answer is, very badly. The Royal Commission on Labour, in the 1890s, showed that women in the cotton industry fared best. They could earn as much as 24s a week in Lancashire. Other industrial workers earned less: in silk weaving, women took home 7s in a good week, in carpet weaving, 10s–14s 6d. Woollen weavers, if female, always earned less than men, and in the West Country had to be content with 10s–14s a week. In the laundry trade, in London, a girl doing high-class work could earn 16–22s for a week of 12-hour days, but a mere 10s–12s further down the hierarchy. These were all 'good' jobs; as you go down the employment scale to 'rough' factory work, cleaning and homework, wages sank to well below 10s a week, with women clothing workers, for example, earning only a few pence for each completed garment. Women in white-collar trades like teaching earned little more, while those in shops or offices often earned less than the semi-skilled factory worker.

To put these wages in perspective, for they changed very little between the 1890s and the First World War, it is worth bearing in mind that in London the rent on one small room could be 3 or 4s a week, a loaf of bread cost about 2½d, half a pound of butter was 7d, meat 6d–8d, milk 2d a pint, and 4oz of tea, 4d. Many women and children lived largely on bread, marg and tea – the cheapest foods – while the protein went to the male breadwinner.

Why were women's wages so low? This is a complex question, and one which was widely discussed in the years immediately before the war. A number of possible reasons were given, and they came up again during wartime debates on the same question – not all of them were altogether logical! It was widely claimed that women were paid less because they 'needed' less money, as they were not breadwinners .The fact that a number of women *were* breadwinners, or made an essential contribution to the family income, was conveniently ignored by those who claimed that women's 'standard of living' was lower – not only did they need less food, but they had fewer financial commitments, according to these speakers. In fact, this was a meaningless idea, since men were not paid on the basis of how many children they had, or whether they were married or single, but it remained a common excuse for paying women lower wages, and for failing to take the question of women's pay seriously. It was also claimed that women did less complex work, or that when they were doing similar jobs to men, their work was less satisfactory. This claim does not stand up to investigation either. Women's work, as we have seen, was often highly complex or tiring, but they were always paid less than men in comparable jobs. In fact, as Edward Cadbury stated in his book on women workers in 1906, most female workers were paid less simply because they were women.[23] They were caught in a vicious exploitative circle in a time when decent wage levels depended upon strong trade unions, or the possession of much sought-after skills. Once women were established in low wage trades, it was almost impossible for them to break out of this position, given that these industries were often non-unionised, and were frequently over-crowded. While the National Federation of Women Workers and the Workers Union recruited many women in the years immediately before the war, most men's unions were not interested in having female members. Women's wages only concerned them when they were a threat to men, and by and large their policy was to keep women out of men's trades if possible.

It is true to say that for women, this was quite disastrous. There was no point in being ambitious if no union would take you, and no employer employ you, on 'men's work'. Most women's trades were 'dead-end', and as long as working days stretched out before you with unchanging monotony, it was tempting to feel you could put up with it only until marriage. Many employers commented on how 'docile' women were, and how tolerant of boring work. This was because they often assumed the work was temporary, and hoped they would escape through marriage and motherhood. In reality, one kind of drudgery was exchanged for another, and the burdens carried by working-class mothers make most of us now wonder how they managed to survive physically and mentally. Until just before the War they could not even look forward to a pension, and old age was often dreaded as much as sickness and unemployment at a time when the destitute finished up in the workhouse.

Changes were afoot, spear-headed by the suffrage movement, in which working-class as well as middle-class women participated. If anything, middle-class families, with their more striking division between male and female roles, were disturbed to a greater extent than working-class families. The cloistering Victorian ideology of a middle-class woman living in domestic bliss, surrounded by a large family and obedient servants, was being eroded. The spread of academic education for girls and young women, and expanding employment opportunities for educated single women meant that Beatrice Potter (later Webb) and, 20 years later, Vera Brittain, believed that by working hard they could break out of a stultifying provincial environment — however much their families hoped for a more 'conventional' life for them. The slowly growing numbers of women who went away to teacher training colleges, as well as the tiny number of women who went to university, treasured the experience, like Helen Pease who described going to Cambridge just before the war as 'absolutely marvellous. Nobody who goes to college now can realize what it was like.'[24] This was despite the fact that female students were chaperoned, and that the University would still not confer degrees upon women.

But although some women felt hopeful about the future, tradition was re-inforced in many ways. Even the academic girls' secondary schools had to include domestic science in the curriculum after 1909, while those in charge of working-class girls' education saw themselves as preparing girls to be obedient domestic servants, and good wives and mothers — not to be a permanent part of the paid labour force. As Carol Dyhouse, in her book on girls' education puts it, 'Women were expected to occupy themselves in providing an environment — a context in which *men* could live and work.'[25] The world of employment before 1914 was curiously dominated by men — engineers, tramdrivers, rural labourers, police, managers, bank clerks, businessmen, were all male, while women's work was often invisible or classed as unimportant. Domestic work above all was under-rated, and was simply seen as women's duty. The 'mothers of the nation' were not supposed to be ambitious, or to want anything other than a comfortable home, complete with husband and children to look after.

This view was shared by many men, whatever their class, and was used as much to denigrate the middle-class feminists as to keep women in a ghetto of low-paid occupations. Ironically, for all their interest in mothers' pensions, a minimum wage, medical care, etc. the labour movement too shared many of the prevailing assumptions. Ethel Snowden, a socialist, outlined her vision of woman's place:

> . . . married women with children will not work in the factory; at least not until the children are out of their hands. They will not wish to do so, for they will be free and their children will claim them.[26]

Although many suffragettes and suffragists fought not only for the vote but for the widening of job opportunities for women of all classes, the aim of the Labour Party was still to give the working man enough money to support a wife and children at home, not to shake up the labour market and let women enter as equals. Although seldom admitted, this belief in women's fulltime domestic role was often accompanied by a scant regard for the work they did do, and a conviction, amongst all classes, that women were not really capable of doing much else.

The war was about to make men think again about what women could, or could not, do at work. It did not alter their belief that women alone were responsible for the home life of the nation.

CHAPTER 3

DILUTION: WOMEN IN MEN'S JOBS

Dilution ... the introduction of the less skilled workers to undertake the whole or part of work previously done by workers of greater skill or experience, often, but not always accompanied by simplification of machinery or breaking up of a job into a number of simpler operations ...
G. D. H. Cole

THE EARLY MONTHS OF WAR

In August 1914, the death of an Austrian archduke in Sarajevo plunged the continent into war. Britain entered the conflict as a direct result of Germany's attack on Belgium. Some people looked on with despair, wondering what this conflict was really about, and European labour organisations clung vainly to the hope that workers of different nations would refuse to fight their brothers. Others were gripped by war fever, and in an atmosphere of intense anti-German feeling many thousands of men joined up in the first few weeks of war. On 5 August, the prime minister, Asquith, called for volunteers, and within 5 weeks 200,000 men had heeded his call. On 1 September alone, 30,000 men signed up.[1] It was debatable whether many of those who joined really knew what they were fighting for – the image of gallant little Belgium resisting the German bully was exploited by the press, and the army needed only jingoism or patriotism to drive men into its ranks. Certainly they had no idea what they were letting themselves in for. Britain had a small professional army, the B E F (British Expeditionary

Force) in 1914, and a powerful navy, and it was assumed that the former, backed up by volunteers, would rapidly bring an end to the war. The government shared this view. Trench warfare was completely unexpected, and only occurred as new, more sophisticated weapons made cavalry battles impossible. Mobile armies would return later in the twentieth century, once tanks, aircraft and light weaponry allowed, but in the transition period, armed with deadly guns but little means of defence, the evenly balanced armies dug themselves in along the Western Front, and fought for mere yards of territory in bitter and bloody battles.

During August and September 1914 the war was having an immediate and serious effect on the economy. Industries with European links were cutting back on their operations, fishing fleets withdrew from the North Sea, the wealthy cancelled orders for clothes and jewellery in a sudden patriotic desire to economise. Unemployment was rising rapidly, and women were badly hit, as they made up many of the domestic servants or workers in the so-called luxury trades who were losing their jobs. Men had the 'opportunity' to enlist, and many did so. Wealthy women who wanted to do something for the war effort were taking up voluntary work, and started to knit or sew for the troops. Working-class women, meanwhile, had no other jobs to turn to. Women's unemployment stood at 190,000 in September 1914 and only dropped to 139,000 in October.[2] It occurred to no one that this could be a temporary problem, and charities set up relief works to help destitute women – the most famous of these, Queen Mary's Workrooms, being set up by the Central Committee for the Employment of Women, a body which included well-known names from the Women's Trade Union League and Women's Labour League, like Mary Macarthur, Susan Lawrence and Margaret Bondfield. Here, women were employed sewing, and the suffragette Sylvia Pankhurst was quick to point out that they were paid only 10s a week, a 'sweated wage'. The government did nothing about women's unemployment, and certainly did not consider the idea of using women on men's jobs in industry. The idea of intervening in employment was totally alien to it, and the assumption was that market forces should be left to take their course. Indeed, at this time, most government and military men thought that women should simply 'stay out of the way' while

2 Mabel Davidson (*left*), of Southampton, one of the rare women tram
drivers, with her conductor

men fought; the limit of women's support was supposed to be knitting for the troops, or possibly nursing them. Ray Strachey, a feminist, later told how when Dr Elsie Inglis approached the War Office with an offer of fully equipped medical units for France . she was told to 'Go home and keep quiet', as commanders did not want to be bothered with hysterical women: women doctors were still not approved of in many circles.[3]

But times were changing fast. As men enlisted, many businesses found themselves short-staffed, and with surprising speed women were taken on in shops, offices and banks to replace them. Many also took over small concerns left by husbands, fathers or brothers, like window-cleaning, gardening, van-driving, or shopkeeping. At the same time, government contracts for uniforms and kits to equip the fast-growing volunteer army led to an increase in work for women in the woollen, tailoring and leather-goods industries – here they began by doing standard 'women's work'. As bus, tram and train companies took them on, and they became road-sweepers, lift attendants, and messengers, women became increasingly visible in city streets, and journalists gawped at the sight of so many doing 'men's work' whether it was the 'conductorette' on the trams, the 'petrol nymph' driving a motor car, or the 'street housemaids' sweeping the roads. Women's unemployment duly dropped to 75,000 in December 1914, and 35,000 in February 1915, but they were still doing very little 'men's work' in industry.

Early 1915 was the turning point for women's employment. By that time it was obvious that the war could last for many months to come, and there was a growing munitions shortage. The introduction of licensing hours for pubs was a direct result of Lloyd George's accusation that workers were sometimes too drunk to be efficient, but it was becoming quite clear that any real increase in production would have to come from changes in workshop practice and recruitment of more workers. The bombardment of German forces had to be kept up – and by 1915 it was clear that this was going to be an expensive business in terms of both arms and men: 75,000 men had been killed by the middle of the year, and it was claimed that more were dying because of the shells shortage.[4] However, increasing production was not that easy. Many skilled engineers had enlisted in the first months of war, and could not be released from the army. A skilled worker took years to train, and the nation did not have years. The government wanted to introduce women into munitions production fast, organising workshops so that women could replace absent men, and 'release' others for the army. The answer lay in altering the way armaments were produced.

The government was thus forced to take action in an unfamiliar field. Its attempt to organise a register of women volunteers was disastrous. Within 2 weeks, 33,000 women had registered at labour exchanges as requested, and there were 110,000 women on the books by the autumn. However, there was no organisation for actually handling so many applications, and the labour exchanges only managed to find jobs for 5,000.[5]

But in 'organising' industry, the government was far more successful. Lloyd George, prime minister from May 1915, took the lead, and the coalition government became involved in the recruitment, training and management of munitions workers for the rest of the war. The state organised the terms and conditions of women's work in the chemical and metal trades, and influenced many other industries by encouraging their use on work 'customarily done by men', to use the key phrase of the time.

Women were accepted with great reluctance into most skilled trades. The first trouble from engineering workers had come as early as November 1914, at Vickers, where skilled men had objected to setting up machines for some new women recruits. (It should be made clear that tool setting was an important part of skilled work, and was always to be a bone of contention.) This dispute was settled by the Crayford Agreement the same month, allowing women on repetition work only.[6] After further murmurings of discontent, the Shells and Fuses Agreement of March 1915 led to women or boys being allowed to operate semi- or completely automatic machines in munitions – this was not skilled work, though it might have been done by adult men before. The Treasury Agreement followed soon afterwards, made between the government and 35 trade unions, and with this, women or boys were allowed to do *parts* of a skilled men's work, leaving the fully skilled tradesman to do the remainder. This was the beginning of widespread 'dilution' –

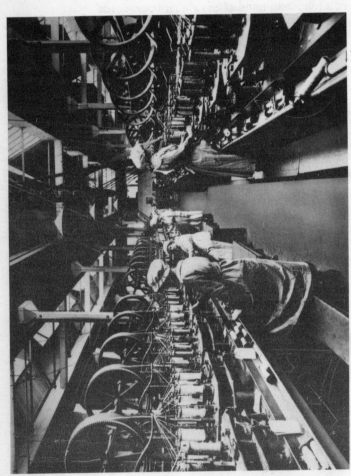

3 Workers at Pirelli Cable Works, Southampton

... the introduction of the less skilled workers to undertake the whole or part of work previously done by workers of greater skill or experience, often, but not always, accompanied by simplification of machinery or breaking up of a job into a number of simpler operations.[7]

The government's primary concern was obviously with dilution in engineering and ammunition factories, and Lloyd George accelerated the process with the Dilution Scheme of October, which eased more women on to semi-skilled work, and the Substitution Scheme in 1916, which moved more women on to skilled processes.[8] No women trade union leaders were involved in these discussions, however, although a number of experienced and articulate trade unionists like Mary Macarthur and Gertrude Tuckwell would have been more than happy to take part at this stage. From the outset this was an arrangement between government, employers and male trade unionists.

Also in 1915, the Ministry of Munitions came into being. This extraordinary body brought over 90 leading businessmen together as government advisors, and rapidly grew into a vast and efficient machine for organising dilution. By 1918, it employed 65,000 people – many of them women clerical workers! It was designed to handle all aspects of the training, health and management of munition workers, plus the transport of weapons and workers, the building of factories, and anything else to do with the industry. It was dedicated to sweeping aside old management and union practices for the duration of the war, and succeeded in doing so. Through it, the state also became an employer, as the Ministry eventually owned 250 factories, and ran another 20,000, which were in fact privately owned – these were known as Controlled Establishments.[9] Needless to say, the fact that so many businessmen were involved in its administration caused much suspicion in the labour movement.

The establishment of the Ministry of Munitions in June was followed a month later by the first Munitions Act. This confirmed that female labour should be allowed into work from which women had been excluded before the war, and introduced the infamous 'leaving certificate'. Without leaving certificates issued by their employers, men and women could not find work with another munitions firm for the following 6 weeks. So workers could not seek factories which paid higher wages. Such was the unpopularity of the certificate that it was eventually scrapped in 1917, after it had been blamed as one of the causes of the rash of strikes that year. But this act, together with the 5 'L' circulars issued on aspects of dilution, paved the way for the flooding of women into munitions.[10] The skilled engineering union, the ASE, was forced to allow women into certain jealously guarded jobs, and was in return given some guarantees about pay (though this was to be a constant source of dispute), and promised that women would be removed at the end of the war.

Other non-munitions unions also made reluctant agreements on the use of women on work 'customarily done by men', aided by pamphlets issued by the Board of Trade, and so women moved into some of men's work in woollen and worsted, bleaching and dying, hosiery, china, brick, woodworking, boot and shoe, brushmaking, electroplating, printing and banking jobs.[11] Local agreements were made in some other areas, and women were allowed into mulespinning in the cotton industry in Oldham, Bury and Rochdale, while Preston resisted their incursion for as long as possible. But everywhere there continued to be arguments about precisely what work women should do, and what they should be paid.

The major expansion in women's employment therefore came from 1915 onwards, and their success at work enabled the government to introduce conscription for men in January 1916. Exemption for skilled men was cancelled in April 1917, by which time women were more and more involved with skilled work in engineering. It is an unfortunate fact that women's skill and enthusiasm made conscription possible.

WOMEN IN MEN'S JOBS

The bald figures for women's work show much. In July 1914, there were 3,276,000 women in industry (not including many homeworkers or those in small workshops), plus about 1,600,000 domestic servants. By April 1918, the total stood at 4,808,000.[12] This meant there had been an increase of about 1½ million women in the industrial labour force. Some had come straight from school, or had never worked before (including some middle-class volunteers), many others had come from domestic service (which lost 400,000 workers during the war) or the clothing trade; a number had retired from paid work on marriage, and now returned to industry. In engineering, the proportion was said to be as high as 40–60 per cent across the country.[13]

'Where the women came from' was a matter much discussed during the war, and investigations showed what trades they had worked in previously. The London General Omnibus Company discovered that by far the largest number of the women workers had been domestic servants (1,245), the next most common being dressmakers (355). Interestingly enough, they included 208 former munitions workers in their figures, showing that some women preferred life in the open to work in factories. 293 said they had 'no paid occupation' before, but some of these would have been married women returning to work.[14] Armstrong Whitworth meanwhile discovered that amongst their 12,000 munitions workers 3,486 had come from home, 2,513 from service, and 1,158 from shopwork.[15] A small proportion of those 'from home' would have been middle class, but not many. These figures were fairly typical of the war industries, and are confirmed by a description written by a woman overseer for *Common Cause* in 1916:

> The examination branch is completely filled by women from the trained industrial classes, the domestic-servant class, and a great deal by married women. Let me tell of the professions of those I personally know. I can think of three fever nurses, two dressmakers trained at Debenham & Freebody's, a showroom woman from a very high-class millinery shop, two cooks, a lady's maid – all in good situations – a parlourmaid from a house in Cavendish Square, two sisters who kept a boarding house with their mother but find it more lucrative to be at the Arsenal, a waitress, a laundry-maid who has been at one place for fifteen years, several clerks, two or three married women with no children, and several more with children of school age . . .[16]

The largest increases were seen in the chemical and engineering trades which made up the munitions industry; here

4 Group portrait of four Birmingham munition workers

women numbered about one million in 1918. They were employed in vast numbers by the national filling factories. For example, Gretna had 10,867 women working there in 1917, 5,000–6,000 of them living in hostels on site, while Woolwich Arsenal, which employed virtually no women before the war, had 9,484 in 1916, and 24,719 by December 1917, working in an industrial complex $3\frac{1}{2}$ miles wide and $2\frac{1}{2}$ miles long.[17] The proportion of women in the national shell factories rose from 13 per cent in 1914 to 73 per cent in July 1917, before starting to tail off in the last year of the war.[18] Here women eventually did almost every job available, making and filling shells and cartridges, labouring, cleaning, catering, driving, and storeroom keeping. Much work in munitions was 'repetition work', and women were largely on automatic or semi-automatic machines. But they did also learn some skills in engineering, which included the production of many kinds of weapons, and although they were frequently only taught part of a job, and never had the chance to become all-round engineers, their skill should not be underestimated. They also became valuable workers in the rapidly expanding optical instrument industry (now the nation could no longer use German and Swiss suppliers), and in the aircraft industry, where they were used as carpenters and needlewomen.

Numbers in other areas of industry were smaller, but nevertheless significant. In commerce, women numbered 496,000 in 1914, and 820,000 in 1917; in banking and finance, there were only 9,000 women in 1914, and 63,000 in 1917; in the civil service, the rise was from 65,000 to 163,000.[19] Much of this work was clerical, and women had been moving into this area before the war. It is depressing to see that one bank manager questioned in 1915 reported that women were not trusted with confidential information,[20] although as time went on, women were given more to do, and there was some opportunity for educated women to take responsibility. But for the majority of women, the work was mundane; the increase in job opportunities did not mean that the jobs themselves were interesting. The same was true of the work in post offices and shops throughout the country, where numbers also rose.

There were more varied jobs in transport. Women were taken on in large numbers as bus conductors, ticket collectors,

5 A group portrait of some of the women gas fitters in Southampton

6 Frances Stockdale, former domestic servant, who was an Ordnance Survey
worker in France during the war

porters, carriage cleaners, and, eventually, bus drivers (though never train drivers). The Great Central Railways reported that only 417 women were employed in 1914, and 5,434 by 1917.[21] Overall, the number of women working on the railways shot up from 9,000 to 50,000. Similarly, the number of women working for the London General Omnibus Company rose from 226 to 2,832, and they were used as conductresses all over the country.

Women also spread into 'men's work' in many other trades, including those like the cotton trade, which was actually depressed by the war. In the pottery trade, tailoring, food processing, boot and shoe, and leather, they learned parts of men's skilled work; they worked in shipbuilding, as crane drivers, labourers, plumbers, electricians and carpenters; they worked again as surface labourers in mining areas which had banned their labour years before, and became gas fitters and foundry workers for the gas and coke companies. Throughout industry, they took on clerical work and van-driving, even being entrusted with the horse-drawn vans of the Royal Mail. Here they worked a 72-hour week, and it was said that they not only spoiled their animals, but that they were excellent at running the home for sick horses![22] They did not do exceptionally heavy labouring, or work underground, however.

The vast army also spawned its own particular service industries. Women carpenters built 37,000 huts in France for those behind the front lines. As professional nurses and doctors (including Elsie Inglis, eventually) turned their attention to the wounded at home and abroad, they were supported by thousands of VADs (members of the Voluntary Aid Detachment, under the auspices of the Red Cross), who took on domestic work and basic nursing. In addition, from 1917 onwards, the Women's Army Auxiliary Corps (the WAACs) did much of the cooking, cleaning, clerical work, typing and driving for the army. These women were provided with uniforms, and even posted to France, but their work was very much 'traditional' female labour, and there was no question of them taking part in the conflict. Figures rose to a maximum of 40,000 in November 1918, with 8,500 abroad, and there were also smaller numbers of women in the WRNS and the Women's Royal Auxiliary Airforce, who did similar tasks, though the WRNS also did more interesting work like coding and de-coding, as well as working as electricians and tele-graphists.[23]

Also in uniform were the women of the Land Army. Many rural labourers joined up in the early months of the war, and farmers were short of workers – a problem as the need for increased food production became urgent during Germany's blockage of ports. In 1915, the Board of Agriculture set up Women's War Agricultural Committees, to organise recruit-ment, and in February 1916 the Women's Land Service Corps was founded. Agricultural Colleges ran short courses, and some special training centres were set up. In 1917, the Corps was succeeded by the Land Army, whose uniformed members were supposed to be a well-trained force, mobile enough to be moved around the country to those areas most in need of them. The idea of such work was very popular with many middle-class women, and there were 40,000 applicants within 2 months (of whom only 5,000 were chosen, although numbers later increased to 23,000). By far the largest number went into dairying or general field work; a few took up ploughing, thatching and shepherding.[24]

The women's police also had a distinctly upper-middle-class image. Although numbers here were small (only 617 in the Women's Patrols in 1917),[25] this marked the beginning of women's entry into the police force. The Women's Police Service was used by local authorities and factory owners to check passes, search workers for dangerous items like matches in areas dealing with explosives, and generally police women outside factories and hostels. They were paid out of a private fund, and worked alongside their male counterparts, but had special responsibility for anything to do with women and children.[26] The Women's Patrols were made up of volunteers, and policed the streets and parks in towns near military camps, hoping to deter prostitutes, and stop young women from hanging around waiting to meet soldiers.

In this way, women spread through large areas of employ-ment previously barred to them, and took up the work offered with alacrity. Such was the popularity of the new jobs that traditional employers lost women to munitions, transport and other 'war work' which offered better money and more interesting work. The Rochdale cotton manufacturers in 1915,[27] and the London dressmakers in 1916,[28] alike increased

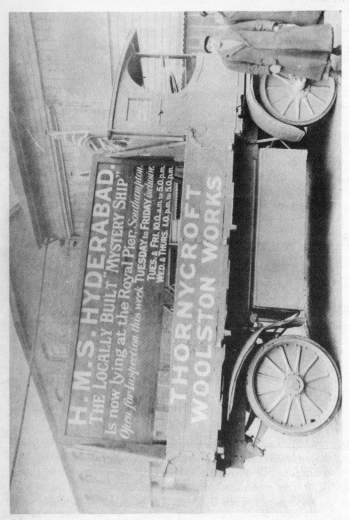

7 Women van drivers at Thorneycrofts, Southampton

wages and tried to lure women back into their old jobs – with little success.

THE MEN'S REACTION

As thousands of women were moving into war work, and were seen to be 'doing their bit' to keep the country going, they were heaped with praise by the press. Articles were often patronising and lightweight, as many writers were more interested in how pretty their subjects were than in the nature of the work. Such descriptions as the following, from the *Daily Mail* give some idea of the tone:

> Overalled, leather-aproned, capped and goggled – displaying nevertheless the woman's genius for making herself attractive in whatsoever working guise – some 18 women are being trained in the Nottinghill Gate workshops of the Women's Service Bureau . . .[29]

This article must have been galling enough at the time to those feminists who ran this particular workshop for training skilled women welders! As the writers of the 1916 Factory Inspector's report so scathingly said:

> It is permissible to wonder whether some of the surprise and admiration freely expressed in many quarters over new proofs of women's physical capacity and endurance, is not in part attributable to lack of knowledge or appreciation of the very heavy and strenuous nature of much of normal pre-war work for women, domestic and industrial.[30]

Most male workers however, did not share this enthusiasm, and many trade unions did their best to keep women out. A few examples will show the kind of attitudes women were up against.[31] The engineers' union, the ASE, was forced to accept women into men's work by the terms of dilution, but remained hostile to their use, and refused to allow them into the union beside men. Their journal told members about one triumphant victory by the Leeds branch in March 1917. There, the men had objected to the use of women working on trams (as engineers, not conductors), and demanded equal pay for them. Instead, employers removed women from the work in question, and the journal reported that 'this was more satisfactory than any award could have been.'[32]

Many men on the railways viewed women with resentment when they were brought in on the 'easier' parts of manual labour, and in particular were annoyed at the number of women who took up ticket-collecting, since this was seen as a 'soft option', and a good path to promotion.[33] Also in the field of transport, the Amalgamated Associaton of Tramway and Vehicle Workers attempted to resist the incursion of women drivers – 'on the grounds that it is highly injurious to women and threatened the welfare of future generations, while in many districts driving by women was a danger to the public.'[34] They successfully passed a resolution at the TUC in 1916, asking the Home Secretary to revoke the licenses of women conductors as soon as the war ended – '. . . so that the men can resume their work and the women can find better work elsewhere, under conditions that will not be harmful to their moral welfare.' Similarly, Liverpool dockers took action to remove women labourers in 1916 (this was seen as a triumph of labour against capitalism), and the Yorkshire miners strongly resisted the use of women as 'pitbrow' workers in their area on the grounds that 'we think a woman's place is in the home, looking after house, husband and family . . . .'[35] The spinners of Preston did their best to keep women out of their mulespinning rooms, even while other areas of Lancashire were accepting them, claiming that conditions meant that 'it is not a suitable occupation for young girls and women'.[36] In other trades, like tailoring and leatherworking, women were successfully kept off certain processes.

Concern for the health and welfare of the mothers of the working class was often given as a reason for excluding women from hot, heavy or dangerous work, and probably there were those who quite genuinely believed some kinds of work were bad for women. However, there were other reasons for men's hostility. Agreements over women's pay were inadequate, even in the engineering trades, particularly as the nature of 'skilled work' remained murky. Men were therefore worried that they would be displaced by cheaper female labour after the war, and it was all too true that women's wages were nearly always

8 Women workers in the coal yards of Southampton docks. They are still wearing skirts, though many coal delivery women wore trousers.
(Courtesy of Mr John Horne)

lower than men's. Only if it could be proved that women were doing the work of a fully skilled tradesman were they given equal piece- and time-rates in engineering. Good money could be earned by women on skilled or dangerous work – the highest wages for women in Woolwich Arsenal in 1917 were £6, for boring and screwing, or £6 6s as a tool-setter in the fuse factories, but these were not typical.[37] Elswhere in munitions, they were supposedly paid equal piece-rates on 'men's work', and were guaranteed a minimum wage of £1 (later 24s) for a 48-hour week on time-rate by the terms of the government circular L2. But the whole system was open to abuse, and many employers went to great lengths to prove that women were actually doing 'women's work' once processes were altered, or to stop money from women's pay packets for a succession of reasons. One article in the *Engineer*, the employers' trade magazine was much-quoted at the time, and showed why the men were much concerned about their future jobs and wages. The author began by explaining that women did not seek permanent jobs in industry, for 'the prospect to which a man looks forward is to earn enough money to keep a wife; the prospect to which a woman looks forward is that *he* may succeed.' This meant, he continued, that women were difficult to organise into trade unions, and if they could be persuaded to see sense they could defy those unions and stay in the industry. Women were a poor investment if they went through apprenticeship, and then left to marry, but as casual labourers on sophisticated machinery, they were very valuable. Existing wages were high because they were based on the false assumption that long training was required. Women and youths could take over from the skilled tradesman, at cheaper rates, as 'the fact of the matter is really, not that women are paid too little – or much too little – but that men are paid too much for work which can be done without previous training.'[38]

Fears were shared by men in other industries, where women were nearly always paid less; even when they had an equal basic rate, they usually had a lower war bonus. This was common in the transport industry. Similarly, they were paid less in clerical and white-collar trades. The government did not set a good example here, as it insisted on paying its female clerks not only less than the men (respectively 20–25s as opposed to 20–40s), but less than they could earn in private industry, where women earned 20–40s on very similar work.[39]

In spite of the competition from war industries, pay-rates in the standard women's trades remained low; for example there were complaints that a Belfast cotton mill paid women only 10s 6d for a 55½-hour week, while the women's rate on hand-grenade making was only 2¼d an hour, lower than that set by the Trade Board for tin-box-making, a sweated industry, and Pirelli's Cable Works in Southampton were paying a mere 1¾d an hour![40] Sylvia Pankhurst reported wages as low as 1s 8d for inserting 400 eyelet holes in a soldier's kitbag – which was outwork – giving one woman the grand sum of 5s 7d for a 47-hour week.[41] But although it was clear that women's usual low status helped depress wages in any other industry they entered, most unions were only interested in women's wages when there was a danger that they might undercut men. (The National Federation of Women Workers and the Workers Union, organised respectively for women and non-skilled workers were exceptions to this for obvious reasons.) Men's unions were, however, quite prepared to back women with strike action if their own careers were affected. When women transport workers struck for equal 'war bonus' in August 1918, they were supported by one of the main unions, and it was freely acknowledged by these men that the struggle was for men's security as well, since women were highly satisfactory as bus and tram conductors, and were likely to be kept on after the war if their labour was cheaper. Throughout the war, skilled men faced a dilemma. On the one hand, they wanted women to have equal pay for their own safety. On the other, they resented women earning good money, and particularly disliked married women earning high wages, as it was felt that they should be suported by their husbands, or did not 'need' good wages. They saw the solution as being the removal of women from their particular trades.

Ironically, although they were often earning less than men, women were in general pleased with the wages on offer, which were often higher than anything they could have earned before the war. Women's average pay in 1914 was 13s 6d a week; by the end of the war it was 30–35s.[42] Although these figures disguise many variations between industries, and inflation swallowed up some of the increase, there was still a real improvement in women's wages.

9   This group of WRAFS at Northam, Southampton, dismantled damaged aircraft

But although economic reasons played their part in women's unpopularity, there were other causes too. It was hard for skilled men to believe that women could do similar work, after they had spent their lives accepting the current view of women as careless, temporary workers; Barbara Drake, a contemporary writer on women in engineering reported that when men were shown some highly accurate pieces of workmanship they at first refused to believe that women had done the work.[43] In addition, from 1916 onwards, women were increasingly used to 'free' men for the army. Skilled men (much to the anger of general unions) evaded conscription for most of the war, but as women learned new jobs these men lost their privileged position. No wonder they resented women.

Ironically, many employers were not that keen on employing women either, and had to be persuaded by the Ministry of Munitions to experiment with their labour. Their views of women's work were mixed, depending on the nature of the work and their own prejudices about women's capabilities. As one writer said at the time:

> Opinions expressed on women who were replacing men vary
> so greatly that it is a temptation to state that women's
> success depends on the skill with which suitable women are
> selected, and the type of management under which they are
> placed.[44]

Throughout the war, there were debates on how 'successful' women's work was. This may seem a meaningless argument, as women's labour certainly kept the country going, but it was important for the current pay debates, and for women's future. Employers who claimed women's work was less successful than men's could pay them less. At the same time, if their performance was good enough to be profitable, they might find themselves kept on after the war.

While it was commonly agreed that women did not do very well on exceptionally heavy work, where if they were used at all they replaced a smaller number of men (for example, 5 women might do the work formerly done by 4 men), on almost every other aspect of their work there were disagreements. A report on employers' attitudes in the early part of the war showed that women were rated lower on initiative, self-reliance and ambition. They were, however, said to be more conscientious than men, while there were very mixed views on concentration and accuracy.[45] Quite simply, different firms allowed women a varying amount of training, supervision and responsibility. The report mentioned above is a catalogue of prejudice. In the heavy-metal trades of Sheffield, for example, it was reported that:

> In no case in this group of industries were women found taking the place of managers or foremen, although in certain works they are employed as chargehands; an official of one works which had experimented with forewomen gave his opinion that 'women are useless except under male supervision; women will not be "bossed" by other women.'[46]

Liverpool had no women on skilled work except in the munitions industry, under male supervisors; in Leeds many employers would not let women set their own tools, and while there were some favourable reports of them, 6 firms in particular had their doubts . . .

> . . . in one it was frankly said that women's work was very expensive, that they were not nearly as good as men, and were quite unskilled: in this case, a small number of women were employed among a considerable number of men, no special supervision arrangements were made, and the firm seemed to accept the idea that women could not be expected to be as good as men as an established fact and to consider their employment as a temporary expedient to be treated with good-natured tolerance; no attempt was made to train them or give them an interest in their work.[47]

Of course the amount of training also varied from firm to firm, and the government never took this over completely, although it did set up 9 instructional factories and workshops, and 40 schools for engineers. For most women in munitions, and all women in other trades, training was on the job, and they often had to pick up what they could with indifferent supervision.

Opinions on time-keeping were mixed too. Some employers said that women were worse than men, while others accepted that wartime strain led to higher rates of sickness, and domestic work inevitably led to absenteeism. Thus one manager from Woolwich Arsenal, having described women's 12-hour working day, and commented on the long travelling distances to work, wrote:

> This, coupled with home difficulties such as the care of children, shopping, cleaning, etc., renders the lot of many women an extremely difficult one, and an average loss of attendance only 50% in excess of the male employees, must, in such circumstances be considered good.[48]

This was a realistic view.

Whenever possible, as we have seen, employers used the fact that women were traditionally low-paid to reduce wages, even if women were doing 'men's work'. This was partly to increase profits, of course, but once again there was another dimension. Many employers and managers shared their own workmen's opinions, and thought that women did not need high wages, and should not expect them. Such views are typified by the words of one employer, when questioned by the Women's Service Bureau about why the women they had trained were getting less money than the men they worked beside – 'If I paid these women on piece work they would earn £3 a week and the men would not like it. Some of them have incomes, and £1 should suit them nicely.'[49] The awful thing is that the manager was probably right about the men's possible response. It was this very issue which divided the two vehicle workers' unions during the 1918 strike for equal pay. One, as already mentioned, supported women's claim, as they did not want to be undercut. The other did not, because members felt that the women were earning quite enough already, given widows' pensions or separation allowances.

Employers were in complete agreement about the success of women on repetition work, however. Although some criticised women for their lack of ambition and initiative, it was this very 'docility', as it was termed, which appealed to those who wanted a workforce which was both willing and able, and very tolerant of boredom. As a result, women were in fact little threat to the truly skilled tradesmen, as employers still preferred to use men on responsible work, and would go back to using them once the war was over. In other trades, the future was mapped out: there would be a struggle for work in some areas where men and women's performance was very similar, like transport, unless the men's unions were strong enough to expel women after the war. And there were some jobs which men would leave to women with little fuss, like factory work on automatic machines. Clerical work, semi-skilled work in factories, shop work, and professional jobs lay in a grey area, where the post-war future was hard to predict.

CHAPTER 4

WAR WORK

THE RESPONSE TO WAR

The last chapter showed how women across the country moved into war work. In this, and the following chapters, we go on to look at the experiences of individual women as workers. Their descriptions come from memoirs of the time, and the recent interviews made by the Imperial War Museum and the Southampton Museum oral history projects.

In the Second World War, women were to be conscripted into industry or the forces; in the First World War they had some kind of choice. What made them flock in thousands to the munitions factories and transport companies? Money was one obvious answer, and it was true that women's wages on 'men's work' remained much higher than those earned on 'women's trades'. Lilian Miles, then a 17-year-old from Exeter, remembered that she and her friends saw posters up asking for workers, and a whole group of them travelled up to Coventry together: 'Well, I think we really came because we thought we were going to get big money, which we were very disappointed over.' She and her sister had a nasty shock. On 30s a week, they discovered that after paying for their hostel and food they had each had 4½d left 'And the second week it was almost as bad. But we skimped on the food. We didn't have as many [food] tickets. So we did get a bit more pocket money . . .'[1]

She was not the only one to travel hundreds of miles in the hope of good wages. Others came to England from Scotland, Wales and Ireland, like Isabella Clarke, from Belfast. At the age of 16 she went into a filling factory, choosing this work because it paid the best money.[2] Throughout the war, women were rumoured to be earning fantastically high wages. These, as one warworker said, tended to 'melt away' on examination. Having described wages in her own factory at the beginning of the war (between 15s and 19s 6d basic, plus bonuses), Monica Cosens, a middle-class volunteer, went on to write:

> All this makes it difficult to believe that the preposterously high wages sometimes quoted as being earned by 'munitions hands' exist. Whether there is any foundation for these reports I cannot say, but I have never been able to discover any girl worker whose wage could be regarded as excessive . . . [3]

But to many women, who had been used to the low pay of dressmaking or domestic service, even those tolerable wages seemed more than adequate, and those on higher wages were delighted. As one Southampton woman, who had worked at the government rolling mills there, recalled – '£3 a week and . . . we thought we were the richest people in Southampton.'[4] With overtime, she earned £4 – ' 'Course that was joy. We could go out on the town on that.' Throughout the war there remained great contrasts in women's wages. Current rates in the sugar, confectionery and food processing trades were around 13s a week at this time, and any munitions worker would earn considerably better pay than that. However, there was more to war work than money.

For many women, the war offered the chance to escape – from home, or from hated jobs. Lily Truphet, for example, was a housemaid on 5s a week, working for an unpleasant employer (who used to weigh the vacuum cleaner bag to see if she'd done a good enough job), and she went to Woolwich Arsenal for both the money and the freedom. Many others left service with great relief.[5] Florence Thompson had been a weaver, while her mother was a charwoman; both of them threw up these traditional female jobs to go and work in the same factory. Looking back, Lilian Miles saw the war itself as useless, but for herself, it was 'like being let out of a cage'.[6]

Others spoke of the need to do something for the war effort. Working-class women obviously needed paid work anyway, but a number of those interviewed said they went into munitions particularly to help the troops. This was one of Elsie Farlow's reasons for moving from weaving to munitions – she

10 Women crane drivers (with one man, perhaps their supervisor) at the government rolling mills near Southampton

11 Southampton crane driver, complete with breeches and soft hat.

thought it was the 'right thing to do' – and Mrs Hunt's reasons for leaving shop work to become a crane driver.[7] Dorothy Haigh, who worked at the same rolling mills, also mentioned this feeling: she was married, with a baby to look after – but the money was needed, and she felt she was 'doing her bit'.[8] Certainly many girls in their teens accepted the risks of munitions work not only because they did not really understand the full danger (as they now admit), but out of a sense of patriotism. As Caroline Rennles said, rather self-mockingly, 'Oh, I wanted to die for my country then, you know . . .'[9]

L.K. Yates, writer of a fine piece of wartime propaganda, *The Woman's Part*, talked of the motives expressed by some of the women in one workshop, and these were probably fairly typical: a woman toolsetter (skilled worker) from a military factory was working for the war effort; the mother of 7 sons in the army took pride in doing her own kind of work for the war; the stewardess from a torpedoed boat worked out of hatred for the Germans; and one wife had taken over her husband's job while he went to the Front.[10] These women would have worked amongst many others with less clear motives but the others too were spurred to hard work by the thought that any munitions shortage would affect the fighting men badly.

Middle-class women did not have the same financial needs, but some excelled in patriotic fervour. They were encouraged to work by the mood which gripped the country in the first few months of war – and as war charities mushroomed, if they did not care for paid work, they could knit socks, collect food, or raise money for war orphans. Caroline Playne, in her social history of the time, wrote:

> It became almost a disgrace to be found at home, it required
> some justifying explanation. It was up to you to show that
> you were a patriotic worker all the time. It was a great
> satisfaction to one elderly lady when a business man allowed
> her to come into his office in the City daily and do her sock-
> knitting there.[11]

The press reinforced these feelings. Naomi Loughnan, a well-to-do volunteer, wrote of how

The papers spoke of shells and tool-setters, of enormous

wages and cheery canteens, happy hostels and gay girl-workers . . . We were sick of frivolling, we wanted to do something big and hard, because of our boys, and of England.[12]

Journalists waged an unofficial recruitment drive, while the government too used the daily press to advertise for women workers. During 1916–17 the munitions industry faced something of a labour shortage, and then articles appeared describing 'the attractive life you will lead if you become a munitionette',[13] while adverts appealed to women's patriotism:

30,000 women wanted at once.
3 Questions to the women of England.
1. Do you realize that an additional 30,000 women are urgently wanted for the national filling factories?
2. Do you realize that every woman who works in these factories is helping to win the War and to save the lives of our soldiers?
3. Will *you* not come forward at once and take your part in this great national work?

Munitions work was undeniably fashionable – upper-class women did *not* go and clean railway carriages, enter the spinning rooms of Lancashire, or sweep the streets – and it was also seen as something of a challenge. *The Lady* told its readers that 'a very fascinating occupation for educated women, whose trained intelligence inspires deft fingers, is to be engaged in aeroplane engine work'.[15] Educated women did heed the call. Monica Cosens began her 1917 book with the words: 'Oh! I wanted – wanted more than anything else in the world to become a "Miss Tommy Atkins" in Lloyd George's Army of Shell-Workers.' A.K. Foxwell, in *Munition Lasses*, talked of her joy in taking part in real war work, 'shorn of comfort, luxury or indulgence'.[16] Naomi Loughnan assured her readers that

Though we munition workers sacrifice our ease we gain a life worth living. Our long days are filled with interest, and with the zest of doing work for our country in the grand cause of freedom.[17]

although this did not stop her saying how boring the fool-proof nature of the machines made such work, a few pages later! All

12 Munition workers, wearing overalls, and badges which identified their
work area (Courtesy of Pippa Richardson)

these contemporary accounts could be seen as mere propaganda – and some women interviewed since have certainly said they joined up just because their friends did; this was Mrs Emerson's reason for becoming a VAD (and she also liked the uniform!).[18] But feelings did run high during the war, and it would be a mistake to assume that many of these women did not mean what they said. Joan Williams' unpublished typescript held by the Imperial War Museum describes how the hardship she endured made her feel that she was doing something real for her country, and others shared this feeling.[19] Others said they enjoyed their work, but that this was partly because they really did think that they were supporting the war to end wars. Sybil Morrison, a pacifist who supported conscientious objectors, remembered that in the early months of 1914, before she threw up her war work, 'It all seemed so much more romantic to be told that you were fighting for the cause – to end all wars.'[20]

Taken to extreme, patriotism became jingoism. Not many women handed out white feathers to men they thought should be in the army, but it did happen, and sometimes feelings of hatred against the Germans were equally chilling. The words of Mrs Humphrey Ward in a piece of wartime propaganda now seem disturbing; in a munitions factory, 'I speak to two educated women, who turn out to be High School mistresses from a town that has been several times visited by Zeppelins. "We just felt we must come and help kill Germans," they say quietly . . .',[21] while the memories of a VAD, who found life in a hospital 'the happiest time I ever spent' also jar. To her, 'it was all so worth while. The men who suffered did so because of their wonderful heroism, not just because they had caught a cold and it had turned into pneumonia or because they had been run over in the street.'[22]

Many women found that, as the war progressed, it became more and more heartbreaking to see young men in uniform going off to fight. One woman told Mrs C.S. Peel:

> I was coming home after a holiday. The time of my train was altered, and I waited, sitting on the platform watching trains full of soldiers going past. Suddenly I felt the tears come . . . all those men . . . those boys . . . one could not bear it . . . .[23]

Awareness of their part in war made some women think very

carefully about the implications of the work they did. Peggy Hamilton, from a prosperous middle-class background, who went into engineering, discovered that munitions work troubled her conscience. Her own friends were dying at the Front, yet she was helping make shells to kill other men.[24] An unsigned typescript, written by another munitions worker, showed that working-class women too shared these feelings. She wrote:

> So on the whole my experience, such as it has been, in a munition factory has been a bright and happy one. Only for the fact that I am using my lifes (sic) energy to destroy human souls, gets on my nerves. Yet on the other hand, I am doing what I can to bring this horrible affair to an end.[25]

Not everyone could reconcile their work with their conscience, however. Sybil Morrison was an ambulance driver in London in the first few months of war, but was not happy – 'I did feel I was taking the place of a man to go and kill and be killed . . .' In the end, she was so appalled to see the crowds laughing and cheering as a German Zeppelin came down in flames – with the loss of the crew – that she decided she could no longer do anything to support the war, and left her job.[26] Others decided to do all they possibly could to help the men who were suffering. Mairi Chisholm and Elsie Knocker became part of an ambulance team at the Front. Once there, they realised that men were dying out in No-Man's Land, far from help, and decided that they could only save them by venturing out themselves. They lived in a shelled house, and carried back wounded men to their ambulance after each battle. Wounded twice, they only gave up after being severely gassed.[27] Another VAD wrote of her feelings, nursing the wounded day after day:

> The terrible suffering of some of those I nursed added to my exhaustion. I think the uncomplaining bravery of the men made it all the more heart-breaking. Probably had I been trained I could have endured it better, for after a time if one is to do one's work one is forced to become less sensitive. I look back on that time with such a loathing of war that remembrance becomes almost a physical pain.[28]

But certainly the worst side of the war passed by many other young women. Strange though it may seem, there were plenty of people who had neither close friends nor relations at the

Front, and could throw themselves into work without thinking too much about the conflict. To quote one woman, Mrs Nightingale, 'It was fun to us to be in munitions.' She took up work in 1914, at the age of 17, and only realised the horror of war when she saw the first wounded soldiers returning.[29]

WORK AND PLAY

What did women like about their wartime work? It should be obvious by now that many of them were delighted with the money, even if most of it went on hostels, lodging or straight to their mothers – in Isabella Clarke's case she regularly sent not only £1 a week to her mother in Belfast, but 5s to her grandmother as well.[30] Most of the women interviewed by the Imperial War Museum in the 1970s, and Southampton Museum in the 1980s, said they liked the money.[31] Although we have seen that many homeworkers were still on appallingly low wages, even those in some of the standard women's trades earned good money – a khaki worker in the East End remembered taking home as much as £2 5s a week, with compulsory overtime, very high wages for the clothing trade.[32] Others put up with indifferent wages not only out of a sense of patriotism, but because they liked the atmosphere of the factories they worked in. For this reason, Dorothy Haigh, an engineer, stayed where she was for most of the war,[33] while Peggy Hamilton, although bored by her first job at Woolwich, where she was doing dull and repetitive work, was pleased with the fact that she was working on an equal footing with so many other workers – 'I felt a curious satisfaction and happiness in being just an ordinary worker pushing my way through the gates with hundreds of others.'[34]

Other middle-class volunteers too were struck by this feeling.[35] Women talked recently of how they were 'happy then', and, as Jane Cox (a needlewoman) said, the war 'allowed women to stand on their own feet. It was the turning point for women.'[36] There was also a feeling of freedom and self-discovery, as women broke away from their old jobs. An ex-servant, interviewed by Common Cause in 1915, told how she

13 The four Grinter sisters, who all joined the Land Army together. They are
dressed in the standard uniform of overalls, breeches, gaiters and soft hats

liked the freedom and fresh air of road-sweeping; this contrasted with her pre-war life when she had to take in washing to supplement her husband's low wages.[37] Mrs Marsh, in the Land Army, said she loved the work and the fresh air,[38] and a woman gas fitter said that these were the happiest years of her single life. Annie Edwards' memories of the summer of 1916 seem to sum up these feelings. She too was in the Land Army, and while harvesting that year found her stays becoming hot and uncomfortable – in spite of wearing breeches, she had still worn a corset up until then:

> . . . when I put the horses in the stable at twelve o'clock I went up in the cake loft and I took them [the stays] off. And close to the farm there was an outside lavatory, you know, where they was emptied every third year or something. They put it on the land for manure. Well, I went and folded them and took them there. And from that day to this I never wore anything at all.[39]

For middle-class women there was also the feeling of seeing life in the raw. A VAD told the historian Mrs C.S. Peel:

> When I was VAD-ing I began in a small country hospital. I was nineteen, very carefully brought up and severely chaperoned. So you imagine that the war seemed to open a new world to me. I passed suddenly from being the kind of girl I was to being a little person who spent her time in hospital freeing from lice the uniforms of the soldiers who were brought in![40]

L.K. Yates reported another kind of discovery made by a woman who had taken over her husband's old job in a munitions factory. He had always complained that the work was very hard, and at home she had catered for his every need:

> At the end of a week she surmised that the task was not so hard as she contemplated; after a month had passed she realized the position. The job had been a capital excuse to secure forgiveness for domestic shortcomings. The wife awaits her husband's return with a certain grim humour.[41]

Women were also pleased with the new skills they learned. Many had to overcome an initial fear of machinery. Elsa Thomas, later an overlooker, reported that when she first arrived for training she was afraid she would never be able to learn the job.[42] Monica Cosens described her trepidation when first let loose on a lathe:

> I did not feel confident to manage that big machine. As long as the shell revolved and the tool continued to cut the rusty coating, leaving it bright and shining beneath, and I could stand and watch it, all was well. But what was going to happen when it came to the end and I had to do something?
>
> The moment to act arrived. Nervously I stretched up my arm to push back the wooden lever.
>
> The machine stopped. It was wonderful. And I had done it. I had gained confidence.[43]

This was quite easy work, but people like Dorothy Poole became skilled engineers, setting their own machines and tool-making,[44] as did Peggy Hamilton, who was trained at a Ministry of Munitions Centre in Birmingham before being dispatched to Southampton. By 1917, she was operating a Churchill grinder, which required a very high degree of accuracy.[45] Mrs Bryant, who worked on a milling machine, remembered it was 'really lovely', and said, 'It was very interesting work, I liked it'.[46] Isabella Clarke, working at the Coventry ordnance factory, performed 'skilled work' and asked for equal pay, 'and they said "no, . . . you can't grind your own tools" '. However, her inspector said he could teach her this in a week. He duly did so, and she found herself making Howitzers. She joined no societies in the factory as she was too involved in her work. Asked whether she enjoyed it, she replied, 'Yes, every minute of it. It was a very happy time and well, everything was very happy, the atmosphere in work and with the people you worked with . . .'.[47]

One group of fully organised, skilled women workers came out of the war – the women welders, trained by the Women's Service Bureau. Snubbed by the ASE, they founded their own society, and fought for skilled status, hoping to carry on with the work after the war. The society had 500 members by 1918. But even those not classed as 'skilled' could be proud of their work. Sarah Pidgeon, who worked on a bottle-washing machine in the brewing trade, alongside women who took on all the physical labour of loading and unloading barrels in the yard, could say when interviewed recently, 'It was real good what we done in that war . . .'[48] Women were increasingly aware of the fact that they were keeping the nation going.

Social life was also important to many, particularly munition workers, who needed to unwind after long hours of tense or repetitive work. Many still remember how they enjoyed going out together, dancing or to the new cinemas, or music hall. Young women spent most of their spare money on clothes, dancing and the pictures (where they could see the Keystone Cops, Chaplin or Mary Pickford, as well as the propaganda films produced by the government) as the women interviewed recently testified![49] A number also commented on how well everyone seemed to get on; as Elsie Farlow, who was one of only eight women in her workshop, said, 'we were all friends together', and they stayed friends after the war as well.[50] She also added that she would do the work again tomorrow if asked.

There was nothing new in factory workers going out together, but the war did provide more money for socialising, and bring larger groups of women together than had been usual in many parts of the country. The need to unwind was probably greater as well. But, contrary to belief at the time, these women still did not go into pubs on their own, and indeed some of them did not go into pubs at all. The changes in social life for wealthier young women were probably more dramatic, as chaperones disappeared, night clubs became more popular, restaurants in the centre of towns were frequented by women clerks out for lunch, and those at work away from home had to get used to life in hostels or lodgings.

Dances were frequently held in the bigger munition factories or hostels, and women were allowed to invite 'a friend in khaki', according to one Woolwich overlooker.[51] It was recognised that musical evenings, singing, dancing and some drinking actually helped keep workers (male and female) happy. Another occasion for relaxation came at pay day, when there was a chance for women to hang around and chat, or go out together, while tea-time at the hostel provided nostalgic memories for some middle-class volunteers: 'The great hour of the day is teatime, when sundry groups gather around various fires and make toast, feeling as if college days had returned,'[52] although it reminded others more of boarding school![53] Buying new clothes went with social life, and Sarah Pidgeon could still,

50 years later, remember what outfits she had bought while earning good money as a bottle-washer, while Elsie McIntyre really did – as the press was always saying of munition workers – buy a fur coat. It was a white imitation fox fur, and it cost 12s 6d.[54]

Of course not everyone had the time or the energy for evenings out. Some were too tired, and others had domestic work to do in the evening. Women in their teens and early twenties had the time and money for such a social life, and this was largely because they were living with their parents or in hostels.

One other thing is very striking about women's memories of work, and that is the ease with which they changed jobs, even when the leaving certificate was still in operation. Many of them did three, or even four, different jobs during the war, while others moved between factories or areas. So, Margaret Adams was a VAD for 6 months, then a Land Girl, and then a van driver with Vickers.[55] Mrs Stephens exmained fuses, then worked on a capstan lathe in various factories, and finally became an airforce motorcyclist, which she loved. Mrs Castle worked on cordite, in a munitions factory, and then joined the WAACs, while, in contrast, Mrs Airey transferred from the Land Army to munitions.[56] Others moved between factory work, the post office and the transport companies. This mobility was quite unknown for women before the war, and goes a long way to explaining why so many found jobs they liked in the end. Their labour was actually in demand – a rare thing for women workers.

WOMEN AND MEN

Some women say how well they got on with their male supervisors or companions at work – Amy May and her female workmates liked their foreman, an elderly man, and had a relaxed enough relationship with him to make teasing and joking with him part of working life.[57] But others had less happy experiences, and faced the kind of prejudice described in the last chapter. When Mrs Stephens became an airforce motorcyclist, the men were not happy. As the only woman there for the first few months, it must have been hard; the male motorcyclists refused to speak to her. Eventually, they 'came round', and some other women were also taken on.[58] Mrs Mullins, a crane driver, remembered that the men at the rolling mills did not want women working there at all, but were obliged to accept them.[59] Once women were actually doing the work, the response varied. Naomi Loughnan's male companions apparently remained scornful, and stayed convinced that women knew nothing – questions about work were discouraged.[60] Others simply behaved badly to the women they worked with. Mrs Airey worked on the land, and the foreman always made sure he gave women the toughest jobs, like pulling up dock plants (which have particularly long roots). So much for chivalry![61] Occasionally, tension led to trouble. One woman, an aircraft worker, was sacked after a man spat tobacco juice in her pocket and she hit him – although the precise cause of this anti-social act is not given.[62]

Most of the hostility came from men's fears about the safety of their own jobs, a fear which many women recognised, and made allowances for. Having said that the men she worked with were 'not very sociable', Elsa Thomas (munitions) was asked if they were actually rude to her. 'Yes,' was the answer, 'They didn't want to show us their livelihood.'[63] Peggy Hamilton remembered that women doing skilled work were not at all popular in her factory, and recalled how one man, who had always been particularly unpleasant, apologised to her when he left, saying, 'I'm sorry I've been a brute to you all this time, but I've got my trade to think of. I've worked damned hard to get where I am, and I hate to see you girls coming in on it so easy.'[64] Dorothy Poole also reported men's hostility, though in her case this was almost certainly because she made her own anti-union views quite clear. Having complained that 'the shop was socialist to a man of the Bolshevist type with a large sprinkling of conscientious objectors and pro-Germans', she went on to write:

> Over and over again the foreman gave me wrong or
> incomplete directions and altered them in such a way as to
> give me hours more work. I took this to be deliberate at the
> time, though I believe now that it was habitual bad

management. I had no tools that I needed, and it was only on Saturdays that I could get to a shop. It was out of the question to borrow anything from the men. Two shop stewards informed me on the first day that they had no objection(!) to my working there provided I received the full men's rate of pay (1/3 an hour). But after this none of the men spoke to me for a long time, and would give me no help as to where to find things. My drawer was nailed up by the men, and oil was poured over everything in it through a crack another night. Had I been satisfied that my work was good I should have been content, but I felt I had not sufficient skill to hold my own against an antagonistic foreman and determined to give up . . .[65]

Isabella Clarke's experience was particularly interesting. As mentioned in the last section, she asked for equal pay, and was at first refused it, as she was not setting her own tools. While the inspector taught her this, only he and the overlooker would speak to her. All the other men avoided her, particularly as she was not a union member. But once she could set her own machine, she applied for equal pay once again, and got it – this time, when she entered the workshop, she was greeted enthusiastically by the men who had ignored her before: 'when I got the rate then of course the men made a bit of a noise with all their spanners and that.'[66] She went on to start a general union branch there herself. In this case, the men's antagonism disappeared once they realised she was really one of the workers, and not a blackleg, but matters were not always so simple. One woman writing to the *Trade Union Worker* in 1917 insisted that many of the men who complained most about women workers discouraged their own wives and daughters from joining trade unions themselves, 'whether it is that they do not like them to be independent, or from some other petty excuse, of course I do not know.'[67] The number of women in trade unions nevertheless more than trebled during the war. In 1914, women trade union members numbered 437,000, and by 1920 they had reached a peak of 1,342,000 – an astonishing rate of increase.[68] Most of them joined the NFWW (National Federation of Women Workers) or the Workers Union, as they were usually barred from skilled unions.

There was also cynicism about women's endurance or skill, and this too was encountered by a number of women. Annie Edwards, Land Army worker, learned how to plough well, and word soon got round:

> So, like, one farm hand from a different farm would go back and tell his boss what he heard at the pub about landgirls who ploughed. Two or three farmers wouldn't believe it. And they'd come on this farm and they'd see me doing it. And one patted me on the back. They said, 'It's really unbelievable . . . .'[69]

Mary Lees, also working on the land, meanwhile found it was her potential employer who viewed her with distrust. 'Old Tapp' had apparently avoided women since his wife died, and she found him waiting for her in the yard when she arrived:

> Still he didn't speak. I thought, well, what the hell's the matter with him. He handed me the sack and the shears. 'Now' he said 'go up the road, first gate on the left down over, under the hedge' he said 'you'll find an old ewe. Her's been dead three weeks. I want the wool.' So I thought, all right, try anything once, that's my motto. So I took them and I went down. And of course, the old sheep, I didn't need the shears. The body was bright blue. So I pulled off all the wool. And I set her up in the hedge. I can see her now with her feet sticking out like that. And I went back. And he was still standing there. I said 'Oh, Mr Tapp I didn't need the shears, because, you see, the wool really came out quite easily. I think perhaps I'd better have a spade hadn't I and bury her/it,' didn't know what it was. And do you know, he looked at me. 'Gor' he said 'you done it?' He said, 'I were testing you. Will you shake hands?'[70]

CLASS TENSIONS

It should be clear by now that the wartime workers were not a homogeneous group. The majority were young and working class, but there were significant numbers of older married women, and a smaller number of wealthier volunteers. L.K.

Yates, in her wartime hymn of praise to women's work, wrote lyrically of the new army of workers:

> They have come from the office and the shop, from domestic
> service and the dressmakers room, from the High Schools
> and the Colleges, and from the quietude of the stately homes
> of the leisured rich.[71]

This was one of the treasured myths of the war – the ready mixture of classes in the workshop. In fact, others estimated that only about 9 per cent of munition workers were upper- or middle-class volunteers,[72] most of these being skilled workers; and Caroline Rennles remembers only 2 wealthy women in her factory at Woolwich, the daughters of industrialists.[73] The proportion was much higher amongst VADs, the Land Army and the police volunteers.

There were bound to be some tensions as women from such different backgrounds came together in the factory. Monica Cosens warned her readers that the volunteer could not go into this situation thinking she could 'improve' the factory girl, and described an atmosphere of teasing, and a certain amount of rivalry; she also said that the lady volunteers were known throughout the factory as 'Miows', presumably because of their accents! She related one incident showing the sensitivity of both sides:

> One day in a lapse of thought a Volunteer provided herself
> with a newspaper on which to cover a greasy bench before
> she sat down upon it. This woman had gained the confidence
> of her neighbours, but for a few days it was shaken. If the
> bare bench was good enough for them it was good enough
> for her.[74]

In her hostel, groups of friends assembled according to the work they were in – the light gun factory, the shell shops, the clerical workers and the canteen helpers. These groups seemed to stick to themselves.

Class was also supposed to show itself in what people wore. As their wages rose, working-class munition workers bought smart clothes, and would not have dreamed of wearing their work clothes in the street – unlike the Land Girls, who took to wearing their breeches off duty as well, while, according to Mrs Peel, for the wealthy, shabby clothes became all the rage.

Monica Cosens, who once put her work cap on by mistake when she went home one evening, found herself the butt of much humour from the working-class girls who saw her.

Wealthy women often isolated themselves to a certain extent, perhaps partly as protection. How could any less-educated woman have broken into the little clique of which A.K. Foxwell became a member as soon as she arrived at her YWCA hostel?

> We had the good fortune to meet with kindred spirits on our arrival last September. A lady, well-known for her social charm, as well as her intrinsic merit, welcomed us and looked after our comfort with the geniality of a hospitable hostess and the sympathy and thought of a mother. We founded an Arts table. It included a niece of Thomas Carlyle, an artist, a sculptor, a writer or two, a niece of Lord Morley's, and later, a relative of Sir Oliver Lodge . . . .[75]

Such volunteers talked with great affection of the ordinary factory workers, but kept their distance socially.

There were also differences amongst the wealthier workers themselves, if Joan Williams is to be believed:

> You could sympathise with a working girl, solely dependent on her earnings, but when you saw a well-fed, well-dressed person, obviously all out for what she could make, while expecting all the kudos of a war worker you felt you could not have struck a more sordid job.[76]

She went on to add:

> I could quite understand the foremen preferring to have real working girls under them to the 'War-Workers', who were apt to make much more fuss when displeased and complain to the higher authorities, without being able to be frightened by any threat of dismissal.[77]

This very feature was commented on by Barbara Drake, a Fabian writer, as being a positive advantage:

> More than once, defective sanitary arrangements or similar abuses have been remedied by the firms owing to the spontaneous indignation and outspoken remonstrance of a middleclass woman.[78]

There was probably something to be said for this.

Occasionally, women found themselves on different sides according to skill as well. The women welders were skilled, and largely middle- or upper-class. When women bench-hands, members of a non-craft union, struck at an aviation works in 1918, for an extra 1d an hour, they found themselves without the support of either the women welders in the building, or the skilled male trade unionists. Not surprisingly, this caused much resentment.[79]

Those interviewing and recruiting women for munition jobs were themselves acutely aware of who was 'suitable' for what job. At Woolwich it was stated that assistant forewomen or principal overlookers should be teachers or university women; overlookers should be 'educated' women; charge hands were to be the most 'capable' of ordinary factory workers; workers on TNT should be reliable, steady and healthy, while shell girls should be strong and mechanically minded; gauging and inspecting should be done by 'refined' elderly women, and canteen work was meanwhile ideal for former charwomen.[80] A.K. Foxwell illustrates beautifully the kind of bias shown by those picking women for work. A middle-aged woman, who is described as a 'Sarah Gamp' type, a washerwoman for the previous eight years, turned up to ask for munitions work at Woolwich:

> A Welfare Worker will probably investigate her case. Such women, if they have merely been unfortunate, may be set to do some good work in scrubbing, and may settle down quite successfully under a firm and kind hand. They regain their self-respect in the knowledge of work honestly done with other workers for the same good end.[81]

Inevitably, in this sort of atmosphere there were prejudices amongst the workers themselves, as some trades in munitions were seen as more 'respectable' than others. Elsie McIntyre, charge hand and later overlooker at Barnbow, worked with TNT, and her skin turned yellow from contact with the poison. She remembered that the women in one of the other workshops would have nothing to do with her girls, so low was their status. They no doubt shared the views of Elsa Thomas, another overlooker in shell-making rather than filling, who never touched TNT, and said that none of her workers would have done such work – '... you must have been d......

hardup to turn yellow, mustn't you?'[82] While she thought the trolley girls were 'coarse', Frank Bradbury, an engineer, went so far as to call the cartridge women 'hooligans'. They reputedly pulled down men's trousers if anyone ventured in their workshops, and were quite unlike the 'respectable' women in the machine shops.[83] Sixty years later, he could still say with feeling that 'they were scum', while no doubt the TNT workers or cartridge girls found their critics bafflingly unfriendly.

So there remained barriers between groups, in spite of the firm friendships which were also made. Even in the midst of war, it was hard for women to escape from prejudice about their status inside and outside the workshops. In spite of the new opportunities, and the new sense of freedom, how far could women really climb out of their traditional role? It is a sobering thought that Laura Verity, a shopkeeper's daughter, gladly went into engineering instead of the classic woman's trade of weaving. But what she really wanted to be, as an intelligent girl in her early teens, was a doctor. This she never had the chance to try.[84]

CHAPTER 5

HEALTH AND WELFARE

CONDITIONS AT WORK

Although there were many things that women liked about their wartime work, this did not mean that life was easy. Against the excitement of new work or surroundings, and the satisfaction of higher wages, should be placed the additional hardship imposed by war. Many women were labouring under exceptional strain in munitions factories, shipyards or transport, and working conditions made a big difference to them. Life outside the factory too had its problems – problems with food or housing shortages and travel, on top of the normal burden of housekeeping, made life harder for most working-class women, while childcare remained difficult for working mothers, and the energy of women from all classes was sapped by anxiety about male friends or relations who had joined the forces. Nevertheless, it should be remembered that for many women life during wartime was no worse than it had been before 1914. For those who had barely survived on very low wages, or had been ground down by oppressive jobs, there were improvements in health and an increase in energy. As one Southampton woman recalled, she had broken down under the strain of life as a 16-year-old maid on 4s 2d a week before the war. 'There was no picking or choosing in those days,' she said, 'I really suffered.'[1] War work had to be better than this. And for those who continued to work in their pre-war trades, life in the factory often changed little during 1914–18, though they shared the travel or food problems of the war workers.

When considering women's health in the factory itself, the government and press of the day concentrated particularly on women munition workers, and to a lesser extent on women in 'men's trades' in general. It was true that here the longest hours were worked, and explosive or toxic materials were frequently used. But women in traditional trades also worked under considerable strain, and received little attention. Mrs Kilford, also interviewed recently by Southampton Museum, told her interviewer that she sewed on buttons for 4s 6d a week to begin with, leaving home at 6.45 in the morning, and getting home at 9.15pm. She later moved on to finishing work (still in the clothing industry), and earned better money, but she had no breaks during her long day except for the lunch hour.[2] Another Southampton woman worked as a delivery driver from 8am to 8pm for 6 days a week, for a mere 12s, cycling to work and back as well![3] In contrast, when she joined the WAAC, she earned £5 a week as a driver. A needlewoman interviewed by the Imperial War Museum recalled that they had no heating, no washrooms, and no medical facilities, while working long hours on uniforms,[4] and countless others across the country worked harder than ever in such mundane trades, arousing very little interest in their work or their health. Priority was given to the health of those whose efficiency at work was vital to munitions production. While the Health of Munitions Workers Committee, set up in 1915 to consider how to improve factory conditions – and hence munitions production, pored over plans for seating, canteens, rest breaks, etc., the writers of a book on the *Girl in Industry* could report that 'the majority of the employers in the clothing trade had never given any consideration to the effects of hours on the health of their operatives. Consequently they were vehement in declaring that a 52-hour week exerted no injurious influence.'[5]

Women munition workers were undeniably working in exceptional circumstances. The Factory Acts were waived for the war period, and they regularly worked night shifts and 6-day weeks. In the early part of the war, 8-hour shifts were rapidly replaced by those of 12 hours, although the government later encouraged the shorter hours again, as it became clear that workers' productivity dropped on the long shifts. Long shifts were usually unpopular, and Monica Cosens, in the book of her experiences as a munition worker, reported the views of her workmates who were appalled at the longer hours:

'I 'ate it! We gets more money, yes, but it's not worth it. An' they says if we gets off at seven we gets a long lovely evenin'. What's the use of a long lovely evenin' to us when we've been standing for 10 hours!'

'It's killin' me.'

'I never knew I 'ad legs. I feels them now.'

'It's too much for anyone. I wish somebody would stop it.'

'It's not too bad by day, but it's the twelve hours of nights that's finishin' us all.'[6]

Only one woman preferred it, because she could actually save £1 a week.

As for night work, ironically, Dr Janet Campbell, for the Health of Munition Workers Committee, reported that this was not that unpopular with women, as it gave them time to shop, earned them higher wages, and gave them longer weekends – which were no doubt used for housework.[7] Most women interviewed recently, by the Imperial War Museum and Southampton Museum, did not mind it too much – they accepted it as part of the job, and some even enjoyed it. Theoretically, overtime was limited to 7½ hours a week, and the total number of hours in a day to 14, including meal breaks, while girls under 16 were not allowed on night work. But a 73-hour week was not uncommon, and permits were readily granted for women's night work and Sunday labour. In engineering, shipbuilding and aircraft work, 11- or 12-hour shifts remained the norm throughout the war. Those on 8-hour shifts in munitions tended to work a 6-day week, plus one or two Sundays in every three.[8]

The experiences of the women who worked in these trades really speak for themselves. Joan Williams, a middle-class volunteer, tells how she used to get up at 5.20am, and start work at 7am. Her hours were 7–12, and 1–5.30pm, with no breaks, and continuous standing. Overtime from 6–8pm was voluntary at first, but later became compulsory. In the early months of the war, they had only one cold-water tap in the entire factory for washing. The work itself gave her inflamed eyes, from grit.[9] Rosina Wyatt, working in Luton, did a 70-hour week for only 30s, and suffered from TNT poisoning (which I shall describe later), an illness which it took her months to get over.[10] Dorothy Poole, at an aeroengine works in

London, also worked from 7 to 5.30, with 2 hours overtime, and reported that the factory was overcrowded, the food was awful, and the workshops were warmed only by buckets of coke – a hazard in themselves. Later, after conditions at this first factory had improved, she moved to another one, and was scathing about this one too:

> Cloakrooms were crowded, noisy, dirty and worse than dirty; the yard was impassable in wet weather and had to be bridged by planks; the tool room was close and badly lighted; the canteen was pandemonium; the food was unpalatable (but that I ate it I should say uneatable) and I could obtain rooms no nearer than 25 minutes walk, which made dinner in the canteen a necessity.[11]

Peggy Hamilton worked in a fuse factory in Woolwich, and travelled there from Blackheath each morning, a journey which took her $1\frac{1}{2}$ hours each way. Her hours were 7am to 7pm, 6 days a week. Later she went to the government rolling mills in Southampton, to train other women, and found herself working a 92-hour week. This was eventually cut back, as it was found to be counter-productive! But they had no canteen until the end of the war, and only one first-aider for the building. She was thankful for the fact that they actually had lavatories.[12]

As factories expanded, conditions usually worsened before they improved. What had been barely adequate for a few hundred men did not serve for thousands of women. Employers who had been used to male workers took some time to adjust to the fact that government demanded better conditions for women. New factories also took time to build, and women often found themselves working in half-finished buildings (like the government rolling mills outside Southampton), or travelling to places sited far from proper transport, trudging through muddy fields to get to work.

Many of the munitions workers were very young, in their mid-teens, and a number of those interviewed recently said they really didn't appreciate the risks they were running when they worked with explosives. They flung themselves into hard physical labour, often without help from lifting equipment or trolleys in the early years – Elsie McIntyre recalled that they threw shells to each other in the Leeds National Filling

Factory.[13] The relatively good money made them accept long hours and fatigue more willingly, and employers were prepared to exploit this. Greenwood & Batley, one munitions firm, was prosecuted for working girls 82 hours a week at one stage, but the government turned a blind eye to long hours and excessive overtime in general. Greenwood & Batley in fact escaped fines, as the local magistrates refused to convict, saying that nothing should stand in the way of munitions production! Twelve-hour days led to fatigue, if nothing more, and could wear out girls who were supposedly in the prime of life. Almost certainly, exhaustion and poor working and living conditions led to the rise in TB which was only really noticed a few years later. Infection was highest amongst young women, and this probably spread in factory, hostel and lodgings.[14]

Monica Cosens, who knew that her own health was strong, thanks to her prosperous background, wrote of her working-class companions:

> . . . it is not only her health she is risking, but her youth as well. As Gran'pa [the skilled supervisor] once said: 'it makes me sad to see the young girls here; they come in fresh and rosy cheeked, and before a month has passed they are pale and careworn.'
>
> Gran'pa is right. There is no doubt that the girls become shadow-eyed and pale, and the effect of working through the night under the glare of electricity adds many wrinkles beneath their eyes, ageing them beyond their years.[15]

Life was obviously very different for the women who blossomed in open-air work, or who were working normal hours in shops and offices. In contrast to the munition workers, women porters, for example, on only £1 a week, were said to be flourishing:

> Health considerations seemed to count first with the women goods porters in their reasons for liking their work. Two who had previously worked as tailoresses were very emphatic in their preference for their new job; one who had worked as a laundry maid in the basement of a big hotel, which she had to leave because she found that the continual artificial light was ruining her sight, said she felt much improved in health now that she was working in the fresh air.[16]

The risks munition workers faced at work included industrial accidents, particularly when they were encouraged to work long shifts at full stretch. A short story, in a book of the time called *TNT Tales*, told of the ironic contrast between a cabinet minister's letter of congratulations pinned up on the wall, and the filthy cloakrooms, lack of drinks, and frequent accidents caused by the firm encouraging the shifts to compete with each other.[17] This was probably not an exaggeration, and women were killed or injured by falling equipment, runaway trolleys or wagons, and badly guarded machinery. Even in the best-run factories accidents happened. Lilian Miles remembered hurting her fingers while doing munitions work – she could not use her hand for 6 weeks, but had to go into the factory and sit around doing nothing, otherwise she would not have been paid.[18] The women at the rolling mills in Southampton cut their hands frequently, and remembered that they kept working; the blood ran away with the industrial effluent. Elsie Farlow, who worked cleaning detonators, had an ulcerated leg which kept her off work for weeks, but remembered that the firm had a special stool built for her when she returned, to ease her leg.[20] Others in the same factory had skin complaints, apparently from the emery dust. Women commented on the unpleasant fumes in the rolling mills,[21] while many engineering operations caused eye problems, or even, as with copper-band turning on shells, cases of mild poisoning.

Working with TNT or aircraft dope was more dangerous. The former was used, as powder or liquid, to fill shells, and was highly explosive. In the 'Danger Sheds' women worked in special overalls, leaving behind jewellery, matches, and even shoes with metal nails in them, in the changing rooms, to avoid striking sparks. Even so, there were several major accidents during the war, the most well-known being at Silvertown, London, in January 1917 when a number of women were killed. None of these were reported in the press, which was censored under the Defence of the Realm Act (DORA): the government did not want to harm civilian morale, or put women off munitions work. One woman interviewed recently remembered an explosion at her factory:

> One day, it was on the 16th of April, some flames started coming along the line towards us, and two men in the shop

got hold of us and threw us outside onto the grass. It was raining like the dickens. They knew something was going to happen. The alarm was going and Queenie, our supervisor, had to go back for her watch. She was blown to pieces. They found her corsets on the line.[22]

Their outdoor clothing was also destroyed in the blast, but the firm gave them no compensation.

TNT was also highly poisonous, a fact often played down by the government. Women in the previous chapter told how they turned yellow when working with it, and this was the first symptom of its toxic effects. Others symptoms followed. *The Lancet* reported that women workers experienced nasal discomfort and bleeding, smarting eyes, headaches, sore throat, coughs, stomach pains, nausea, constipation or diarrhoea, skin rashes, anorexia, giddiness, drowsiness, and swelling of hands and feet.[23] A report on Woolwich Arsenal, meanwhile, stated that 37 per cent of women on shellfilling experienced abdominal pain, nausea and constipation, while:

All workers complained of a metallic bitter taste; some had complete loss of appetite, others stated that they were 'always hungry but never felt satisfied' . . . . Constipation was very general . . . .[24]

In addition, 25 per cent of the women at the Arsenal had skin problems, many found their periods affected, and 36 per cent said they suffered from depression and irritability.

Many said that at the end of the day's work they 'wanted to sit about and cry', others were oppressed with a sense that 'something awful was going to happen', and one woman volunteered that 'if poison had been by she would have felt obliged to take it'. The women definitely stated that their spirits were not usually depressed and the symptoms only occur when working on TNT.[25]

The first deaths from toxic jaundice, caused by TNT, were reported in 1915, and numbers increased in 1916. At least 349 cases of serious TNT poisoning were registered during the war (this did not mean there were not more which went unrecognised), and of these, 109 people died – there was no treatment; doctors simply stood by waiting to see if the patient recovered or not. The press, meanwhile, was encouraged to play down the dangers of TNT, especially once women seemed inclined to avoid the work. A shamefully propagandist article in the *Weekly Welcome*, in 1917, at the height of the labour shortage, told readers that 'The yellow colouring which appears on the skin in no way affects the health, and will disappear when work in this department is given up for a week or two.'[26] Just as dishonest was A.K. Foxwell's passage in her book of the time *Munition Lasses*. She describes the Lady Principal Overlooker of Woolwich interviewing young women for jobs at the Arsenal:

> Occasionally a timid question as to the particular dangers of the Danger Buildings elicits the remark: 'You girls seem to think that we have a little cemetery tucked away in the corner of the Arsenal, where *hundreds* of people are buried who have been blown up. We don't have these excitements here.' . . . .
>
> Then the cheery voice continues: 'However, this is war work, so we don't expect to get a leisurely job. Aren't you willing to do your bit, like the soldiers in the trenches? We mustn't expect *our* work to be easy.'[27]

In this way women's fears were dismissed.

Aircraft dope was also poisonous, and the fumes could kill. It was used to coat the fabric on the wings of the fragile, wooden aircraft of the time, and this work was done entirely by women. As with TNT, the danger was almost ignored by the press, and only trade unions complained about the hazard. Employers hoped to solve the problem by moving women from job to job, and providing good ventilation.

WELFARE

The government was forced to look into conditions in the workplace. This was partly because it had to pay at least lip-service to current concerns about the health of the 'mother of the race'. The poor health of working-class recruits for the Boer War had led to concern about working-class health in general, and there was plenty of evidence to show that women were particularly prone to sickness – thanks to low wages, poor diet, and too many pregnancies. Strong mothers were required to produce the strong sons the empire needed. There had also been decades of debate – intensified in the early years of the twentieth century – about the extent to which married women's paid work affected the health of their babies. These debates did not die away with the war, and there were plenty of people who believed that the effect of so many women in munitions would be distrastrous for 'the race'.

Ostensibly the government was paying attention to all these fears when it formed the Health of Munition Workers Committee, the Women's Employment Committee and the War Cabinet Committee on Women in Industry – which together considered aspects of health in the workplace, and the future of women's pay and prospects in industry. In fact, there was also another, less humanitarian, reason for the Munition Workers Committee. The government accepted that good conditions would lead to higher output, while fatigue led to sickness, absenteeism and lower production. It was vital that munitions production should be kept as high as possible. For this reason, the Committee did not concern itself with the health and welfare of women in any other industry, and indeed skated over some aspects of life in the factory itself.

The Health of Munition Workers Committee, after interviews and investigations, produced a series of reports for employers' guidance. These reports do make interesting reading, particularly as the Committee decided from the beginning that it was not merely interested in the physical side of health, but in the 'mental and moral' aspects, as –

Discontent, apathy, monotony, boredom and lack of interest in life may be just as detrimental as physical ailment and may equally involve irreparable loss in individual fitness, well-being and efficiency.[28]

Significantly, although munition workers included men, the Committee was only really interested in women and boy workers – seeing women as a particular problem (as usual!). They were, as the Committee said, physiologically different, less muscular, and less strongly built than men. They may also have led sedentary or domestic lives which left them ill-fitted for heavy work, and they were known to suffer commonly from poor digestion, anaemia, headaches, 'nervous exhaustion', 'muscular pain and weakness' and menstrual disorders. All of these were the product of both living and working conditions, a combination which the Committee only partly acknowledged; while Janet Campbell, who wrote the medical section of this report, concluded that although women's health could be improved by good nutrition and sensible exercise, they would continue to be at a disadvantage in industry thanks to menstruation and weaker muscles. Over and over again, this Committee emphasised that the physical differences between men and women, and the latters' childbearing role, could not be disregarded.

In the workplace, the Health of Munition Workers' Committee did achieve some changes – although not as many as everyone was encouraged to believe, and some of these were in any case a mixed blessing to women. Hours remained long throughout the war, although overtime dropped in 1917–18, and engineering workshops increasingly moved to a 7 or 7½-hour day instead of 12.[29] But in shell shops the two-shift system remained common, in spite of pressure from the Health of Munition Workers Committee, and evidence from before the war which showed that output often rose with shorter hours. No attempt was made to reduce the hours in non-munition jobs, so bus conductors, tram drivers, needlewomen and others continued to work very long hours for the duration of the war.

Conditions in many munition factories and engineering workshops did start to improve from 1916 onwards. Proper toilets were installed in many munition factories, partly because there were fears that poor hygiene would encourage the spread of venereal disease. Seats and lifting apparatus became more common, new factories were built with rest rooms, good ventilation and canteens, and medical facilities became more usual. Most women and their trade unions accepted that conditions needed improving, and that breaks, recreational facilities and first-aid rooms were to be welcomed. Unfortunately, however, these changes were all put under the heading of 'Welfare Work', and the Health of Munition Workers Committee recommended that they should be organised by 'Welfare Supervisors'. Problems were bound to arise. Welfare supervisors – always women – were in an ambiguous position.

14 The canteen at Pirelli's, Southampton. This looks like a very high-class canteen, with pictures on the walls, and nice cutlery, but women workers were paid low wages here – showing welfare provision did not necessarily go hand in hand with good rates of pay

They were paid by the employer, and were supposed to make life comfortable enough for the workers to keep up production; at the same time they were supposed to convince those workers that they had their interests at heart. In addition, there was resentment at the fact that only women were supposed to need welfare workers – men were deemed to be capable of taking care of themselves through their trade unions – and about the way in which the duties of the welfare supervisors went well beyond the simple administration of canteens, cloakrooms and so on. The Health of Munition Workers Committee recommended that they should also keep employees' records, investigate lost time or sickness, supervise night work, make visits to check accommodation, assist in setting up thrift schemes, arrange educational classes, look into housing and transport problems, and help provide recreation. They should also ensure that only 'healthy and wholesome' (by which they meant morally unsullied) women were employed in areas away from home, and discourage the recruitment of mothers to the factory.

This took welfare supervisors into the homes and outside lives of the women workers, and it was hardly surprising that many people saw them as little more than the employer's spies. They were also supposed to be the moral guardians of the workforce, and the girls' clubs, evening classes and dances they organised were supposed to keep the daughters of the working class on the right track. Writing in the *Women's Industrial News* in 1917, M.C. Matheson said hopefully that most mothers would welcome this kind of supervision:

> She will be glad that someone will support her daughter in her effort not to succumb to evil talk and foul insinuation, to the temptation to join in drinking parties or in pleasures that look harmless to the high spirited girl and are full of peril.[30]

But in reality welfare supervisors were far from popular. They treated the workers like ignorant children, sometimes, like the famous superintendent of Woolwich, Lilian Barker, criticising hats and make-up, often advising them not to spend their money on frivolities, always acting as advisors and guardians. Peggy Hamilton, a middle-class volunteer, saw their role as being similar to a matron confronted by a group of schoolgirls (and she didn't like it). Another worker remembered being annoyed that in the dead of night the women were obliged to go to the canteen for refreshments, being counted past like children by the welfare supervisor who tapped each one on the shoulder, while the men were allowed to brew tea in their own workshops.[31] More seriously, supervisors were seen as undermining trade unions, and extending the employers' control over the workforce. Dorothea Proud, writer of a well-respected book on welfare work at the time, said firmly that it could not be successful unless employers started out by paying good rates to their workers, but this side of welfare was often ignored.[32] It was particularly resented once the government allowed its costs to be deducted from the wage bill. Class conflicts obviously played their part as well. Helen Pease, who worked as an NFWW organiser in a factory in the East End, reported that women did not mind middle-class organisers like herself interfering, as they knew she was on their side – unlike the welfare worker, whose role was quite different.[33] Working-class women did not like being patronised, as one journalist reported in 1917:

> Factory girls are just as sensitive to home truths as other women. They object to comments on their dress and their domestic arrangements from the welfare worker as much as she would object to similar comments from them. One lady made her debut in the factory where very rough girls worked by saying to them 'you want a club, you come from such overcrowded, dirty homes,' and then she was astounded when they threw their lunch at her![34]

The largest filling factories employed welfare supervisors from early in the war, with mixed results. At Gretna, for example, welfare supervisors (who had to be 'educated trained women') were employed to oversee the hiring of all female staff, provide general supervision, and run the 70 hostels and 40 or 50 smaller houses which came under the factory's control.[35] At Woolwich, they ran the hostels, crêches, children's homes and canteens – though many women remember the food as being awful![36] A paper written at the time by the Chief Welfare Officer at Armstrong Whitworth and Co. is very revealing. Twenty thousand women were employed there by 1916, and, wrote, E.B. Jayne, the new welfare officers had a hard time to begin with, as the girls had just won improved pay

15   Mrs Fry and her sister, both tram conductors in Southampton. Notice that
this picture has the same painted backdrop as that on page 33: the
Southampton photographer they visited must have had a standard 'garden'
backdrop for portraits. He obviously had plenty of women transport workers
who wanted their photos taken

and conditions through strike action, and saw the supervisors as spies or goody-goodies. The welfare workers were forced to begin by establishing an overall department, and by visiting bad time-keepers at home. From there they branched out to overseeing the recruitment of new workers, supervising canteens and cloakrooms, keeping workers' records, and running 'thrift schemes'.[37] The job description of a welfare supervisor at Woolwich seems to say it all:

> The general work of the Supervisors will be directed to making regular inspection of the factories with a view to reducing the difficulties caused to the Factory staff through irregularity of attendance, bad time-keeping, slackness, want of good discipline, etc. among the workers. It will be the duty of the Supervisors to inquire into and endeavour to remedy the causes, from which the above difficulties have arisen.[38]

With this in mind they were to help select new workers, keep records, meet newly arrived recruits from the railway station, deal with absentees and bad time-keepers, check the cleanliness of the canteens, supervise lavatories and cloakrooms, recommend candidates for convalescent homes, assist in schemes for the 'general improvement' of the workers. They were also supposed to visit homes, and check whether children were being looked after properly. No wonder Proud wrote that 'to safeguard individual liberty and respect class feelings is the central problem of Welfare Work'![39]

Of course, welfare work also offered employment to middle-class women, and there is little doubt, from the Imperial War Museum reports and records, that most welfare departments took great pride in their work. Welfare supervisors really did seem to feel that they were helping the workers, and were doing a worthy and necessary job. It seems that many did not realise quite how sensitive this area was, and lacked Dorothea Proud's awareness of the problems. From welfare supervision sprang the personnel departments of later years, but perhaps these had more respect for the individual worker than the early matron-like supervisors.

The straightforward factory improvements were welcomed. A good canteen in any trade was appreciated, as some Southampton tram conductors remembered. Monica Cosens too recalled the difference it made to life.

When I first 'signed on' there was no adequate accommodation for meals. It was a choice between sitting in a room far too small to accommodate our crowd, or out of doors in a yard littered with mortar, planks and building materials to be used for the further construction of the premises . . .[40]

Then came the YWCA canteen about which she was enthusiastic:

The Canteen is a long low building filled with narrow chairs and tables. At the far end are two counters, one piled with buns, oranges, sweets, lemonade; the other given up to urns of boiling water, mugs of tea, glasses of milk, whilst above it swings a large blackboard, on which is written the day's list of hot dishes prepared in the kitchen close at hand, and the announcement that 'workers' own food will be cooked at the charge of one penny'.[41]

Some other facilities set up through the workplace were appreciated: one of the tram conductors also recalled a social club which she enjoyed attending, and a garden she worked in in her spare time. Others remembered being supplied with overalls, and free milk, or the provision of films and dancing, but canteens had the most effect – the one at Barnbow was wonderful, it was said![42] Protective clothing was sometimes welcomed, and sometimes seen as a nuisance – caps apparently encouraged lice (something the Health of Munition Workers Committee did not think of), while respirators were uncomfortable.[43] Dorothy Poole remembered that conditions improved rapidly as time passed, and by 1917 the crowded, cold aeroengine works at which she was employed had been transformed by canteens, cloakrooms, heating, stools, rest rooms and nursing staff. Naomi Loughnan, a middle-class war volunteer, regretted the passing of the old primitive conditions (which made her feel that she was really sacrificing part of her life) as factory surroundings improved. Most women welcomed the material gains, no matter how much they disliked welfare supervision.[44]

But while all this was going on, precious little was done in the field of industrial illness. The Health of Munition Workers Committee produced hundreds of pages on the subject of food, overalls, seats, cloakrooms, etc., but did not really tackle the problem of work with TNT. Studies by various doctors and the TNT Advisory Committee led to the conviction that it was absorbed through the skin as well as lungs (the primitive respirators and green veils were useless), and that its grave effects were untreatable. The Health of Munition Workers Committee produced a memorandum on the subject in 1916, in which it recommended good ventilation, washing facilities, medical inspection, no overtime, and the wearing of respirators, overalls and gloves. Many factories duly applied these measures, adding for good measure caps and veils, and free milk for TNT workers. Milk actually had no effect on the illness, but did encourage workers to believe that employers were looking after them – not surprisingly, many of them also thought that the drinking of milk offered them some protection.

From the list of symptoms mentioned earlier in this chapter it seems more than likely that TNT also affected pregnancy, but no investigations were made into this. In spite of all the government's vaunted concern with women's health, and the current fears for the 'health of the race', the dangers of TNT were quietly swept under the carpet. It was accepted, in effect, that women had to become ill, or even die, in order to keep up munitions production, as no really effective protective clothing existed at the time – absorption of the poison could even be encouraged by gloves, collars and cuffs, as it was trapped against the skin.[45] Women, meanwhile, did continue to take work with TNT, though increasingly reluctantly, and the labour shortage of 1916 affected the filling factories more than any other area of munitions, thanks to dislike of the work. Fortunately for the government, the requirement for shells did not continue to increase at such a rate in 1917.

The government's wartime intervention in factory conditions was unprecedented, but the uneven nature of this interference was important for women. On the one hand, the kind of welfare supervision set up certainly encouraged the belief that women were incapable of looking after themselves, and that their employment was somehow different from men's because of special physical weakness. On the other hand, the government would only interfere to workers' advantage to a very limited extent when it came to the matters of long hours and low pay, although both of these had an adverse effect on health. It certainly never considered interfering with women's working conditions outside the munitions industry. Finally, it was clear that nothing should stand in the way of munitions production, not even the death or illness of workers on TNT. The mothers of the race were not *that* important.

CHAPTER 6

DOMESTIC LIFE

THE PROBLEMS OF DAILY LIFE

It is an interesting fact that very little attention was originally paid by the government or employers as to how the women recruited into munitions work (or any other trades which needed them) were actually going to cope with long journeys, shopping, cooking, and childcare outside their long working hours — with the rest of life, in fact. It seems to have been assumed that women would get on with these tasks just as they had always done. But life was made harder for many by the war. Airship raids caused death and destruction in some coastal towns, and as a result, lights were dimmed or put out at night — making accidents in the street common. A surprisingly large number of civilians were hurt by the bombings, with 1,413 killed, and 3,407 injured. East coast towns were bombarded early in the war, while Dover and London probably suffered worst from the airships — the latter experienced 52 raids between January 1915 and August 1918.[1]

Although transport kept going throughout the war, the vast numbers trooping daily or nightly to factories found the journeys cramped and long. As Caroline Playne wrote, 'the dread of the evening struggle in dark streets hung over many workers all the time, adding considerably to the strain of life.'[2] A.K. Foxwell, overlooker at Woolwich, wrote graphically of the daily grind:

In the hot August days the heat was stifling and the dust suffocating; in the wet days of October, and the rampantly torrential nights of November, we waded ankle deep in mud and water, arriving with shoes, stockings and galoshes soaked.[3]

A middle-aged VAD, already tired out by her work, complained that:

> My fatigue was intensified by having to come to hospital by
> train (we were no longer able to keep any kind of
> conveyance) and to return home the same way. And trains
> were few and far between. After a time I took lodgings in the
> town for my spells of duty, which made it easier, but often I
> was so tired that I have felt that I should be obliged when my
> night ended to crawl out of the ward on my hands and
> knees.[4]

In the darkened streets there were also frequent accidents, while
the words of some of the women quoted in the last chapter
showed how long the journeys actually were.

Housing, in the meantime, deteriorated, as all domestic
building came virtually to a halt. There were more houses
demolished than built in London in 1911 to 1915, and just
after the war it was shown that the number of households
sharing a dwelling had actually increased from 15.7 per cent in
1914 to 20 per cent.[5] For those women working far from their
home towns lodgings were hard to find. Such was the shortage
of accommodation that unscrupulous landlords could let rooms
to one lot of workers by day, and one by night – the same beds
were slept in almost continuously. Lodgings were also expensive – up to 12s a week for a single room in the areas most
swelled by war workers.

Then there were the food shortages, as Germany's blockade
of British shipping became ever more effective. There were also
at times shortages of wool, paper, leather, coal and wood. But
here, once again, it is difficult to work out whether life was
much worse than normal for many women workers. After all,
many found themselves with better wages, and more money to
spend on food, while soldiers' and sailors' wives had separation
allowances (12s 6d, plus 2s for each child) which often
amounted to considerably more than their husbands had given
them for housekeeping before the war. The women who had
done sedentary work before 1915, and lived largely on a diet of
bread and tea, now did harder work and ate more food. Family
budgets were often improved when men were away at the
Front.

But some women interviewed recently remember terrible

food shortages, and a lack of much to spend their wages on. Those like Sarah Pidgeon whose parents grew vegetables and reared rabbits and chickens for the pot were lucky, as they were sheltered from the worst of the shortages.[6] Meat and sugar were badly affected, while the government had to fix the prices of butter, margarine, sugar, bacon and cheese. The Ministry of Food was established in December 1916, and by 1917 the government was urging people to 'eat less bread' (not a helpful message to the poor) and ordering restaurants to have 'meatless' days. The queue became a regular sight outside food shops, and economy campaigns urged people not to be wasteful – as insulting to working-class people as the 'thrift' campaigns were, encouraging them to put their savings into war bonds, rather than buy Christmas presents for the children, or treat themselves to a gramophone. Such press campaigns led to one woman writing indignantly to *Labour Woman* in 1916:

I must say I was surprised to read last month of the women in the Labour League being advised to lead the way in *thrift*. Take the lead, Ye Gods! To advise us working women to be thrifty is about the limit![7]

Opinions on queueing itself varied. Mrs C.S. Peel, writing in the 1920s, remembered that:

Anyone who penetrated the poorer neighbourhoods became familiar with the queue. In the bitter cold and rain of that depressing winter of 1917 women and children waited outside the shabby shops common to the poorer districts of all towns.[8]

But Caroline Playne recalled:

For those who took life lightly or had little to do at home, 'queueing' could be an enjoyable pastime, for joking was rife, tales and rumours flooded about and merriment took on the exhilaration of a time of adventure and upheaval.[9]

Probably both pictures had elements of truth in them. What can be said with certainty is that working-class people suffered as a result of such food shortages, while the wealthy were merely inconvenienced, thanks to the greater variety of their diet, and the fact that they could afford more expensive alternative foods.

Of course it was working women who suffered most from queueing. Others could settle down for hours to wait their turn at the butchers or bakers – they could not. They had to fit shopping into their lunch hours (which meant missing a meal), or after work. It is difficult to imagine how exhausting such a life must have been. After a journey to work, many women, married or single, then had to queue for food on the way home, at one of the shops which stayed open all evening, and cook the food when they did get back. As Elsie McIntyre, a shell filler, remembered, once she had queued for meat: '. . . by the time it got to my turn there would be no more meat left, only sausages . . . You went straight into the queue before you could go to bed.'[10] It was quite hard enough for a non-working woman to get meat. One middle-class housewife, who no longer had servants, told Mrs Peel how she queued for ages, hoping for silverside, watching everyone in front of her carry off their meat in triumph:

> But after 20 joints had been carved from one small piece of 'animal', there seemed but little chance of my obtaining my silverside. I approached the butcher furtively. 'Have you any silverside?' I whispered. 'No, no silverside – breast, scrag or bit o' brisket,' he yapped at me impatiently. In those days I was not as experienced a housewife as I am now, and one feels somewhat weak after half an hour spent standing in a butchers' shop glaring at ugly insides. I gasped 'brisket', and then found myself on the pavement clasping lovingly a very minute parcel of stringy meat.[11]

For those with little money and less time, it was much worse. Things got so bad in 1917 that women in Leeds actually threatened to march on food shops, while there was also much unrest amongst munition workers in Woolwich and Glasgow. But even when women got hold of enough food, they still had to cook it for husbands or children, which must have been a problem after a long and stressful day.

There was also the matter of childcare. To begin with, women with babies or young children continued to do as they had done if they worked before the war – they left them with relatives, friends or minders, and if necessary, they went home at lunchtime to feed their babies, as Dorothy Haigh who worked at the rolling mills in Southampton recalled doing day after day.[12] She remembered many women there being married, and no doubt others did the same. A survey done in Leeds in 1916 showed that of 129 munition workers' children (under school age), 83 were left with grandmothers or near relations, 42 with neighbours, 1 with a day nursery, 1 with a landlady, and 1 boarded out.[13] Young married women certainly depended upon their own mothers to help them look after their children throughout the war.

CHANGES DURING THE WAR

Little was done about the problems of travelling itself, but the government did attempt to tackle the matter of long travelling distances and poor housing for munition workers by embarking on a building programme near some of the bigger factories, and subsiding some estates built by private arms firms. At first, they attempted to cope with the large numbers by building temporary hostels and huts, but this was an expensive approach, and it was soon decided to build permanent accommodation which could later be used in peacetime. The most famous estates built were at Well Hall, for Woolwich Arsenal, and Gretna, and certainly these provided some very pleasant accommodation, particularly at Well Hall, which was built on garden city lines. Between 1915 and 1918, 10,000 houses were built on 38 different estates, and 2,800 temporary cottages. But they only housed a few thousand people; the housing shortage remained acute in many areas, and most women workers continued to live in their existing houses, in temporary logdings, or in hostels, which housed 20,000 workers.[14] Opinions on the latter varied. A.K. Foxwell, quoted in Chapter 4, seemed to like hers, while Monica Cosens could say that hers, a converted school, was simply plain, unhomely, and clean. There were complaints at the time of barrack-like regimes, with poor food, little heating, gates shut at 10.30, and no male visitors allowed at all, and no doubt conditions varied a lot. It is difficult to find many personal reports of women who lived in them, though Lilian Miles, interviewed by the Imperial War Museum, recalled she had a very tiny room, and the lights were turned out by 9.30pm. When she moved out to lodgings, she had to share a bed, and was thrown out for complaining about the overcrowding.[15] Others found hostels less unpleasant; Isabella Clarke, in Coventry, reported her accommodation was good, with an excellent canteen, but this did cost her 15s a week.[16] Outside the munitions industry, women lived in much the same deteriorating conditions as before, although of course the Land Army members were billeted, sometimes in big comfortable country houses, and sometimes in less prosperous farmhouses, and the WAACs lived in camps.

The government also made some attempt to stop rents soaring in England by bringing in the Rent and Mortgage Protection Act of 1915, but the general problem of housing was something the Liberals promised to tackle after the war.

1917–18 was almost certainly the hardest year of the war for civilians, and life was made worse by the flu epidemic which started to sweep across Europe, attacking a population which was weakened by 3 years of strain, tension, grief, hard work, and a limited diet. The government had to take food shortages seriously after the increasing number of strikes in 1917 – their spies (literally, as government agents infiltrated unions and labour groups) and the investigators for the Royal Commission on Industrial Unrest all reported that people were growing angry with high rents, bad housing, and food shortages. The Russian Revolutions were a graphic reminder of the fact that war weariness and harsh living conditions were a spur to uprising, and the government could no longer afford to ignore the complaints from the towns. It was this pressure which helped force the government to consider rationing. It is also an interesting thought that, apart from anything else, queues were places were people could discuss their grievances and exchange information – as the war grew steadily less popular and living conditions deteriorated, this was the last thing the government wanted. Particularly disturbing was the alliance of munition workers and their landladies who marched together during the Glasgow rent strike of 1916;[17] the authorities did not want a repeat of this, or further public unrest.

The Ministry of Food had been set up in 1916, and took over 85 per cent of the nation's food supplies. But in spite of severe local food shortages, there was great reluctance to consider rationing until 1917. After an unsuccessful national economy campaign (to save bread and meat in particular), rationing of sugar, meat, jam, bread, butter, margarine and lard finally came in 1918. People also grew used to eating regulation bread, which contained barley, maize or rice flour, along with the wheat, according to what grain was available at the time. There was some attempt to organise a food ticket system for regular customers, but this was difficult to administer, and was dropped. So local rationing was tried at first, followed by national: weekly allowances were for 1½lb of meat per person, 4 oz of butter or margarine, and 8oz of sugar.[18] Unfortunately, rationing did not mean that shops always had enough stocks of these items, and women were still left to go from shop to shop with their coupons when no bread or meat was left. Even rationing did not make food supplies fair – after all, as was pointed out at the time, the poorer you were, the more you needed large quantities of bread to keep fit. As for the meat ration, those on low incomes could not afford the amount allowed to them, and should really have been able to buy extra quantities of other food stuffs to make up for this – but they were not.[19] The allowance of bread was 4lb a week for women, and 7lb a week for men, whatever the rest of the diet was like.

The only more daring attempt to change the nation's eating patterns came with the opening of an experimental National Kitchen in Westminster Bridge Road in 1917, designed to make sure women workers and their children were fed properly.[20] A few others followed, but they never became widespread. Canteens helped those women who had one available, and some children had school meals, but no attempt was made to encourage employers to allow their women workers staggered shifts to enable time to queue, or employ people on a part-time basis. On the contrary, it was even feared that if women worked shorter shifts they might spend more time on domestic work, and wear themselves out! It is worth remembering that it was hard to buy cheap take-away food at this time (apart from chips and pies or fish), and that cooking itself always took a long time, given the kind of equipment and kitchens women had to work with. The middle-class war worker escaped these problems. She did not have to queue for food, or cook and clean. No matter how tired out she was by travelling and by the work she did, she could recuperate at home, or in her hostel, and being single, she did not have to worry about childcare. Women of all classes shared many problems during the war, but this difference in home life was vital. Women in good hostels were also fortunate, as cooking was often not a problem.

The matter of childcare was more sensitive. Most of the members of the government committees believed that married women really should not work outside the home. During the war, their work was seen as a necessary evil, but this did not mean that anything should be done to encourage it in future. For example, the Women's Employment Committee expressed its hope that after the war 'every encouragement' would be made to get married women back to their children, and stated that the 'working woman must be safeguarded as the homemaker of the nation'.[21] Similarly, the Health of Munition Workers Committee stated firmly that 'Upon the womanhood of the country most largely rests the privilege first of creating and maintaining a wholesome family life, and secondly of developing the higher influences of social life.'[22] Thus women had a responsibility for both the physical and moral welfare of the family.

There was a fairly widespread fear that if childcare were made too easy working-class women might abandon their homes for the world of work, leaving behind neglected husbands and children. As one writer in the feminist paper *Common Cause* said (in an article very untypical of the paper itself),

> Where they can get their children really well cared for at a cost to themselves which is altogether out of proportion to what the children receive, the temptation is strong to go out and earn extra money; which involves temptation to the husband to make no effort to meet the increasing needs of a growing family, and in addition is an inducement to the woman to accept inadequate wages because she is not wholly dependent on them.[23]

Perfectly respectable papers like *The Times* carried articles expressing the fear that women workers leaving their children in crêches during the war, and those who enjoyed improved working conditions, might be encouraged to abandon their domestic role by this experience. As one of their journalists wrote in 1916:

It would be deplorable if the measures taken to preserve the health of girls and mothers in the war factories led married women definitely to abandon their homes for industrial work. If their incursion into skilled labour is to be permanent, then we have paid infinitely too high for any immediate advantage to our arms. But we must feel that public opinion, if not the instinct of the women, will restore them, after the war, to their traditional place.[24]

Employers themselves were often doubtful about employing married women because of their domestic responsibilities. The Health of Munition Workers Committee had shown that women's health was most severely affected when heavy work was combined with long hours and domestic labour – which meant married women were worst hit.

When sufficiently hardpressed, women simply had to stay away from work – one overlooker at Barnbow recalled that married women had family responsibilities, particularly washing for large families, which caused absenteeism. This she understood, unlike the employer who complained to the Committee on Women in Industry that women

... stay away more for what are from the point of view of the employer trivial reasons. A day's washing may be a very serious thing for a woman, but to stay away and leave her machine idle for a day's wash does not appear to be anything but trivial to her employer.[25]

Of course mothers quite simply had no choice – Elsa Thomas, the overlooker quoted above, herself had to cut short her training at Woolwich because her small son fell ill with measles.[26]

Welfare workers checked up on absentee women for precisely this reason. As a Woolwich Arsenal welfare worker reported, they were

really there to find out why a girl was doing bad time-keeping ... we could find out if it was the fault of the Arsenal or whether it was her own conditions at home .... if a woman had four or five children and she still tried to come to work, well, if the children were ill, of course she didn't want to go to work .... if she was doing bad time-keeping she was told then either she must find somebody else to look after her children or she must give up her work.[27]

Lack of childcare arrangements could stop a woman from working outside the home, no matter how much she needed the money. One woman explained:

> In the First World War I couldn't go out to work, because I had a baby of two and a half. My husband was working in an army factory. He was only getting 26s a week, and he was supposed to send some to me, but I never received it, so I had to do something desperate. I could have got a job at the Arsenal, but I would have had to do night work. I wanted my mother to look after my baby so I could go to work, but she refused. She couldn't take on the responsibility of having the baby with the bombing going on. So that stopped that.[28]

She took the classic women's option; bought a sewing machine, and made clothes at home for Woolwich workers.

But married women's labour was needed, and just as reluctant employers were obliged to accept them as workers, a cautious government was eventually forced to intervene to a very limited extent in childcare. From 1917 onwards, the Treasury was prepared to pay up to 75 per cent of the cost of day nurseries for munition workers, and 7d per head, but Leeds had no crêche until 1918 (for a mere 40 children). Most other towns had no childcare facilities at all, in spite of the fact that local authorities were, from 1914 onwards, able to pay 50 per cent of the cost of infant welfare centres: these were not nurseries, but they did offer medical facilities and 'advice' to mothers. In the meantime Sylvia Pankhurst's East End Federation set up a nursery, largely for local munition workers, in the Mother's Arms (it was an old pub), which catered for about 40 small children. She said this inspired a number of other private nurseries, but they cannot have catered for many.

Large government-run or controlled factories were really the only workplaces to install crêches – by 1917 there were 108 day nurseries across the country, looking after 4,000 children.[29] This was simply a drop in the ocean compared with the numbers of women actually working. Nor did anyone suggest crêches for the children of women who were not working in munitions – they were regarded as a necessary evil for war workers alone. None of the women interviewed recently had used a crêche, and although it was probably true that some of them were very useful to working mothers, it is difficult to see them as significant to the majority of women. Almost certainly it was hoped that the war would end before the problem really had to be tackled, and this is precisely what happened. The government managed to pay lip service to the idea of the importance of the mother of the race and her future offspring while evading direct financial responsibility or 'interference' with family life. The Maternity and Child Welfare Act of 1918 offered hospital treatment, lying-in homes, and nurseries as a possibility, but paid no attention to the particular needs of working women.

WOMEN'S 'MORALS'

The existence of welfare supervisors, and the words of those who criticised the very idea of crêches for working mothers, both show that there was much distrust of working-class women. By and large, they were held to be in need of moral education and guardianship; like servants, they needed 'watching'. So, young women in the factory were to be organised into clubs and classes, discouraged from wearing awful hats and make-up, and taught how to be quiet, obedient workers. Working mothers, meanwhile (who were supposed to need educating on matters of childcare and home-keeping, and who were the subject of the National Baby Week Campaigns of 1917 and 1918, designed to 'save every savable child'), also had to be kept an eye on. According to one's point of view, they had to be watched to make sure they did not neglect their children for their work – or their work for their children. They were just as likely to be criticised for either!

The war intensified this mistrust, and brought in new fears about women's 'morals'. Concern was expressed that long hours working with men, journeys to and from work at night, and the existence of large numbers of soldiers in barracks near big towns, would all lead to a rising tide of immorality and illegitimacy. Sylvia Pankhurt puts it well:

War-time hysterics gave currency to fabulous rumour. From

press and pulpit stories ran rampant of drunkenness and depravity amongst the women of the masses. Alarmist morality mongers conceived most monstrous visions of girls and women, freed from the control of fathers and husbands who had hitherto compelled them to industry, chastity and sobriety, now neglecting their homes, plunging into excesses, and burdening the country with swarms of illegitimate infants.[30]

As a direct result of this concern, a plan for the 'surveillance' of soldiers' and sailors' wives was dreamed up. In October 1914 an Army Council Memorandum on the 'Cessation of Separation Allowances and Allotments to the Unworthy' was issued, and a letter was circulated to chief constables by the Home Office. This asked the police in each area to gather lists of the names of wives and dependants of soldiers and sailors who were in receipt of separation allowance –

.... and though it is hoped that there will not be many cases in which such extreme measures will be necessary, the Secretary of State is confident that Local Committees may rely upon your cooperation in their endeavour to ensure that relief shall not be continued to persons who prove themselves unworthy to receive it.[31]

In other words, those women even suspected of being drunk, or consorting with other men, were to be investigated, and if necessary their separation allowances were to be stopped. There was an outcry about this scheme, and the War Office hastily issued a revised order, which was also made known to the press:

When a woman is arrested for being drunk and incapable, drunk and disorderly, or drunk in charge of children, she shall be detained at the police station until sober. If she is the wife of a soldier or sailor, the station officer will not proceed with the charges, but will appeal to her better nature, warn her of the serious consequences, including the loss of .separation allowance that must ensue if she persists in such irregularity of conduct, and urge upon her to prove herself worthy of the husband who is away fighting for his country.[32]

But the police still had the power to enter women's homes, and tick them off for unwifely behaviour, and although it was finally agreed that the separation allowance could only be cut off if women were *convicted* of an offence, this still would have been a serious blow to women with no other means of support. Also, the suspicion remained that wives with any money of their own to spend might be profligate – Hartlepool went so far as to ban soldiers' wives from pubs in 1917.

At the same time, the new Women's Police Patrols took to checking streets, parks, pubs, and even houses in large towns, in areas where it was feared that women might seduce young soldiers, or succumb to men's advances. There were fears that a large army might encourage prostitution (although the army's attitude to prostitution was highly ambiguous, as it was also assumed that men would 'need' prostitutes sometimes), and the Military Commander for the Western part of Britain issued an order banning some women from Cardiff's pubs between 7pm and 6am, and Cardiff's streets from 7pm to 8am. A similar order was made in Grantham, and a quotation from one of the policewomen ordered to investigate the houses of local women gives an idea of the atmosphere of the time:

> We were asked to deal with the women and children and to help keep the girls in their houses. Just as we went there [Grantham] the General had issued an unhappy order, by which women were to be kept in their houses from 8 o'clock in the evening until 7 o'clock next morning in certain districts . . . .
>
> A Defence of the Realm regulation gave us power to go in the women's houses and to see if the girls were in bed, and to see who was in the house. We found that the women were getting large quantities of drink and were entertaining the men in their houses instead of being out on the streets, and, as we pointed out to the military authority, that was doing more harm than if the women had actually been in the public houses and in the streets where people could see them. We turned hundreds of soldiers and girls out of these houses, and reported it to the military authority and to the Chief Constable, with a result that the order restricting women was taken off.[33]

The order was also lifted in Cardiff, but not before 5 women had been arrested for being out of their houses during this curfew, prosecuted under the Defence of the Realm Act, and given 62 days imprisonment each.[34]

The women's police often took over where the welfare supervisors left off. They reported that they had performed the following duties:

> *With Women.* We have warned them of soliciting, protected them from undesirable attention from men, and have advised and helped them when they have appealed to us.
> *With girls.* Cautioned them for behaving in an unseemly manner with male companions. Warned them of evil consequences. Sent them home when found loitering about late at night and in undesirable localities.[35]

But was the First World War really a time of sexual ferment? For all the fears, the answer seems to have been no. The marriage rate rose slightly, but the divorce rate remained stable at 0.2 per 10,000 population, exactly the same as 1910, only rising in 1920 to 0.8.[36] (Though divorce was so hard to come by for most people that these figures do not really mean much.) Figures for illegitimacy are confusing. Numbers of illegitimate children per 1,000 live births rose by 30 per cent, which may seem quite high. However, the birthrate fell during the war, so fewer women actually gave birth to an illegitimate child; indeed, the illegitimacy rate per 1,000 women (rather than births) fell from 8 per cent in 1911 to 7.6–7.7 per cent during the war.[37]

Obviously, social life for many women changed during the war – married women, with husbands away, went out with friends, young women had more money to spend, as we have seen – but the effects of this have been exaggerated. Mary Agnes Hamilton's words about the loss of 'old ideals of chastity and self-control in sex' during a time when 'life was less than cheap'[38] have often been quoted, but many women workers seem to have remained very cautious in their dealings with individual men. Caroline Rennles remembers that sometimes a group of them would take an afternoon off from munitions work, and go out with some American or Canadian soldiers, towards the end of the war, and that they were very kind to them – but this simply seems to have been part of group social life. They remained very moralistic about those who had become pregnant, and when Lilian Barker went round the Woolwich Workshops asking for contributions of 1s each from everyone as a collection for pregnant workers, '. . . we all refused because you know we thought it was disgusting for girls to be pregnant in those times . . .'[39] Miss Barker stopped their sugar rations instead! Others would have nothing to do with soldiers:

> I went dancing a lot, at the Elephant and Castle. There were plenty of boys there. I was blonde then, and I'd get stopped under the lights. They'd remember my hair. I'm easy to get along with if people are straight with me, but you've got to have a safeguard before you go intimate with men like that. If they turn rough, you've got no proof. I never went out with soldiers.[40]

These are the words of a woman who was a waitress during the war. A woman clerk, meanwhile, told Mrs Peel about the problems from the men she worked with, who were 'very ready to be saucy', but altered their attitude 'if they found you didn't appreciate it'.[41] Mary Lees, who worked on the land, had more problems with farmers proposing to her than propositioning her, which she said got to be 'an awful bore'. Her solution was to beg a photo from a goodlooking friend of her brother's in the army, and present this at opportune moments, telling suitors they were too late as this was her fiancé.[42] A number of Land Girls did in fact marry farmers!

Of course, a hasty marriage could disguise illegitimacy, and Laura Verity recalled that when anyone in her factory got married people suspected the woman of being pregnant. Single women told her when they were, and if possible they went to Bradford for an abortion – abortions were still common, but dangerous, and she remembered girls dying from those that went wrong. Abortionists were usually found through neighbours, family, or other informal contacts, and Laura Verity herself had one friend whose sister acted as untrained abortionist. Those in her factory who did have their babies put them out to nurse, or left them with their mothers while they went back to work: they found life hard, as opinion was still against them. She also remembered a big row at work when a girl who had an abortion hit a foreman who made advances to her – he had assumed that once she had slept with one man she was open to any other.[43]

Men's attitudes were often the problem. Assuming that prostitution was necessary, the military authorities even suggested resurrecting the notorious Contagious Diseases Act, repealed years before after public protest (it introduced draconian measures of control over prostitutes while doing nothing about men's roles in the cycle of infection) – though fortunately this did not happen. But certainly some soldiers took advantage of wartime 'romances', and left some women literally holding the baby. Sylvia Pankhurst quotes a letter from one such man, approached after a baby was born to a local woman:

> I met her in the latter end of January and kept company with her for about 6 weeks . . . she is not the class of girl for me . . . I am shortly leaving for the Front, and am putting the affair in my mother's hands. She is in possession of all the dates, and should they tally with the birth of the child, I have instructed her to make a small allowance for the maintenance of the child.[44]

A woman clerk at Woolwich docks described how women would write in complaining that their husbands were 'carrying on' with someone else – or even worse, that their husband had stopped their separation allowance because he had moved in with another woman.[45] There were evidently men who took advantage of the war, but this was really nothing new, any more than illegitimacy or adultery were. Marriages were bound to be put under strain, and there were certainly affairs, pregnancies and separations as a result of the stress of war, but it is hard to find out what people really thought about any changes in their relationships – this is something people were not so willing to talk about openly. The woman who told Mrs Peel that 'It's the only time since I've been married as I and the children's 'ad peace. The war's been a 'appy time for us' cannot have been the only one relieved at her husband's absence![46]

Middle-class women probably experienced more changes in their day-to-day life than did working-class women. As we have seen, young women were out late at night, were unchaperoned, and lived in hostels or lodgings that they would never have seen in ordinary circumstances. But there is no sign that they produced thousands of war babies either! Indeed, it might be said that given the tensions of war, and the breakdown of 'separate spheres' for the sexes, everyone was remarkably restrained.

Still, the scaremongering persisted, and attitudes to the WAAC produce one final example of the fears which seemed to exist around the whole idea of women's sexuality when free of 'normal' restraints. The women's forces were in a strange situation. They worked next to men who were destined to fight, although they themselves never lifted a gun. And like the army, they were made up of a mixture of classes, with middle- or upper-class women as the officers. Perhaps surprisingly, they were allowed to mix quite freely with the soldiers. One woman reported that when she got to France –

> . . . we were assembled in the drill hall and given the 'gen' on Camp life. Much to my surprise we were informed that we could make friends with the troops, but were advised to choose carefully. I had not anticipated that this would be allowed, but like so many other girls it was here that I was to meet my future husband.[47]

Such socialising led to genuine romances, or some fleeting relationships – but almost inevitably given the mood of the time, it also led to a mass of accusations about women's conduct. A Commission of Enquiry was set up to look into these in 1918, and it was decided that 'We can find no justification of any kind for the vague accusations of immoral conduct on a large scale which have been circulated about the WAAC.'[48] The rate of pregnancy and VD amongst the WAACs was very low. However, facts often do not dispel rumours, and just as the First World War was often described as a time of great sexual freedom in later years, so the poor reputation of the WAACs lived on to affect those women who wanted to join up 20 years later.

CHAPTER 7

DEMOBILISATION 1918–20

ARMISTICE

Vera Brittain, in *Testament of Youth*, remembered vividly the Armistice:

> When the sound of victorious guns burst over London at 11am on November 11th, 1918, the men and women who looked incredulously into each other's faces did not cry jubilantly: 'We've won the War!' They only said: 'The War is over'.[1]

For many people, disillusionment with the war had set in early. What they had hoped would be a minor skirmish in Europe, 'over by Christmas' in 1914, had turned into a long and bloody battle. The early volunteers had soon discovered there was nothing glorious about this war; life in the trenches was so horrific that many of them found it difficult to talk about when home on leave. It was impossible to convey a picture of the desolation, the mud, the decomposing bodies, and the feeling of futility experienced as they 'won' a few yards of land and advanced, or lost them again and retreated. By 1916, when conscription was introduced, it was clear that this war could go on for years, and it was becoming difficult to remember what it was about. No wonder the British press, encouraged by the government, printed constant tales of the Huns' vicious behaviour; the public had to be reminded that this war was worth fighting; and that their menfolk were dying in a good cause.

It has already been said that 1917–18 was a bad year. The food shortages were at their worst, it was a cold winter, casualties on the Front still rose inexorably (British casualties numbered 300,000 in Germany's spring offensive, and those of her allies and enemies alike were equally high), while from the middle of 1918 the flu epidemic was claiming lives at home. Anti-German feelings were whipped up to a yet higher pitch by such 'patriotic' papers as *John Bull*, which led the calls to 'Hang the Kaiser', and 'make Germany pay'. People were tired of death, blackouts, food shortages, and 'making do'; they longed for a return to normal life. When 1918 began, few wondered whether this year might see the end of the fighting – there seemed no end in sight. Continuing industrial unrest, including the big transport strikes for equal pay, led the government to fear further strikes and disorder in the months to come.

Vera Brittain felt no sense of joy when peace arrived, only numbness – she had lost all the men most dear to her. Other bereaved parents, wives and children felt similarly stunned. Helen Pease was in Stafford at the time, and remembered no celebrations there. 'Everybody seemed to be walking up and down the streets saying "Is it really over, is it really over? Perhaps he'll come on home after all".'[2] But as it slowly sank in that the war really had ended, the celebrations began in London, and by the evening of November 11th the streets were full of crowds, waving flags and rattles, dancing through the night. The main feeling was one of relief that at last people could return to normal lives. Asked whether people were excited because they had won the war, or because it was over, Mary Lees, who was out in those crowded streets, unwittingly echoed Vera Brittain's words – 'Oh, because it was over . . .'[3] But what came next?

Politicians, journalists, trade unionists and writers had been pondering on 'post-war reconstruction' for several years. Government committees considered women's role in the light of their new jobs in industry, every book on women's work expounded on the future, while books like that edited by Basil Worsfold on 'war and social change' appeared, allowing experts to debate to their hearts' content. All too often they started from the idea that radical changes in society had already taken place as a result of the war, and that the process of social change would continue unchecked when peace came. Even the hard-headed trade unionist Mary Macarthur could write with confidence:

> Of all the changes worked by the war none has been greater than the change in the status and position of women: and yet it is not so much that woman herself has changed, as that man's conception of her has changed.

It was a naive approach, shared by a number of those who both approved or disapproved of these changes. Women's wartime jobs and apparent independence were supposedly signs that their role had been 'transformed', class barriers were said to have been broken down in the trenches and the factories alike, as men and women from different backgrounds had 'pulled together' for the nation. Many thought that working-class men and women had been politicised by their wartime experiences, and that they would demand better jobs, houses and pay as a result. This paragraph from one writer of 1915 is typical of the time; of the troops he wrote:

> They will return from the war seasoned men and thinking citizens. . . . There has been a breach with the past: new tastes have been acquired, new ideas of life and its realities have come to birth, new demands for self expression will come from thousands of lips.[4]

Very similar things were said about the 'new' women workers. To quote one employer:

> These women will not want to return to their domestic duties after the war. The widening of women's sphere and outlook is a phase greatly accentuated by war conditions; and, although it will be modified when peace comes, it will never go back to what it used to be.[5]

These changes were sometimes welcomed by those who wrote about them, and sometimes deplored, just as some hoped for further reform after the war and others feared discontent and industrial unrest. The Russian revolution was an example which inspired hope or fear, according to the politics of the observer. But few doubted that change had already occurred. At the same time, Lloyd George and the Liberals were promising that Britain after the war would be a land fit for heroes, and that housing and social welfare would be a priority; in effect he was saying that the people would be rewarded for their struggle. The General Election, called with almost indecent haste at the end of 1918, put Lloyd George back in power – having won not only with promises of social reform, but with guarantees that reparations would be extracted from the defeated Germany. Many election candidates had shamelessly exploited anti-German feeling, and had won the votes of those seeking a scapegoat for the four years of hardship they had just endured.

It was accepted by the government that the demobilisation of warworkers and soldiers would be a problem. Hundreds of thousands of women would lose their wartime jobs; equivalent numbers of men had to be released from the army and navy, and would in turn be seeking work. The Ministry of Reconstruction had set up two bodies, the Civil War Workers Committee and the Women's Employment Committee to look at the demobilisation of women in particular, and their possible post-war unemployment problems. The former early decided that 'preparations must accordingly be made by the Government for assisting such workers to return to their former employment',[6] and advised that the organisation of women's employment should be through labour exchanges. Sidney Webb, who was on this Committee, campaigned hard for a month's paid holiday for women munition workers when peace was declared, partly to ease the industrial chaos which instant dismissal would cause, and partly as some kind of reward for their hard work – but this idea was not popular with the majority of the Committee. When fellow members Susan Lawrence and Marion Phillips (Labour Party stalwarts and supporters of women's rights) pressed again for this holiday, saying that women deserved it in view of the effect on their health caused by long hours and wartime stress, the chairman of the Committee blithely replied that it was not necessary, since the reports of the Health of Munition Workers Committee showed that women's health was good. This kind of refusal to acknowledge women's interests was ominous for the future.[7]

The government did make some attempt to forecast employment trends, and a scheme of 'out-of-work donation' was planned, paying 24s a week to men and 20s to women. The

Wages (Temporary Regulation) Act was also passed in 1918, fixing wages for 6 months after the Armistice, in an attempt to ensure that earnings did not plummet in the post-war chaos. But apart from this, very little was planned, and ex-munition workers were supposed to be content with a free rail pass home, 2 weeks' pay in lieu of notice, and the fact that they would all receive out-of-work donation. This was of some help in the days and weeks following the end of the war, but it did not help women find work. The government made no attempt to ease matters by allowing their contracts for clothing or army equipment to continue for a few weeks longer, and backed out of controlling the armament industry as quickly as possible.

Matters worsened steadily in 1919. Firstly, soldiers did indeed return to their old jobs (and were released from the army much faster than the government had anticipated after threats of mutiny around the country). Women were also displaced by men who had never served in the forces, as it became increasingly unacceptable to employ women in 'men's work'. Secondly, a brief post-war boom, which had enabled some women to hold on to jobs in engineering, shops and transport, was succeeded by a slump in 1920. It became hard for anyone to find work; 2 million were registered as unemployed in July 1921, and the rate of female unemployment was higher than male. Some training schemes were set up for unemployed women, but these were in dressmaking, housecraft or other 'women's trades'. Life was made worse by the fact that out-of-work donation did not last indefinitely. It was reduced after 6 months, and then replaced altogether by national-insurance-related dole. When benefit ran out, the unemployed had to resort to the workhouse for poor relief. The effects on women's unemployment were drastic.

WHAT HAPPENED TO WOMEN WORKERS?

First, two quotations. This is Vera Brittain again, writing several years after the war:

Today, as we look back, 1919 seems a horrid year,
dominated by a thoroughly nasty Peace. But when it came in,

it appeared to an enchanted world as divine normality, the spring of life after a winter of death, the stepping-stone to a new era, the gateway to an infinite future – a future not without its dreads and discomforts, but one in whose promise we had to believe, since it was all that some of us had left to believe in.[8]

And these are the dry words of the Z8 report on employment figures for July 1919:

The placing in domestic occupations by the employment exchanges, which were not apparently more numerous during the first three months of Armistice than in the corresponding period a year earlier, were, in the following 6 months about 40% greater in 1919 than in 1918.[9]

The two quotations together really sum up this period. First came the relief, and the sense of returning to normality, during which time unemployment did not seem too serious to those women who lost their jobs. War workers were, after all, exhausted after years of long hours and few holidays, and 20s a week was just enough to live on while they looked for new jobs. Six months later, after benefit cuts (to 15s after 13 weeks), and the bullying of labour exchanges, women were once again accepting jobs in domestic service. There was little other work available, and they could not survive on reduced or non-existent benefit.

Women's experience did of course vary from trade to trade. Most munition workers were laid off in 1918, but some managed to hang on to jobs in general engineering for a few more months, despite the Restoration of Pre-War Practices Act, which had promised that such work would revert to men in peacetime. A limited number of women also stayed in aircraft work, glass and printing for a short time, or moved on to what was formerly regarded as boys' work, as labourers in the iron and steel industry, or manual workers in the docks, leather trade, sawmills, and brewing. They were rapidly dismissed from transport, but some remained as booking clerks on the railway, and delivery drivers for small firms – these were less likely to be bound by union agreements, and more likely to keep on a familiar face. Many women did stay in offices and shops – work which was becoming less popular with men anyway.

Some women certainly left their jobs willingly. Married women with children, whose husbands returned to civilian life, were often relieved to abandon such a strenuous existence, while most middle-class munition workers had no intention of remaining in such work beyond the war – although a few women engineers were quite determined to carve a niche for women in this profession, and founded the Women's Engineering Society in 1919. They were amongst a number of educated women who wanted to open up trade, commerce, industry and the civil service, and were to battle on the 1920s and 1930s. The government had pinned its hopes on the peaceful withdrawal of women from the labourforce, or at least their 'return' to the women's trades as soon as the War ended. However, this did not happen; 494,000 women were registered unemployed by March 1919, and they made up two thirds of the unemployed by May.[10] Ironically, unemployment amongst ex-servicemen did not turn out to be a problem – priority was often given to them by employers, over both women and non-serving men.

Women's unemployment then dropped drastically – to about 29,000 by November 1919.[11] What had happened to them? The answer is, they had been systematically pushed off the unemployment register, and been forced to give up paid work altogether, or to take work in the unpopular 'women's' trades, especially domestic service and laundry. This was a calculated action, taken by the government and its agents, the labour exchanges, and backed up by an unpleasant and hysterical campaign in the national and local press.

The process of persuasion began early. Lilian Barker, the formidable supervisor at Woolwich Arsenal (who seems to have run the place rather in the manner of a firm headmistress faced with unruly pupils), spoke to all the women laid off after the armistice:

It was pointed out to them that their first duty was to the soldier – the man who had done his bit for the past 4 years – and who would now be wanting to return to his normal occupation.

They were then told about local job vacancies, including domestic service – which, they were assured, had changed much over the war, as mistresses had learned to 'appreciate' good servants, and treat them with consideration.[12] The Woolwich workers were not soothed by this kind of assurance, however, and about 6,000 of them still marched to the Houses of Parliament to protest, and appeal for work. (They received one month's paid holiday, and assurance of benefit, for those made redundant, as their reward.) Most woman laid off, in any area of the country, were nevertheless determined to resist domestic service, whether or not this had been their trade before the war. They were looking for factory work, preferably using some of the skills they had learned, and they wanted reasonable wages. The *Daily Chronicle* questioned the women signing on at one labour exchange, and reported the case of one ex-munition worker, who had formerly been earning 37s 6d a week, but did not expect such good wages again:

> 'But I feel so pleased the war's over that I'll take any old job again.'
> 'Domestic service?'
> 'Except that,' she laughed.[13]

The daily press complained increasingly that women were not taking domestic and laundry work. There was a 'shortage' of servants for the middle classes, and women were simply refusing the jobs when offered; they were thus 'taking a holiday at the public expense', to use one popular phrase of the time, which has strange echoes of the accusations made about the unemployed in today's Britain. There was also work available in weaving and dressmaking which women were reluctant to take – weaving, once regarded as a good trade, fell from favour during the War, as weavers experienced the higher wages of munitions, or the greater freedom of outdoor work. Those who wished to recruit servants in the Kingston-on-Thames area even agreed to a sort of servants' contract, whereby the minimum wage would be £20 per annum, with guaranteed leisure periods, half a day a week off, part-time work on Sundays, one week's paid holiday every 6 months, and a written agreement of conditions.[14] Whether this increased the number of applicants in the area is another matter, but it seems a little unlikely, in view of the results of a quick survey by the *Woman Worker* (newspaper of the NFWW) outside a labour exchange in February 1919. Asked if they would take work in service, 5 per cent said they would, if wages went up to £40 pa, servants could choose their own clothes, and two half-days were free a week; 30 per cent agreed to the idea if they could live out, with a guaranteed hourly rate and double time on Sundays; 65 per cent said they would not take the work in any circumstances.[15]

But journalists continued their propaganda battle. There were many unskilled women claiming benefit who should not be, reported the *Manchester Evening Chronicle* in March 1919; the genuine work-seekers had to be weeded out from the 'dodgers'.[16] The *Manchester Dispatch* meanwhile assured its readers that the unemployed figures really were not as bad as they seemed; they should not include all those women who went to work for the first time during the war, after all.[17] The *Aberdeen Free Press* complained of women 'loafing about idly',[18] and the *Evening Standard* criticised 'slackers with state pay'.[19] A writer for the *Daily Express* made the common complaint that many 'unemployed' women really had husbands to support them or pensions to live on, and so should not be claiming benefit,[20] while an ex-serviceman wrote to the *Hull Daily Mail* deploring the fact that women were still in men's jobs, and that although there were plenty of jobs available in domestic service '. . . they won't have that. They would sooner fill a man's place while he walks about the street looking for a right to live.'[21]

Increasingly, the attacks on women were two-edged. Firstly, they should not be hanging on to men's jobs, and should give way to soldiers; and secondly, they should not be unemployed, because there were really plenty of jobs available to them. So, they were either traitors to men or scroungers on the state. This unpopularity would have been quite bad enough in itself, as it led to the abuse of women in the street ('When are you going to throw your —— job in, and let your men come back?' were the words hurled at one woman who wrote to her local paper to complain in April 1919[22]), and encouraged the further displacement of those women who had managed to keep their jobs after the war – steadily gas workers, shipyard workers, pitbrow workers, coppersmiths and scientific instrument makers found themselves eased out in the early months of 1919. But the government's own policy on women workers made life far more difficult for them. The benefit cut after 3 months meant that spring 1919 saw many women with less money. From that time onwards women all over the country were urged by labour exchanges to take domestic or laundry work. If they refused, their benefit was cut completely. (Unemployed men, meanwhile, could only be offered jobs in their usual trade.) Suddenly, four years in an engineering workshop or an aircraft factory counted for absolutely nothing; everyone knew that women were naturally suited for domestic work, so this was the work they were supposed to take. This policy was strongly supported by the press, although there were some journalists who attacked it. As one such writer in the *Liverpool Daily Post* put it:

> One would think to hear some people talk that the whole problem of women's unemployment is to be solved in the near future by a general 'back to the kitchen' movement on the part of ex-munition workers. Certainly the ordinary man in the street holds that view, but it is not the true one. It is simply a belated survival of the old myth that women's sphere is the home, and if she does not happen to possess one of her own she had best make herself useful in someone else's.[23]

More typical was the *Morning Post*'s smug report in April 1919:

> It has been found necessary to restrict, and in some cases stop, unemployment benefit pay to demobilised munition workers in Sheffield. Three hundred women who have refused to accept work in domestic service have been suspended from all benefit.[24]

The labour press was full of examples of women who had been refused benefit, and had taken their cases to the Court of Referees to appeal. This did not do much good. *Labour Woman* reported that in one week in Manchester alone 1,000 appeals against suspension were turned down.[25] One writer has since estimated that between 1918 and 1921, 81 per cent of women's appeals failed, because they had refused jobs in service or the laundry trade.[26] Even the Chief Inspector of Factories Report of 1919 said that '. . . interesting work is being taken out of their hands, and they are steadily being forced back into the routine of their hitherto normal occupations.'[27]

It is worth looking at some examples of this harsh treatment. A widow with one child, writing to the *Woman Worker* in

March 1919, told how the Camberwell labour exchange had offered her laundry work at 17s a week, then service, if she would put the child in a home, and finally wood-chopping at 17s 6d a week; she was told she would be reported and lose her benefit if she took none of these.[28] A group of girls in Manchester were suspended when they refused to work in a factory for 6s a week.[29] Occasionally, individuals managed to convince the Court of Referees of the justice of their case – a former shop assistant, who had been an aircraft worker during the war, was offered a job as nurse-housemaid, living out, for 12s 6d a week. She turned it down, saying she needed more time to look for work, and the Court agreed. Another woman, with children, went for a job as cook in a coffee house, at £1 a week, and was told to come back 2 weeks later. When she returned, the cook's job was gone, and she was offered bar work at 14s–16s a week. She turned this down, as she was already paying 18s a week to a childminder, and her appeal was allowed, as her expenses meant the job was unsuitable.[30] These wages, by the way, should be seen in perspective. Inflation during the war meant that by 1919 a skilled bricklayer was earning round £4 a week, while an unskilled male labourer would be earning about £3. The £1 a week classed as necessary for survival in 1914 would have grown to around £2 a week by 1919.

The government was not even prepared to help women through the Trade Boards, which had been set up to fix minimum wages in the lowest paid sectors of industry. In June 1920, the rate for general laundry work was fixed at 28s a week, the equivalent of 12s 6d in pre-war terms. Laundry workers gathered to protest, at the Central Hall Westminster, demanding £2, holidays and shorter hours, but only gained a slight increase in pay. Nor did educated women escape the new attacks on women's pay. In 1918, the LCC offered male teachers a wage rise – but not female.[31]

The slump began in 1920, and simply worsened women's employment prospects. Women's unemployment rose faster than men's, and pay rates in some trades, including engineering, were cut. Unfortunately, the traditional fields of women's work like clothing and textiles were hit badly, and there were layoffs here too. Through all this, married women fared particularly badly. On the one hand they were discriminated

16 This young Southampton girl drove the bread van shown here throughout the war, but had to give up when the men came home

against by the national insurance benefit which replaced out-of-work donation, as they had to have been in work, and paying N I stamps immediately before the war in order to be eligible. On the other they were excluded from the few government training schemes for women which were set up. In 1921, the LCC decided to sack all married women workers, unless they were doctors or teachers (where presumably there were staff shortages). This meant that all married women cleaners and domestic staff found themselves out of work, even if divorced or separated. By 1922, married women were in any case excluded from claiming dole, unless the total family income came to less than 10s a week.

Nevertheless, in spite of all this pressure, the number of servants did not return to pre-war levels – which says much for women's determination. One reason for this is shown by some figures assembled by Deborah Thom, on employment in the Woolwich area.[32] These are the comparative employment statistics for women:

	1911	1921
Service	4679	4451
Textiles	2663	1913
Commerce	1404	4260
Industrial	677	2964
	9423	13588

Here, as in many other urban areas, women had found jobs in new industries – light manufacturing – and factories which had no agreements with men. They also stayed in a number of white-collar jobs in shops, offices, insurance companies, and banks, where employers were happy to keep them. Clerical work was clean, respectable and mundane; it became seen as ideal work for unmarried women to do for a few years before marriage and 'retirement' – voluntary or enforced. Their low wages left them open to the accusation of being 'pocket money workers' and under-cutting men, but for many office jobs there was little competition from men anyway.

Earlier chapters have quoted from the experiences of a

number of women interviewed by the Imperial War Museum and Southampton Museum in recent years. What happened to them after the war? Mostly they left their wartime work with regret, but with surprisingly little bitterness. One woman, a bakery delivery driver (with horse and cart), said:

> I cried when I had to come off the round. I didn't think it was fair; but of course men were coming home from the War and men wanted jobs. So to see a girl driving round with pony and cart was not in it.[33]

She went home to help her mother with the housework. One shell filler said she was sorry to leave the work, but knew that it was only temporary. Mrs Stone, a farm worker, Mrs Bell, who worked at Pirelli's, and Mrs Gregory, an engineer at Avro, all went into service. The latter said she would have loved to have stayed on, but it was only fair for her to leave. Mrs Mullins, who worked in the Government Rolling Mills, became a nurse on one of the Southampton liners, but left to get married – something she regretted later; 'that was the end of my working days, unfortunately.' One munitions worker, later post office assistant, went back to tailoring. She was quite pleased to get back into what she saw as a good trade, just as Mrs Brady was happy to return to dressmaking, which she enjoyed. Mrs Kilford stayed in office work, which she had moved into during the war, while Mrs Barnet, a telegraph operator, retired from work with some relief as she had a child to look after. Mrs Hayes, a transport worker, had to leave the trams, to her regret, and took up cleaning instead. Mrs Ottaway, a van-driver, became a bakery van-driver after the war, but left to get married. Many women stayed in employment, but found their jobs less interesting – for example, one woman gasfitter had thoroughly enjoyed her work during the war. When the men came back, she was moved on to inspecting gas mantles for a living, which she found very boring, and was not sorry to leave when she married. Mrs Bryant had worked inspecting, cleaning and repairing guns sent back from France, and then became a milling machine operator. She was laid off at the end of the war, and found work in a shop. She was laid off again in 1919, as returning men took back these jobs too, and wound up packing uniforms – she left this as soon as she could. Several other women made unemployed did not look for paid work at all, but went home to help around the house.[34]

Mrs Mortimer's recollections are perhaps most interesting of all, however. She had worked in munitions, and on demobilisation was sent by the local labour exchange for a servant's job in Bassett, a prosperous area of Southampton. She had in fact been in service before the war, but, quite straight-faced, told her prospective employer that she knew nothing about serving at table – and thus successfully avoided a job as parlour maid. She was then offered the post of housemaid instead, but, on being told she would have to help with the mending, said innocently that she could not sew (although she could), and that offer was withdrawn. But of course she got her card signed by the employer to prove that she had tried to find work! She spent 16 weeks on the dole, and finally became a store-room attendant at a local hospital.[35]

The women interviewed by the Imperial War Museum had similar experiences. Some went back to traditional trades, like weaving or needlework. Others stayed unemployed for some time. Jane Cox made her living by sewing at home once her children were born, earning 8s 6d a week, and said, with feeling, 'things were bad after the war, very bad. I mean, people of this day and age can't have any conception of what it was like. It was bad.' Caroline Rennles, a Woolwich worker, was one of those who marched to Westminster to protest in 1918, and said with some bitterness, 'they threw us all out on the slag heap'. Isabella Clarke went back to Ireland, and took on another 'man's job' as a flax dresser. Laura Verity was one of the rare few who stayed on as a mechanic for 2 years, but had to leave because her throat was irritated by the work. She went back to housework, and part-time work in a shop.

Nearly all these women were laid off, and many of them spent some time unemployed. When they did find work, it was often something which they did not find interesting. A few found work they liked, but most put up with domestic service, or the kind of repetitive work deemed suitable for women. There is no doubt about the fact that many of them would have stayed in industrial or transport work if they could, or would have taken additional training had it been offered to them – but it was not.

VIEWS OF WOMEN'S ROLE: LIFE RETURNS TO 'NORMAL'

The wartime debates about women's future role seemed very far away by 1920. Women now had the vote, if they were over 30 and property owners, but they had not abandoned husbands and children for exciting jobs, they had not gained equal pay, they were not moving into skilled work. They had been forced back into a role in industry very similar to their pre-1914 one, and while many of the women themselves, and their middle-class feminist sisters, may have regretted this, other people were relieved. Unemployment benefit was an expensive drain on resources in a country already severely affected by 4 years of war; the government could not afford to pay the non-contributory out-of-work donation for long, and nor did it want the national insurance funds burdened by too many unemployed women. At the same time, employers of servants, laundry companies, and dressmaking establishments all depended upon a ready supply of cheap labour – they needed women who would take low-paid work, and the government's policy provided them with such women. The trade unions acting for workers in the 'men's trades', meanwhile, were all too pleased to see the interlopers disappear. Although only the unions in munitions had a formal agreement with the government, employers in other trades often willingly dismissed women, either because of pressure from unions or public opinion, or because they themselves thought that women were not worth the trouble of keeping on. In many cases, the largest women's union, the NFWW, allowed this to happen: they too believed that women had a moral obligation to retreat from men's jobs. This was partly because many of them shared the still-prevailing view in the labour movement that the comfort of a working-class home was best provided by a well-paid man, and that ideally married women would not want to work while they had children anyway. The continuing campaign for 'mother's pensions' which had begun several years earlier, was itself based on this idea; what woman would go out to work if she could be paid to do her proper job in the home? To quote one delegate at the NFWW conference in 1920 – 'If the mothers had pensions they would stop at home, and that would reduce unemployment.'[36] Feminist bodies like the Women's Industrial League did not agree, and campaigned for better training, and the opening up of opportunities to all women – but such was the mood after the war that it seemed to many that all wartime gains had been lost.

It was hard indeed for women who had been told that they were helping to win the war to accept that they were now parasites on society, and should 'go home' and stop taking the bread out of men's mouths – the contrast between wartime and post-war propaganda still seems extraordinary. Monica Cosens finished her book, *Lloyd George's Munition Girls*, with these words:

> And last of all, the Nation – what will it think of Miss Tommy Atkins when the War is over, and it has time to stand still, to look back and to think how these light-hearted, gay, simple-minded children – for that is what they are – have borne the heat of battle, how they fought smiling all the time, no matter if the day was hard and long?
>
> Then it will be the turn of their country to shake them by the hand and echo the words spoken by Mr Tommy Atkins: 'It's great what you have done!'[37]

This is not what 'the Nation' in the guise of the press chose to say. Instead, let me give one final contrasting quote from the *Evening News*, just two months after the war ended. Talking of unemployed munition workers, the writer added:

> These women are not wearing out their shoe leather to any great extent looking for work. Many of them would do their best to dodge a job if they saw one coming. (4/1/19)[38]

Nevertheless, criticised though they were, and constrained by poverty to go back to the old jobs, this did not mean that all the beneficial effects of war work disappeared completely. Many women had a new sense of self-worth – no matter what jobs they found themselves in, they could speak with pride of their past work. Women interviewed recently still retain that pride. They remember how they were once good mechanics, or crane drivers, or tram drivers. They became used to handling machinery, or a plough team, or a bus, and that feeling of satisfaction was important.

The war experience should also have demolished once and

for all the myth that women were in some way responsible for their own poor job status. After 1918 they had tried to get good jobs and hold out for decent wages, they had wanted training, and they had attempted to avoid the female ghettos. The fact that they were forced to take such work was not their fault. However, the myth of the apathetic, docile woman worker – who lacked ambition and would willingly undercut a man – remained an enduring one. It was too convenient to perish so easily.

Part Two
THE SECOND WORLD WAR

I thoroughly enjoy my four hours working in the afternoon. I'm all agog to get here. After all, for a housewife who's been a cabbage for fifteen years — you feel you've got out of the cage and you're free. Quite a lot of the part-timers feel like that — to get out and see some fresh faces — it's all so different, such a change from dusting. I think the war has made a lot of difference to housewives. I don't think they'll want to go back to the old narrow life. (Mass-Observation, *The Journey Home*, 1944, p.58)

17   May English, the young tram conductor on page 9, returned to work as a
      bus conductor in the Second World War

CHAPTER 8

WOMEN BETWEEN THE WARS

WORK

A girl born in 1918 at the end of one holocaust would have been 21 at the start of the next, assuming that she survived the flu epidemic of 1918, the slump of the 1920s and the depression of the 1930s. Her experiences of those years would have been heavily influenced by the niche in society into which she was born. Class was still important in inter-war Britain, even though its precise economic boundaries were becoming harder to define. This was especially so as far as women were concerned. The occupational class of increasing numbers of women, such as clerks, typists or teachers, was different from that of their fathers or husbands, many of whom were manual workers of various kinds, yet a woman's class position was recorded in the Census as that of the (male) head of her household. In spite of the blurring of economic boundaries, however, British society was still scored by social divides, as Mary Lee Settle, a young American volunteer in the Women's Auxiliary Air Force, discovered in 1942 on meeting her fellow recruits:

> It was the first glimpse of the stratification, almost Chinese in
> its complication and formality, which covered everything
> from a hairdo to a state of health to sugar in tea and by
> which each Englishman holds himself apart, himself his
> castle, from his fellows.[1]

The First World War had done little to alter the visible signs of class.

A minority of girls spent the years before their twenty-first birthdays entirely at school or at college. Only about 15 per cent of girls aged 11 to 17 went to secondary school in the 1930s, the norm being to stay within the elementary system till the school leaving age of 14. Even fewer went into higher education: by one estimate only 0.5 per cent of all girls who reached the age of 18 during the 1920s.[2] These young women had (like Vera Brittain or Winifred Holtby who both went back to Oxford after serving as VADs in the First War) to be clever, determined and to have families which were willing and able to support them financially into adulthood. For them there was a possibility of entering one of the professions. The number of women doctors increased during and after the First World War from 477 in 1911 to 2,580 in 1928. The number of women in the professional classes of the civil service was creeping up, too, though most of the 28,000 women employed there in 1939 were in the clerical grades. There were only fifty women in the better-paid and higher-status administrative grades in that year, and there were complaints that the selection procedures were stacked against women. Numbers in the professions which the Sex Discrimination (Removal) Act of 1919 had 'opened' to women were still pitiful. For example, there were a mere 82 women dentists, 21 women architects and 10 women chartered accountants in 1928. The vast majority of professional women were either teachers or nurses, of whom there were 134,000 and 154,000 in 1938.[3] Both teaching and nursing were considered 'good' careers for girls, although conditions could be rough under some employers, equal pay was non-existent, and the marriage bar, introduced into many public services as a cost-cutting exercise in 1922, presented work and marriage as incompatible alternatives.

So working life was not easy even for the relatively privileged well-educated young woman. Feminist organisations like the National Union of Societies for Equal Citizenship were campaigning to enlarge her opportunities in the male professional world by demanding 'a fair field and no favour'. In other words they wanted the removal of the practice of regarding most professional jobs as male preserves, and recognition of the right of women to compete on equal terms with men, for equal remuneration. The 'equal rights' feminists inevitably ran into conflict not only with men, but also with some women trade unionists such as the members of the Standing Joint Committee of Working Women's Organisations, who saw the promotion of women's interests in industry in an entirely different light. In their eyes women in industry should not be treated as if they were men. They thought that differences in their physique and social roles meant that women needed special protection as women, in the form, for example, of shorter hours and prohibitions on heavy work. Equal rights feminists, on the other hand, were worried that this type of protection would lead employers and trade unionists to bar women from all sorts of better paying jobs and equal pay with men. In contrast, although committed to raising women's wages through collective bargaining, some women trade unionists supported the male demand for a 'family' wage and did not prioritise equal pay on the grounds that it would be better for wives and mothers not to have to go out to work.

The employment prospects of the majority of girls who left school at 14 depended greatly on what was available locally. Jobs for women in clerical work were increasing, especially in large cities like Liverpool, Manchester and London. There were 124,843 women clerks in 1911 and 565,055 in 1931.[4] The advocacy of a friend or relative coupled with the claim to come from a respectable family helped in the scramble for these much-sought-after jobs. A sympathetic Church Deaconess secured the 15-year-old Helen Forrester, desperate for a job, the post of telephone operator at 12s 6d a week in the offices of a charitable organisation in Liverpool. In the absence of any training in the intricacies of a switchboard she was rapidly demoted to 'office girl' at 10s a week, a job to which she clung in spite of an exhausting round of errands all over Liverpool and the lecherous advances of lift attendants, since the alternative was a return to the role of household drudge.[5] A shorthand and typewriting qualification was a valuable asset in the restricted female labour market. Only $2\frac{1}{2}$ per cent of typists were men in the 1930s, but although such work was stereotyped 'women's work', beneath the superior aptitudes of men, and was paid as such, women were criticised for taking it in the Depression, as if by doing so they were robbing men of jobs. 'Better Pay and Smarter Clothes for Women: Unemployment and Patched Pants for Men' ran the newspaper headline to an article on women secretaries in 1934. Young city women could also find employment as shop assistants, another occupation in which the numbers of women had risen since before the First World War, from about 300,000 in 1911 to about 400,000 by 1931.[6] Such jobs varied greatly in the degree of status, gentility and pay attached to them as between, for example, the family corner shop and the large department store. The custom of requiring women to resign on marriage ensured that women working in shops and offices were either very young women expecting to have short careers, or older spinsters for whom this was their life's work. Some tension between the two groups was perhaps inevitable.

Many of the newer, 'lighter' manufacturing ventures of the inter-war years, like the tobacco, confectionery and electrical goods industries, followed a similar policy of employing young, unmarried women. Around 90 per cent of the women in these industries were single and under 35.[7] Women's industrial wages were about half of men's, and girls under 18 earned half as much again, so they were an economical option for any employer. Pay and hours varied from trade to trade, but adult female earnings of 30 shillings for a 48-hour week were officially fairly standard in 1935,[8] though employers in laundries, catering and retail shops were notorious for extracting 60 hours a week or more from their women workers. Women were not supposed to work at night under the 1937 Factory Act, but numerous employers claimed 'permissible exemption' status. As the preference for a youthful female workforce suggests, these jobs were not regarded as skilled, nor were they expected to lead anywhere. Edith Hall, who was born in West London in 1908, wrote, 'I must have had seventeen jobs by the time I was seventeen, leaving each, as I thought, to better myself . . . but I never did.' In her part of London the firms which lined the Great West Road, like His Master's Voice, and lampshade and sweet factories, took on school-leavers, but advancing years made these jobs harder to obtain. Edith describes the reaction of her friend Molly:

> She was beautiful and the dew of the morning shone in her eyes. She was seventeen and could not understand that here she was, young and not wanted. 'No, nothing today', the time-keeper would tell us as we went from factory to factory.[9]

Yet when she and Molly were working, they would be abused

in the street with taunts of 'Girls taking men's jobs'.

The long-established textile industries of Lancashire, York-shire and industrial Scotland were in Vera Brittain's eyes 'the chief as well as the best trades employing women'. Textile and clothing together absorbed about 1.2 million workers out of a total of some 6 million 'gainfully employed' in 1931. There was a tradition of married women working: 36 per cent of women textile workers were married and about a third were over 35 in 1931. In some branches of the industry, notably weaving, trade union organisation was strong, and women's earnings were above the female average. The same was true in branches of tailoring like mantle and costume-making, and in hosiery and boot and shoe manufacture, and these trades were among the few in which women were regarded as skilled. However, the Depression hit cotton and woollen manufacture hard. There was much short-time working and unemployment, and the textile workforce as a whole was shrinking. Informal networks operated between overlookers and parents, through pubs and neighbourhoods, to secure places and training for prospective girl workers, though not all were enthusiastic entrants. For example, Adelaide Shaw from Halifax remembered her intro-duction to the local mill as a 14-year-old:

> The men that were the overlookers used to be looking out for
> girls that were leaving school and two or three asked my
> mother if I could go and work in their mill . . . I wasn't very
> strong . . . every now and then I had to have a month nearly
> off poorly. I think my dad realized I wasn't very strong but I
> don't think it was ever thought you could do anything else.
> They were poor and they needed the money.[10]

Family pressure on young girls to contribute to the domestic budget was given a special edge in these years. Over 3 million men were unemployed in 1933, and the earnings of all members of a household were taken into account in the application of the means test to the dole. Thus a young woman could find herself forced by the state to support her father, a reversal of the expected roles, which could have a disturbing effect on them both.

The production line and methods of organising processes 'scientifically' in order to maximise output were introduced into many factories between the wars. Like the piece-work system, they were designed to produce an intense pace of work, which was conducive to accidents. Women, being largely un-unionised and on the lowest paying work, were particularly vulnerable. In 1936 the 14-year-old Betty Ferry was stitching the sleeves of army greatcoats for 55 hours a week at a firm called Silberstons in East London.

> This was a right sweat firm. It was rush from the time you went in till the hooter sounded for home time. Nobody hardly ever spoke to each other. I was hurrying up one day when my finger went under the machine. This gave me quite a shock.[11]

Safety precautions were still minimal in many workshops and factories in spite of the attention drawn to the problem in the First World War. Doris White wrote of being peppered with metal splinters when needles and poppers broke at the Canda Manufacturing Company where she worked in the late 1930s, and a woman who worked in a lampshade factory described how,

> The girls were expected to do needlework and paint with frozen hands and terrible chilblains . . . the air was often filled with fumes of spirit dye . . . and the girls breathed it in and got coloured nostrils, but they dare not complain for fear of losing their job.[12]

Hence the campaigns of women trade unionists to obtain industrial protection for women workers, with a view, they argued, to its eventual extension to men.

The least protected of any women workers were domestic servants. Edith Hall interspersed her numerous factory jobs with a spell as a 'general', that is a maid of all work, in big and small households near her home in West London.

> A 'general' was expected to do all the housework, preparing the vegetables and the cooking. I had to be up at six-thirty in the morning and clean the master's shoes and get the children's clothes ready for school. I was small for fifteen and their own daughter, who was thirteen, had reached pubescence and I had not; I was never treated as a child in any way, or even as a young person. When my master or mistress went out at night, I was expected to stay up in case one of the young children woke and called. I was left plenty

of ironing to do and silver to clean just in case I got sleepy; then up again next morning early.[13]

Employers' assumptions that they owned their servants, body and soul, were increasingly resented, and occasions of particularly blatant exploitation bitterly remembered, as for example when an invitation for Edith to stay to Christmas dinner turned out to mean a gobbled meal from the draining board followed by all the washing up. Vera Brittain wrote, 'There is probably no occupation in which the worker is still so emphatically regarded as having a "place", and that a very inferior one.' As we have seen, women who had done industrial work in the First World War were loath to go into service after it, and where there were alternative types of work they were eagerly seized. But in some areas, like the north-east, South Wales and many rural districts, there was simply nothing else, especially in view of the decline in the practice of employing women on farms, except as seasonal labour. Successive governments continued to see domestic service as the solution to female unemployment, and the numbers of women in service increased by 16 per cent during the Depression, from 1.1 million in 1921 to 1.3 million in 1931. But although 800,000 women continued to live in, there was a shift towards non-residential work in institutions like hospitals, schools and office premises, where conditions did not resemble slavery quite so much. Official domestic training centres were set up in big towns, but when the Pilgrim Trust interviewed girls at a centre in Liverpool they found little enthusiasm for their work as such. Asked about their prospects, nearly all the girls said they wanted to get married, preferably to someone rich.[14]

MARRIAGE

Marriage must have seemed an attractive alternative to many young women in low-paid and unskilled jobs, and the social expectation that this was a young woman's natural destination was enormous. Margery Spring Rice, who wrote up the Women's Health Enquiry undertaken in the 1930s as a book called *Working Class Wives*, wrote:

Throughout their lives, they have been faced with the
tradition that the crown of a woman's life is to be a wife and
mother. Their primary ambition therefore is satisfied.
Everybody is pleased when they get married, most of all the
great public, who see therein, the workings of nature's divine
and immutable laws. If for the woman herself the crown
turns out to be of thorns that again must be Nature's
inexorable way.[15]

Marriage had the attraction of freeing a young woman from
the bonds imposed by her parents, to set up house with a
husband of her own choosing and to start a family. Some
historians (like Jane Lewis) have commented on the decline of
the 'patriarchal' marriage, in which the husband dominated a
household geared to serve his needs, and the rise of the
'companionable' marriage in which husband and wife jointly
made crucial decisions like where to live and whether to use
contraception, visited the pub or cinema together, and even
shared some of the household tasks. Companionable marriages
were more comon in areas where it was normal for both
partners to be in paid employment, as in the case of the
weavers of Preston or Burnley, and they may have been on the
increase in the middle classes, for example where the wife had
given up a professional job in marrying.[16] Even though she
might get help, however, it was highly exceptional for the
responsibility for domestic management to lie anywhere other
than with the wife in the 1930s, whatever class she belonged to,
and households abounded in which husbands' and wives' roles
were rigidly separated. In dockside, shipbuilding, mining, and
engineering communities and on farms throughout the country,
arduous and exhausting work for men was typically accompanied by hard drinking and the expectation of wifely
submission, with the threat of violence never far from the
surface. In such marriages the criterion for a 'good husband'
was not one who helped with the washing up, but one who
'never laid a finger on us'.[17]

It was possible for women who suffered brutal husbands to
obtain a judicial separation and a maintenance order through
the local magistrates' courts, but divorce was expensive and
difficult to obtain. Before the First World War feminists pressed
for an end to the Victorian double standard under which a wife

could be divorced for adultery but a husband could not, and they finally achieved this equalisation of the law in the Matrimonial Causes Act of 1923. But cruelty, like insanity and desertion, did not become grounds for divorce until another Act was passed in 1937. With each liberalisation of the divorce laws there was an outcry about the undermining of the sanctity of marriage and the imminent disintegration of society. Such feelings were especially entrenched in some middle-class circles. For example, Katharine Chorley, who grew up in a comfortable suburb south of Manchester between the 1900s and the 1920s, wrote that her father would not allow her mother to receive Mrs Green, a respectably married neighbour, because either she or her husband had at some time in the past been involved in a divorce. The First World War played a part in unbending Katharine's mother, who 'met Mrs Green on various war jobs and liked her', but it was only after Mr Chorley was in his grave that she went as far as to exchange calls. Katharine observed that most couples in their circle struggled with 'the maintenance of a marriage at almost any cost'.[18] But in spite of the enduring social opprobrium, a growing number of couples took advantage of the increasing accessibility of divorce to put an end to unsatisfactory marriages: the number of divorces in England doubled between the wars from 3,041 in 1920 to 6,092 in 1938.[19]

Throughout society there was much wifely ignorance about what a husband earned, and of course husbands decided how much of their wages they would 'tip up' to the wives. Some feminists, worried by the total dependency of the wife, argued that she should be paid a wage by the state, or have a legal claim on a fixed portion of her husband's wage, others that a family allowance was essential for her well-being and that of her children. Mary Sutherland (later the Chief Woman Officer of the Labour Party), replied to these arguments, 'From their fervent advocacy, it would seem that all married women are married unhappily, and to the same man – one who is not a very noble specimen of his sex.' In fact, she said, most industrial women were satisfied with a mutual 'understanding about money' between themselves and their husbands, and rather than state intervention they wanted higher male wages.[20] However, even in households where mutual agreements were honoured, the fact remained that the housewife had to make her allowance stretch over the needs of the entire family, including the breadwinner, who enjoyed privileges of pocket money and leisure denied to her. Not surprisingly, there was much secrecy on the part of wives about how they managed the family finances, especially about the debts they incurred, and money tensions were a major source of marital friction.

Many wives resorted to supplementing their allowances with earnings from all sorts of sources, from pawning possessions to taking in washing, children, lodgers or outwork, gathering sticks to sell, or going out charring. Sometimes the work had to be done in secret, so great was the man's stake in the notion that he could 'provide' and that a woman's place was in the home. The Women's Health Enquiry collected some pathetic examples of working-class women literally penned into their homes, like the woman who had five babies in five years and whose husband refused to allow her out until, finally, she had a nervous breakdown. This woman's comment was, 'It isn't the men are unkind. It is just the old idea that we should always be at home.'[21]

This is not to say that most women were the silent sufferers of domestic oppression. Within segregated marriages women often dominated their sphere in both practical and moral terms, and derived support from kin and community networks which could operate if necessary to contain and control a husband's abuse of his power as well as a wife's deviation from the standards expected of her. But all the same, for the 90 per cent of wives who were not engaged in fulltime paid employment in 1931, fundamental economic power lay with him.

Even though a full day in the mill or factory followed by shopping, cooking, cleaning and caring for a family was still seen by many working women as a burden to be avoided if economic circumstances permitted, the proportion of married women working rose slightly in the inter-war years from 13 to 16 per cent of all women in paid work between 1921 and 1931. If employers were willing to take them on, there were married women who would work. This was true not only of manual work, where economic necessity could be seen as the driving force, but also of white-collar work like teaching. Following the London County Council's removal of its bar in 1935, increasing numbers of women teachers opted to stay in teaching after marriage: by 1939 the number of women resigning was only one tenth of the 1935 level.[22] There were evidently middle-class as well as working-class women who desired (for whatever reason) to reduce the extent of their dependency in marriage.

In areas and occupations where convention permitted it, like the textile towns, married women workers included mothers, who managed in much the same way as working mothers had before the First World War. The vast majority who were not in a position to employ a nanny depended on neighbours or kin for childminding, since the day nurseries run by the Ministry of Health under the Act of 1918 were not numerous and were in any case supposed to rescue the children of the very poor from neglect, rather than provide a service for mothers going out to work. Although labour-saving technology was being applied to domestic work, its advance was slow. Manufacturers' priorities in marketing products like gas and electric cookers, irons and water-heating systems, were to raise the consumption of gas and electricity, so the cost of buying and running these items was high. The salesman's targets were housewives in the new suburbs growing up around large towns like London and Birmingham during the building boom of 1933–8, rather than working-class wives.[23] One estimate placed two-thirds of working-class families in homes built before the First World War, half of which were insanitary,[24] and the Women's Health Inquiry found that only 10 per cent of working-class homes had an internal water supply, let alone any labour-saving devices. No doubt, whether they were in paid work or not, women welcomed them when they could get them, but vacuum cleaners and washing machines were more common in relatively well-off households (where they might be used by a maid) than in the households of mothers in manual work.

Overall between the wars, working wives and especially working mothers were still unusual. Like their predecessors in the First World War and before, they had to plan housework carefully, particularly the family wash, and fit it around paid work early in the morning, late at night and on Sundays. As a Preston woman said of life for them between the wars 'it was all bed and work'.[25] The convention that marriage was a woman's normal fulltime occupation was still very strong.

A population imbalance of about one and a half million more women than men in 1921 meant that there was a shortage of potential husbands throughout the inter-war years. About 18 per cent of women aged 20 to 45 never married in this period. But all the same, single women were mocked as social failures. As Winifred Holtby wrote, the words 'frustrated' and 'spinster' were still commonly combined, and both she and the childless wife 'are led to believe they are missing out in a fundamental way'.[26]

The young woman's desire for freedom from conventional constraints, expressed in the 'flapper' fashion of the 1920s for short straight dresses, cropped hair, serviceable shoes, cigarettes and sexual freedom was satirised in popular songs. Edith Hall remembered one called 'Just a girl men forget':

> Dear little girl they call you a flirt,
> A flapper with up-to-date ways,
> You may shine brightly, but just like a lamp,
> You'll burn out one of these days.
> Then your old-fashioned sister will come into view,
> With a husband and kiddies, but what about you?
> You'll soon realize that you're not so wise
> When the years will bring tears of regret
> For when they play 'Here comes the bride'
> You'll stay outside,
> Just a girl men forget.[27]

Winifred Holtby, Cicely Hamilton and other feminists stoutly defended the independent single woman, especially the teacher or doctor who 'although they lacked husbands, seemed to get on well enough and find plenty of interest in life'.[28] Furthermore, numerous single women workers were supporting older parents or other kin. Hence the anger of women civil servants or teachers, for example, at the male assumption that they were only working for pin money and were not 'breadwinners' in their own right. Holtby wrote that the spread of knowledge about contraception meant that many were not celibate, but simply avoided motherhood. Such views were risqué for the time, however. The churches still regarded sex as being for procreation only, scandal surrounded Marie Stopes' publications advocating sexual pleasure for *married* women, and in the 1920s she was involved in several major court cases over her advocacy of the use of birth control.[29]

Family limitation was practised more widely, however, in the inter-war years than ever before. Middle-class family size had been falling since the mid-nineteenth century, from the typical Victorian family of over six children per marriage to an average of about two, and in the inter-war years working-class families became smaller. Where the necessary knowhow came from is rather mysterious, since the whole subject of the reproductive system was shrouded in embarrassment and official restrictions on the spread of information about contraception were tight. A woman's life had to be in danger before most doctors would introduce her to methods of birth control, which by the late 1920s included the sheath, the cap, the sponge, pessaries and douching, in addition to the age-old techniques of coitus interruptus and abstinence. But the supply of rubber contraceptives was increasing, and so was the motivation of many couples to limit their families. The decline of infant mortality meant more children per family were growing up, and the raising of the school leaving age to 14 in 1918 prolonged the period of their economic independence on their parents. Women of all social classes appear to have desired to avoid both the repeated pregnancies of their mothers and the dangers reflected in the stubbornly high rate of maternal mortality between the wars. The overall fall in fertility rates varied from occupation to occupation. The biggest families still characterized the most segregated families, like those of miners, farm labourers and domestic servants, and smaller families were more common where both partners did paid work, like textile workers, or where the wife had done work involving plenty of contact with other women before marriage.[30]

In most families numerous children took a toll of their mother's health, in both bearing them and in stretching the family's resources to provide for them. The Women's Health Enquiry suggested that women were not much healthier during the inter-war years than they had been before, in spite of the introduction of National Insurance in 1911. Only women in insured employment (about half of those in paid work) were entitled to medical attention without charge, and women neglected their own nutrition and health for the sake of providing for their families. Women in their thirties and forties were becoming old before their time due to untreated problems like dysmenorrhoea, anaemia, headaches, haemorrhoids, rheumatism, varicosity and prolapse.

WAR

One of the things which was different about the inter-war years from the period before 1918 was that women now had a political voice. Women over 30 at last had the right to stand and vote in parliamentary and local elections and the first woman Member of Parliament, Lady Astor, was elected in 1919. In 1928 an equal franchise with men was won, voting age for men and women being 21. The political affiliations of women in politics were spread over all parties, and, as we have seen there were differences of view among feminists, particularly over the degrees of protection and equality merited by women's work and family roles, but nevertheless it is not too much of an oversimplification to identify two main causes in which women used their new political influence: welfare and peace. The horrifying evidence of the neglect of women during and after childbirth made the improvement of local and national provision for women's welfare, particularly maternity care, an urgent priority. Upper-class women like Lady Astor and Lady Rhondda had more time and money to devote to public life, but the MPs and local councillors of the inter-war years included some women from middle- and working-class backgrounds who worked hard on these issues, such as Ellen Wilkinson, MP for Middlesbrough and later Jarrow, and the councillors Selina Cooper of Nelson and Colne, Annie Barnes of Stepney and Hannah Mitchell of Manchester.[31]

The other political objective of particular concern to women in the inter-war years was the campaign for international peace, and many women in politics were both feminists and pacifists. Perhaps the two best known were Ellen Wilkinson who became a Labour MP in 1924 and Eleanor Rathbone who sat as an Independent from 1929 to 1946. As well as campaigning on welfare issues, including family allowances (to which Eleanor Rathbone devoted her political career), both campaigned for the League of Nations to be made an effective peace-keeping body. Many women who did not hold political office but were well-known intellectuals, like Vera Brittain, Dora Russell and Frances Partridge, promoted the same ideal.

During the 1930s there was a growing feeling of international menace as fascist dictatorships were established in Italy,

Germany and Spain and fears grew that the League of Nations was incapable of doing the job for which it had been set up. As well as threatening war by their relentless pursuit of new territories, these dictatorships worried feminists because of their savage repression of minorities like Jews and communists, and their growing emphasis on restricting women's sphere to the home and the reproduction of the 'master race'.

Pacifists confronted a dilemma. Did appeasement of the dictators come within the principles of international morality, or should they be resisted which would inevitably mean war? Appeasement, which meant agreeing to the seizure of parts of other countries on the understanding that expansionism would then cease, was the policy of the Conservative governments of the 1930s, but public disquiet grew when Neville Chamberlain came back from a conference with Hitler in Munich in September 1938 declaring that 'Peace in our time' had been obtained by permitting the Nazi annexation of a large part of Czechoslovakia.

Many of the fifteen women MPs in 1938, including Ellen Wilkinson and Eleanor Rathbone, declared themselves anti-fascists, thereby aligning themselves with the rearmament campaign and dropping their pacificsm. Indeed Edith Summer-skill, a medical doctor who had been drawn into politics through her concern for maternal and child welfare, won a by-election for Labour in West Fulham in 1938 on this platform.[32] Dora Russell, deeply concerned during the 1930s about the consequences of Nazi oppression, also decided that pacifism was irrelevant in the face of fascism, while still deploring 'the restless drive for power and destruction' in the West, that produced war.[33] But some women, while opposing fascism, could not abandon their pacifist principles. Vera Brittain, as we have seen, lost all the men closest to her in the First World War, her brother, lover and friends, as well as experiencing at first hand as a VAD in France the mutilation and disfiguration inflicted by shelling and gas attacks. Frances Partridge was married to an ex-army officer whose experiences of trench warfare convinced them both that killing was an unacceptable method of solving political problems. At the price of social ostracism both remained staunch pacifists throughout the war.[34]

The summer of 1938 was also a turning point in the

government's acceptance of the need to prepare for war. Women figured in its plans, in acknowledgment both of their usefulness in the First World War, and the extensive devastation within Britain expected to result from the techniques of waging war which had been developed since then, involving the use of fighter planes, bombers and fast-moving tanks armed with machine guns. In May Sir Samuel Hoare, the Home Secretary, asked the redoubtable Dowager Marchioness of Reading, widow of the Viceroy of India, to form 'Women's Voluntary Services for Air Raid Precautions', officially launched in June 1938. The WVS was intended to provide back-up for Civil Defence, specifically by training women to protect their own homes and families in the event of air attack or invasion, though they were not to wield weapons, something considered far too unfeminine. During 1938, over 32,000 women enrolled, mostly recruited initially through a personal network of better-off, married women, emanating from Lady Reading's address book.[35]

Simultaneously, the War Office decided to revive the idea of an auxiliary service staffed by women to support the men in the army with catering, clerical and storekeeping services, as the Women's Auxiliary Army Corps had done in the First World War. Since it was still peacetime the new body was modelled on the Territorials, a reserve force of male volunteers who engaged in regular training in order to be available for instant mobilisation if war broke out. It was called the Auxiliary Territorial Service (ATS) and was initially staffed by women with links with the Territorials, mostly wives and daughters of soldiers, many of whom had been WAACs in the First World War. It was led by Dame Helen Gwynne Vaughan who had all these qualifications. By June 1939 the political situation was so menacing that the Ministry of Agriculture decided to resurrect another women's organisation of the First World War, the Women's Land Army. Lady Denman, who was also Chairman of the Federation of Women's Institutes, took on the task from her country seat in Sussex.

So the nuclei of all three, the WCS, the ATS and the Land Army, were formed by 'local great ladies' who recruited the first officers from among their own ranks. Problems of class and age inevitably arose as the services grew. In particular, it became apparent that there was a yawning gulf between the

First World War veterans and the generation which had grown up since. As one young woman put it, 'People who were in the last war are a nuisance. They are always saying: "We did this or that" – but we can't go back.'[36] The world of 1939 was indeed different from that of 1914, yet there must have been a sense of déjà vu for many older women as Britain rolled inexorably towards another war with Germany.

Nazi Germany invaded Poland on 1 September 1939. This time Neville Chamberlain honoured his pledge that Britain would not tolerate any more German expansionism and on 3 September he issued a declaration of war. A small British Expeditionary Force was sent to France and the navy began its six-year game of cat and mouse with German submarines round the British coast and in the Atlantic. But the scale of the war at this stage was very limited. In particular the devastating air raids on the civilian population did not materialise as predicted. Although the reaction of many women to the declaration of war was to want to do something useful, they were given few opportunities. War-oriented activity was still largely confined to women with cars, time and money who were able to rush about the counties organising the WVS, the ATS and the Land Army.

The prospects of the majority of women workers at the beginning of the Second World War were as discouraging as they had been at the start of the First. The immediate effect of war was a rise in women's unemployment. Because so many women worked in consumer industries such as textiles, clothing, pottery and boots and shoes which, as in 1914, cut their workforces in the face of the threat war posed to their markets, there were more women out of work during 1940 than there had been in 1939, whereas the number of unemployed men fell.[1] In spite of this apparent waste of womanpower the process was officially encouraged, especially by Churchill's Coalition Government which ousted the Chamberlain Government in May 1940 on the grounds that greater state intervention was necessary in order to gear the country up for war. It was assumed that if 'non-essential' industries were

...trated in a few firms, factory space and resources would became available and workers would be freed for employment in more important industries like munitions. But the process did not work as smoothly as this. For example, 20,000 women were 'freed' from the cotton industry during 1940–1 but only half of them found new jobs, in spite of the urgency of the war situation, especially after the hasty British retreat from Dunkirk in May 1940 which ended nine months of 'Phoney War' and introduced a real threat of Nazi invasion.[2]

Women who wanted to help to resist such an invasion were not welcomed either. The 'Local Defence Volunteers', rapidly officially reorganised as the Home Guard, were formed under the shadow of the invasion threat, but women were not allowed to join, so strong was both the ideology of the male defender of women and children and the antipathy to women bearing arms. Edith Summerskill, MP, was eventually permitted to become a member of the House of Commons Home Guard because she was so insistent, and in 1943 obtained the right for women to serve as Home Guard auxiliaries, but they were still not supposed to use weapons. Women who wanted to do agricultural work faced considerable discouragement too. At a call from the Ministry of Agriculture, 30,000 enrolled in the Women's Land Army in August 1939 but after training many of them had to return to the queues at the labour exchanges, and even by Christmas 1941 only 20,000 were in regular employment on the land, fewer than the number enrolled in 1918.[3]

Things were not much better for women with educational qualifications, who hoped they could be of service. Elaine Burton, an unemployed administrator, responded bitterly to the statement by Ralph Assheton, Parliamentary Secretary to the Minister of Labour, that the large number of unemployed women was 'an asset' which would become useful later in the war. She wrote, 'Has Mr Assheton any conception of what it means to be an "asset" living on fifteen shillings a week dole for seven months?'[4]

Gradually the government wanted to make use of its 'asset', but became increasingly perplexed about how to do so. Having shrunk from all but the most marginal intervention in the mobilisation of women in the First World War, it had little experience upon which to fall back. However, by the beginning of 1941 industrialists and government departments were complaining of a growing labour shortage leading to production hold-ups and even to the deaths of soldiers in North Africa, where fronts had been opened up against the Italians.[5] How could such a situation arise at a time when there were still over a quarter of a million women out of work?

One of the causes was that employers were loath to alter the employment practices which they had re-established since the First World War. Most jobs in skilled engineering and the higher grades of the civil service, for example, and almost all jobs on the land, were regarded by employers, workers and trade unions as 'men's jobs'. But it was not only the wisdom of giving women work regarded as skilled or heavy that was at issue. Many employers had to be convinced all over again 'that women were no less competent than men to carry out some of the less skilled processes' in spite of the fact that women had been widely employed in manufacturing industries on repetition processes throughout the inter-war years.[6] But even where employers did commonly hire women, in electrical engineering, light metal work and the retail trade, for example, they were (as we have seen) used to taking on only those who were young and single. Elaine Burton was showered with letters from older married women complaining that their offers of service were rebuffed by employers to whom women over 35 represented an unfamiliar and unwelcome addition to the labourforce. It seemed incredible to her that employers were so short-sighted that they could find no use for these women. The Ministry of Labour's suggestion that industrialists should take on Irishwomen, the principal source of immigrant labour in the Second World War, struck employers as even more outlandish, their prejudices against women now bolstered by stereotypes of Irish unreliability, drunkenness and immorality. Even in 1942, at least one labour manager desperate for new workers left a young woman sitting in the employment exchange rather than take her, when told that she was Irish.[7]

In the early months of 1941 at a time when Britain was suffering the Blitz and battling alone against Germany and Italy without the help of either Russia or the USA, the government came to a conclusion it never reached during the First World War: it could no longer wait for women to be employed spontaneously on the scale required. Under the stolid but persuasive influence of Ernest Bevin, ex-trade union leader and now Minister of Labour, the wartime coalition government assumed responsibility for women's mobilisation. The first official step was compulsory registration. This meant that from March 1941 all women aged 19 to 40 had to register at employment exchanges so that the Ministry of Labour had a record of what they were doing and could direct those considered suitable into 'essential work'. Recognising the reluctance of many employers to take on women, the government simultaneously issued a regulation known as the Essential Work Order (EWO) which bound them to take and keep the women workers compelled to enter war work in this way. Most of the 350,000 women who were unemployed in January 1941 had found jobs by the end of the year. By October 1943 only 24,000 women were registered unemployed.[8] The EWO prevented workers from leaving work without the permission of the National Service Office (a Ministry of Labour official) but, though a constraint on a worker's freedom, the order was not loathed as much as the leaving certificates of the First World War had been, partly because the employer had to guarantee certain standards of pay and conditions and partly because National Service Officers usually let women go if they claimed that they were needed at home.[9]

Officials were worried that women's conventional domestic responsibilities would prove major obstacles to their recruitment for war work. They were uncertain about whether to try to push women into work regardless of their home ties or whether to grant exemptions, and if so on what basis. For nine months the Woman Power Committee, a very active wartime caucus of women MPs, had been urging the government to listen to women's ideas about solving such problems of mobilisation, but feminism was distrusted and the female parliamentary presence was small (there were no women in the Wartime Cabinet) so up to now they had been ignored. They brought the matter to a head in March 1941 with a debate in the House of Commons on 'Woman-Power'. Under this pressure the Ministry of Labour rather reluctantly turned to women's representatives for their advice, calling into being an official Women's Consultative Committee. Its nucleus was two women MPs, Edith Summerskill (Labour) and Irene Ward (Conservative), and it also contained trade union and labour women, and representatives of women's voluntary organisations.

All members of the committee were adamant that single women without dependants should be directed to work wherever they were needed, even if it meant travelling a long way from home. Even though women MPs were angry that the principle of equal pay was not written into it, the committee endorsed the National Service Number 2 Act of December 1941, the only piece of wartime legislation conscripting women, under which single women aged 20 to 30 (extended to 19 in 1943) became liable for military service. But they were much more cautious about compelling wives and mothers to work. On the committee the concern of inter-war feminists about the hard work and poor health of working-class women who bore a double burden and the conventional views of the representatives of women's voluntary organisations about the place of the wife and mother combined to ensure that no mother of children under 14 living at home would be directed into war work. The committee also thought that many other housewives would be fully occupied at home, and therefore not available for outside work, and they invented the 'Household R' category of exemption for the guidance of interviewing officers. Such was the respect for the domestic role that even a woman running a 'small household' of only one other adult than herself, with domestic help, was exempt, suggesting that the government would do little to spread the burdens of war evenly over women of different classes. Women in the 'Household R' category were regarded as 'non-mobile', that is they could not be directed to work in factories at a distance which would require them to leave home. However, the interviewing officer could decide whether to direct such women into work locally.[10]

Later, as the labour shortage bit harder, it was decided that there were many exempt housewives who could be directed into part-time work, which was officially organised for the first time in the Second World War. At first employers were reluctant to recruit part-timers, who struck them as having an inappropriate view of the factory as 'a place where you can drop in for a spot of work just when you feel like it'. But state intervention changed this. A Control of Engagement (Directed Persons) Order issued in April 1943 increased the numbers of part-timers to nearly one million by the end of 1943. The pool from which women could be directed into employment was also enlarged by raising the age limit for women's registration. By the beginning of 1944 all women up to the age of 50 were supposed to have registered, in spite of protests in the press that this amounted to the 'conscription of grandmothers'. Employers had no choice but to take these 'older women' in spite of their earlier prejudices against them, and the proportion of women workers coming from each age group up to 50 became more equal than it had been before the war.[11]

Even women who were considered unsuitable for part-time work because they lived in rural areas and had household responsibilities were being drawn into war work by 1943. A scheme of engineering outwork was developed under which work as diverse as the assembly of engine parts and instrument panels and the sorting of small components muddled during raids was farmed out to local centres or women's own homes. It was a government-sponsored version of the long-standing exploitative homework system.

The decisions of the Women's Consultative Committee set boundaries on the compulsory powers of the state, but all women, including mothers of young children, were urged to volunteer. However, there were clearly many men who did not believe that the 'angel of the house' should be encouraged to spread her wings even in wartime. Originally it had been proposed that childless married women who were living alone should, like single women, be conscripted, but the Chiefs of the Armed Forces argued in Cabinet that servicemen were deeply opposed to any conscription of women because they did not want their wives and sweethearts to be placed in danger.[12] This argument ignored the fact that in a war involving the persistent bombing of civilian targets almost everyone was in danger. A wave of children was evacuated at the start of each new phase of bombing: the Blitz of September 1940 to June 1941, the 1942 Baedeker raids on historic towns, the renewed air attacks on London and other big cities in 1943 to 1944, and the V1 and V2 flying bombs and rockets of 1944 to 1945. But the attempt to evacuate pregnant women and mothers with small children in September 1939 was unsuccessful, the mothers returning rapidly, preferring the perils at home to the isolation and loneliness of life in a 'billet'. In consequence most women in the major towns of Britain had been subject to the horrors of the Blitz for over a year before conscription was introduced.

Other evidence suggests that men bewailed the compulsory war service of women because of its more immediate threat to conjugal relations. Mass-Observation, one of the first opinion-research organisations, collected the comments of ordinary people on the subject, up and down the country. For example, a Cardiff woman told them, 'My husband's said he'll come out of the Army if I go into war-work.' And a man in Bradford, aware that mothers of young children were exempt from all forms of compulsion, proposed that his wife should become pregnant as a matter of priority. He and others claimed that the call up of married women would lead to the break-up of homes, but it is clear that the loss of the services they were used to getting from their wives was uppermost in their minds. 'Men coming home on leave will find that they can only see their wives for an hour or two a day. Men in reserved occupations will come back to cold untidy houses with no meal ready,' lamented an air-raid warden. Another man felt that a wife in paid work, especially munitions, would 'degrade him in his position'. Sometimes reluctantly, in the knowledge that they were missing out on both fun and money, women tended to defer to their husbands' wishes in the matter.[13]

Some women were critical of the ease with which wives were exempted from compulsory war work, arguing that men did not need looking after as much as the war effort needed women. For example, one woman reported to Mass-Observation in 1941:

> A friend in her twenties went to Labour Exchange on Friday for interview after registration months ago. 'I see you are married. Does your husband come home to his mid-day meal?' 'Yes.' 'Very well, I expect you have enough to do so we won't keep you.' The larger lunacy again.[14]

There was a sharp edge to the criticism when it was felt that wealthier women who could afford servants were being let off lightly. But on the whole working-class women regarded compulsion cautiously. Married women were worried that the weight of domestic work which they bore personally would not be taken into account, and that too much would be expected. 'It's all right for them young ladies with butlers and chauffeurs who don't have to worry their sweet little heads about keeping home,' commented a Coventry woman about joining the Forces. Others indicated that though they would like to 'do their bit', and though they needed the money in view of rising prices, they did not see how they could possibly participate, unless employers altered the hours of work typical of industry, and the government provided far more help with domestic work such as shopping, cooking and childcare. The government, however, introduced compulsory registration first, and only after March 1941 did its ministries turn their attention to the vital question of women workers' domestic burdens. Another Coventry woman summed up the dilemma when describing how she had requested part-time work at the 'Unemployment Bureau' as she called it, in November 1941, but had been rebuffed: 'They could give us full-time work but we would get war in our homes if we took it.'[15]

Married women were particularly fearful that they might be expected to move away from home. The official decision that they would not be regarded as 'mobile' as long as they were maintaining their husbands' homes does not appear to have been very clearly communicated. Unmarried women were the Ministry of Labour's target, constituting its most desirable category of 'surplus unskilled mobile woman labour', available to be sent anywhere.[16] Nevertheless there was a burst of protective moral outrage from Scottish male MPs about the transfer of young Scotswomen to English munitions factories at the rate of 400 a month by January 1942. They claimed that the Scots girls were not properly supervised, billeted or paid, but the nub of their criticism was a nationalistic possessiveness about 'their' young women. David Kirkwood said in Parliament, 'The Scots as a nation will be wiped out if denuded of their womenfolk.' Whether or not the government took this seriously, the number of Scotswomen transferred dropped to 40 a month by the end of 1942.[17]

Quite apart from men's preference to keep them at home, many single women hotly resented the feeling of being 'moved about by powers like pawns in a game of chess between Titans' as a General Manager's secretary put it to Mass-Observation. Complaints ranged from those of the Bradford girls who said they did not want to sleep in single beds in the Midlands when they were used to sleeping two to a bed in Yorkshire, to the careful explanations of women to whom life in the parental home represented both a set of binding responsibilities and an opportunity for economic and emotional security. Young women were understandably irritated to be sent away only to discover that their places had been taken by other girls directed far from home.[18] Many such women looked for ways of avoiding direction far afield, for instance by taking any local work which might be considered 'essential', even in laundries. There were rumours of hasty marriages, quick conceptions and the recall of evacuated children. It was, after all, children under 14 who were the ultimate barrier to state interference. In their presence the decision about whether to work belonged incontrovertibly to the woman herself and not to the government. This kind of anxiety did not occur in the First World War, because women were not obliged to take up war work in the same way.

Few women spoke enthusiastically about leaving home to go into war work. In fact one third of a sample of married and single women 'apparently free to go into war work' in October 1941 said they were definitely unwilling to do so, mostly because of their domestic work or dislike of leaving home.[19] Those who were keen tended to be girls from better-off homes, in some cases accustomed to 'mobility' (if only between home and boarding school) but more often anxious to experience a bit more of life than convention normally granted to the middle-class daughter. For example, Joan Welch was a secretary before the war, living at home:

> My brother had already been called up to go in the RAF, and
> I was a bit jealous really. I wasn't very happy at home,
> because my father had such a strict regime . . . I was always a
> bit shy and reserved . . . and I thought it would probably be
> better to go into the services.[20]

Such girls tended to join the relatively small and select Women's Auxiliary Air Force, the Women's Royal Naval Service or the Women's Land Army, rather than going into the ATS or munitions, sometimes against the wishes of parents who would have preferred their daughters to have remained 'sheltered'. Mrs Grange's grandmother helped her join the WAAFs with promises that she would 'see to' her family afterwards, though her mother still managed to reduce her to tears at the station, and Mickie Hutton Storie's mother burnt

18   Joan Welsh in WAAF uniform in Trafalgar Square (Courtesy of Age
Exchange Theatre Trust)

her application forms twice before she escaped via the employment exchange into an ATS Searchlight Regiment. Shirley Joseph, whose account of her experiences as a Land Girl was tellingly entitled *If Their Mothers Only Knew*, had a phlegmatic response to her mother's reaction: 'I listened patiently to her warnings of every imaginable misfortune, from sitting on strange lavatory seats to being out after dark, and then began to do my packing.'[21]

Theoretically, women conscripted under the National Service Number 2 Act had a choice between the services, Civil Defence, the Land Army and industry. But in practice the usual destinations were the ATS and munitions where shortages were most acute, so to get into one of the others it was important to apply as a volunteer well before being called up. The WRNS had a particularly 'well-bred' image. It was composed entirely of volunteers each of whom was supposed to provide three satisfactory references, and alone among the services it was not subject to military discipline, which meant that loyalty rather than the threat of court martial was supposed to keep its members in line. Internal discipline was as strict as any girls' boarding school, however. One Wren remembers being put on a charge of mutiny for daring to suggest that the time of the weekly pay parade should be changed so that the Wrens would not miss the bus into town for the evening cinema show. Officials discussing discipline problems in the ATS said that in comparison the WRNS was 'like a Sunday School'.[22]

In contrast to the glamour associated (not altogether appropriately) with both the Wrens and the WAAFs, the poor image of both the ATS and the munitions factories did not help their recruitment. The ATS was seen as the 'Cinderella service', its status symbolised above all by its uniform which was khaki-brown compared with the smarter navy- and airforce-blue of its sister services. A reputation for immorality hung over it, deriving in some people's eyes from the 'camp-follower' image of the WAACs of the First World War ('the groundsheet of the army'), though all the women's services were the targets of such comments at times, as if a woman automatically abandoned moral restraint when she put on a uniform. 'Up with the lark and to bed with a Wren' and 'Backs to the land' were among the bawdy sentiments directed at the WRNS and the WLA. One woman reported that she had mentioned to her doctor that she was thinking of joining the ATS. 'He said "Don't you dare!". He had seen an ATS camp. Spent their time in the bar with the men.' Another young woman said, 'Oh, I couldn't join the ATS. All my friends would think I was one of "those".' Women received contradictory messages. Uniforms (especially trousers) were supposed to rob them of their femininity, so magazine advertisements urged them to compensate with lavish use of cosmetics, yet they were simultaneously publicly condemned for making themselves 'cheap' by such means. A young man commented candidly that the image of service-women's low morals resulted more from soldiers' rapacity than anything the women themselves did.[23]

Factory work was considered monotonous, and factory women a 'rough lot' by some of those outside. Daughters quoted their mothers' memories of women going 'barmy' after a few weeks on repetitive work in the First World War, and others claimed to know that there was 'a very low class of girls in the factories now'. In addition to fears that repetitive work would drive you mad in uncongenial company, there were suspicions that hold-ups and delays due to poor management meant that, in spite of the wartime emergency, there might not be a lot of work to do.[24]

The doubts and fears of potential women war workers were frequently not allayed by their first visits to the employment exchange, some of which were hastily set up in church halls or (in the north) in weaving sheds. Officials were told to do everything they could to make each woman feel that she was doing voluntarily what was in the best interests of the country. But there were frequent complaints from women that short shrift was given to their personal circumstances and even to their special skills and qualifications. It was particularly galling to older women when their employment exchange interviewers were 'inexperienced girls', some of whom certainly felt out of their depth after the sheltered world of the girls' secondary schools they had just left. Tension between women of different generations was considered a sufficient barrier to recruitment by 1943 that the Ministry of Labour changed its rules so that interviewers had to be over 30.[25]

In the First World War women's decisions about whether to enter war work or not were based on individual conscience and economic need. The official machinery of compulsion for women was entirely new in the Second World War. Women's reactions to the prospects of being sucked up by it were eagerly documented by organisations like Mass-Observation and form fascinating reading.[26] The reluctance of many women to join up which this evidence brings to light has been overlooked in the patriotic versions of wartime history produced since, but it is important not to let the balance swing too far the other way. Large numbers of women did offer their services before compulsion was introduced: 155,000 women volunteered for the auxiliary services during 1941 and the number was nearly as great in 1942. Many women who did not volunteer nevertheless accepted direction and conscription without complaint, as a necessary step in the process by which the country geared up for war. For example, over three-quarters of the women who had not joined war work in the autumn of 1941 said they would not mind going when conscripted.[27] However, even willing volunteers were not spared difficulties, and several women writers felt it necessary to defend women from the criticism that they were waiting passively to be told what to do in 1941–2, by pointing out that such a response was the natural consequence of the rebuffs to women volunteers in 1939–40, when neither the government nor industry had been ready or willing to receive them.

In spite of the set-backs, by 1943 there had been a huge change in the pattern of women's employment. Even though women aged 18 to 50 continued to be directed into work through the employment exchanges, call up under the National Service Act was suspended towards the end of 1944, because the government had enough women where it wanted them. In all, 1,500,000 more women were working in 'essential industries' in 1943 than in 1939. These included every branch of engineering, as well as chemicals, vehicles, transport, gas, water and electricity and shipbuilding. Nearly 600,000 more women were working in commerce and national and local government, 500,000 were in Civil Defence and over 450,000 women were in the forces. The Women's Land Army had grown to 80,000. As during the First World War, these women had mostly moved from industries like textiles and clothing, and from services like waitressing, shopwork and above all personal domestic service, which never recovered from this depletion. Once again even those women recruited from the home had mostly worked before, usually prior to marriage, in a typical 'woman's trade'. There were a few whose last job had been in munitions or the WAACs in the First World War, for the 17-year-olds of 1916 were only 44 in 1943. Only about 6 per cent of women war workers had come straight from school. The thoroughness of the mobilisation of women at the height of the Second World War is indicated by factors such as the rise in the numbers of working women in areas like Durham and South Wales, where few had been in paid work pre-war, and by the increase in the proportion of married women in the workforce; whereas only 16 per cent of working women were married in 1931, 43 per cent were married in 1943. It was estimated that at least 7,750,000 were in paid work in that year, and it was believed that if part-time and voluntary work were taken into account, fully 80 per cent of married women and 90 per cent of single women were by now contributing to the war effort.[28]

CHAPTER 10

DILUTION AGAIN

Once again, not all men were delighted at the prospect of women joining them in the factories. Skilled engineering work had returned to being a male preserve after the First War and there was a repetition of the abuse to which women dilutees had been subject then. As in 1914–18, men's feelings were concerned with the impact that an influx of women would make on their wages and status. Men feared that employers would pay women less for doing the same work, and that men undercut in this way would be pushed into the Army, even though a Schedule of Reserved Occupations, drawn up in 1939 because of the chaos caused at the start of the First War, prevented most skilled men in the munitions industries from being called up. Men also feared that they would not earn enough if paired with a woman because she would go too slowly, or alternatively that women would bring piece-rates down by working too fast. Some men refused to help women who had 'taken a man's job' like acetylene burning in the docks which involved carrying heavy gear around, even though they would give another man a hand. In one Birmingham factory men on the night shift expressed their disapproval of the fact that a woman worked on 'their' lathe on the day shift, at a lower rate, by loosening all the nuts on the lathe before they knocked off. Needless to say this was dangerous as well as having the effect of slowing the woman up while she put it right next day.[1] All men were not as openly hostile as this, but Mark Benney, an aircraft worker, described the apprehension with which he and his workmates regarded the arrival of the first women workers during 1942:

One day a signwriter appeared in the shop. A new washplace

had recently been completed, and on its door he wrote the word 'Women'. On the doors of the two old washplaces he wrote the word 'Men'. This caused a great deal of talk.

It was in February that the first batch of women arrived. Fred's massive shoulders dropped perceptibly when he first heard the news of their coming; and when they were distributed about the detail shop he breathed a deep sigh of relief.

But it was short-lived relief. The following week, an apologetic clerk from the Personnel Office brought us Mrs Stone.

We looked at her. She was in bright blue overalls, and wore them with an air. A slender, dark-haired woman with carefully made-up face. When Fred asked her what she could do her make-up splintered into a sudden smile and she said: 'Not much I'm afraid, but I can learn.' She had a sharp voice, unaffected. Fred shrugged despondently and told Danny to find a job for her.

We looked at her, nine of us, for days, as though we had never seen a woman before. We watched the dainty way she picked up a file, with red-enamelled fingertip extended as though she were holding a cup of tea. We watched the way she brushed the filings off her overalls after every few strokes, the awkward way she opened and closed her vice, her concern for the cleanliness of her hands, her delicate, unhandy way with a hammer. Sometimes she would look up from her work and see us watching her, and throw us one of those sudden splintery smiles. Behind her back we had great fun mimicking her; to her face we treated her with an almost desperate punctilio.[2]

In the Second World War the government refrained from passing legislation on dilution. Rather than having another Munitions Act like that of 1916, Bevin preferred to encourage the trade unions and employers' associations to enter into voluntary agreements about the 'relaxation of pre-war practices' concerning the employment of women. His own position as an ex-chief of one of the largest unions, the Transport and General Workers Union, helped to give the unions confidence that the agreements would give them the safeguards they wanted, and by 1943 the vast majority of unions had made 'extended employment of women' agreements, covering work in a long list of trades, including boot and shoe manufacture, corn-milling, engineering, iron and steel, railway service, work on trams and buses, baking, cast stone manufacture and work in royal ordnance factories. The unions which did not make such agreements were generally the most exclusive craft unions, like the National Union of Sheet Metal Workers and Braziers, whose members still did not believe that women had even a temporary place in their trades.[3]

The usual formula of the agreements was for women who were replacing men to start by earning a proportion of the men's rate, and to graduate to the full rate in stages over a probationary period. Employers insisted that women must be able to do the work 'without additional supervision or assistance' before they qualified for the top rate, which gave them a much-used loophole for avoiding paying women as much as men. An Amalgamated Engineering Union representative complained about this at the Royal Commission on Equal Pay in 1945: 'The not infrequent result is that women capable of setting their machines are forbidden to do so, or that the woman's day is not complete unless a forman or chargehand addresses a few words of good cheer to her, thereby knocking 20 per cent of her pay packet each week.'[4] Of course a woman paid on such a basis was seen to be much-dreaded cheap labour. All the same, some of the agreements negotiated by the unions did not embody the principle of equal pay. Women replacing men on a list of diverse types of work, including labouring in Admiralty establishments, paint manufacture and the wholesale grocery trade, could never get as much as the men they replaced. The unions which negotiated these agreements were probably relying on a clause common to them all, which stated that women were replacing men for the duration of the war only, and presumably they believed that they had the shopfloor strength to make sure that employers honoured this clause.

Since women were expected to be doing 'men's work' on a temporary basis, the training that they were given was often sketchy or even totally inappropriate. Employers preferred to train women on the job, as they had done in the First World War, and the government did not at first admit women to the new Government Training Centres. But in 1941 it was decided that recruitment was suffering from the menial image of women's war work, and much was made of the fact that they could now come to the centres to be trained. Once inside, however, some women found that the 'training' had more to do with introducing them to factory routine and machinery than with preparing them for skilled work in engineering, and the courses were cut from 16 to 8 weeks in 1942. Women still needed training on the job, and with male attitudes being what they were some had trouble getting any. For example, Mrs Grossman went to work at De Havillands repairing aircraft:

> The training school never taught me anything to do with planes, we were just taught to handle tools, and everything was so different at the aerodrome. A man nicknamed 'Dingle' . . . trained me. He never seemed to be there! I don't know why, but you could never find him. He treated me alright, but he used to think I couldn't do it. He didn't think any of the girls could, but we outshone some of the men.[5]

Things were different in the forces, where the growing shortage of skilled men created an urgent need for women to become fully skilled aircraft fitters, mechanics, searchlight operators and so on, and they were put through rigorous courses. Even here, however, they did not escape the prejudice of men who did not really believe that women should be in the army. Therese Roberts, who was one of a small minority of ATS women deployed at anti-aircraft batteries in the latter years of the war, remembers one male officer who was 'very rough on us. He said "You joined the army. You want to behave like men. I'll treat you like men!" ' But she received a thorough training in how to operate an AckAck gun.[6] Some women in industry also had the benefit of a good course of training, like women welders trained at Welding Rods in Sheffield. Their problem was that the hostility of male workers and employers' desires to avoid shopfloor disputes meant that when they actually went to work they were often given repetitive tasks for which their training was irrelevant.[7]

It was not only women on the shop floor who appeared threatening to men. In 1944 the Institution of Mechanical Engineers admitted its first full woman member, causing a stir in the columns of the employers' journal, *The Engineer*. Correspondents repeated arguments which the same journal

19 Therese Roberts, ATS Anti-Aircraft Battery (Courtesy of Thames TV/
Channel 4, *A People's War*)

had hurled against women in the engineerings shops in the First War, addressing them now to women aspiring to become professional engineers. The world of engineering was unsuitable for women because they would be exposed to bad language and long hours of standing (by implication it did not now matter that working-class women put up with these things daily in the workshops). Moreover, women might undercut the male professional engineer and compete with him for jobs:

> When one reflects on the 'rough and tumble' of shop life, the elegant language of the men, and other items which a woman's delicacy would naturally disregard, heaven forbid that Great Britain should encourage the training of the 'gentler sex' to become engineers. . . . Professional engineers already have too much competition to face, and *après la guerre* – well, 'you never can tell'.[8]

However, though men at the top feared an influx of women to their ranks, they urged the unions to drop their opposition to women dilutees on the shopfloor. The way that dilution worked in the Second World War was much the same as it had been in the First, with the same sort of union alertness to employers' attempts to evade the letter of the law, and determination to see the back of women once the war was over. It was now explicitly stated in many of the agreements that women doing work 'commonly performed by women in the industry' were not regarded as replacing men, and were exempted from everything the agreements stipulated about rates of pay and being temporary. This clause was included in recognition of the increasing numbers of women in many branches of industry between the wars, where they did 'women's work' at women's rates. It was another loophole for employers, tempting them to label any of the wartime work which they gave women as work 'commonly performed by women in the industry'. From women's point of view this meant that they would be denied the men's rate, even if they had in fact replaced a man, and from the workman's point of view it meant that whole areas of work might be redesignated 'women's work' during the war, and be lost to men. Long and bitter were the arguments between union and employer representatives about whether jobs as varied as sweeping up the factory floor, core-making, crane driving, welding and inspection were 'commonly performed by women' in engineering. The difficulties that trade unionists had in convincing employers that, pre-war, 'women's work' had been confined by virtue of women's limited competence to simple, light, repetitive work, led some male trade unionists to see the sense of arguing for equal pay across the board, rather than subscribing to the notion that there were women's jobs and men's jobs, by the end of the war. George Woodcock, head of the TUC's research department, presented this position in his evidence to the Royal Commission on Equal Pay in 1945. He was supported by Jack Tanner, President of the Amalgamated Engineering Union, though Tanner's statements make it clear that the objective was still to prevent women being employed at a lower rate, in preference to men.[9]

The architects of the dilution agreements were men. Women were not encouraged to participate in building the framework within which they were employed during the war, and not surprisingly many women do not really seem to have understood the basis upon which they were paid. The way that wages were worked out in many trades, especially engineering, was notoriously complicated. Rates for skilled, semi-skilled and unskilled labour varied from district to district, and there was a complex web of supplements which often paid more than the basic rate, also agreed on a district basis, involving piece-work rates, time bonuses and output bonuses of which women received varying proportions.[10]

For most women during the war the issue was more pay, rather than equal pay. It was hard enough to work out what they should have got in their own right, let alone in relation to men, and their comparisons were with the workers next to them on the bench (usually women), and with what they had earned the week before, rather than between something as abstract as an average rate for women and an average rate for men in their trade. In her novel *Night Shift*, Inez Holden described the emotional climate among the women on pay night: 'After Alfred had given over each wage packet with the operator's name and the sum enclosed written on the outside, an atmosphere of resentment and hostility went up quickly like a rise in temperature'.[11] The wage packets were always slightly different, sometimes bonuses were included, sometimes they were not, some women had deductions for lateness, while others discovered unexpected extras for piece-work. Resentment was particularly strong when women working side by side on similar machines earned persistently different wages from each other, usually because one was on work classified as 'women's work' while the other was deemed to have replaced a man. Towards the end of the war, women became increasingly inclined to take short sharp strike action over these niggling disappointments, even though strikes were illegal during the war, and the unions rarely supported the sporadic action.[12]

The most celebrated women's pay strike of the war was at the Rolls Royce aero-engine plant at Hillington near Glasgow. Clydeside was an area where women were not strangers to paid work. They worked in textiles, printing and bookbinding factories, for example, at least until they married. But better-paid work in marine engineering and shipbuilding had been entirely confined to men. The war created a demand for all kinds of new engineering component manufacture and assembly work and for a new workforce to do it. Young women were brought in from the Highlands and the Western Isles, and many Glaswegian women like Agnes McLean welcomed the opportunity to swap their old jobs for work on milling, drilling and grinding machines at Hillington, earning about 35 shillings a week at the start of the war.

Agnes and the other women developed skills they did not know they had, becoming, as she put it, 'very neat tidy engineers', but by about 1941 they were thoroughly irritated by the fact that men with no more training or experience than their own, working alongside them, earned substantially more than they did. As she explained: 'They were in three categories, there was skilled men, there was semi-skilled men, and there was unskilled men and others, and we were the others, and we were below even the unskilled.'[13] Her memory is that by now the women were getting about 43 shillings, whereas men on the same work received 73 shillings, and when these men left to join the army and women took their place, the women were not paid more. The unions endeavoured to sort out the issue, but the women became impatient with negotiations that dragged on throughout 1942 and into 1943, and eventually walked out. In the street eggs and tomatoes were thrown at them as well as taunts that they were letting the country down, but as the women stood shivering and uncertain in a local park the men from the factory appeared en masse to support them. Agnes was under no illusion about their motivation. 'Once the men realised first of all it was injustice being done to women being paid less than the rate for the job and secondly they were being used for cheap labour and therefore a danger to the men . . . the men were absolutely fantastic.'[14]

The upshot was a court of enquiry and, eventually, a special arrangement under which every machine was named and allocated to a grade specifying the rate to be paid to its operator.[15] All the same, the concepts of men's work and women's work had not been thrown out of the window. Under the new grading agreement, work placed in the higher grades was paid in relation to the men's skilled rates, in the middle grades pay was related to the men's semi-skilled rates, and in the lower grades it was related to the women's rates. Very few women found themselves placed even in the middle grades, and the vast majority were at the bottom still, but even though it did not represent equal pay, grading did at least mean a rise in the wages that most women received. By the end of the war, with the bonus included, Agnes remembers earning over £5: 'I was quite tickled to show them in the house a five pound note, I'd never seen a five pound note.'[16]

Elsewhere in the country also, women like Agnes became shop stewards and for the first time in their lives started to take an interest in trade union politics and to stand up for their rights both within their unions and with management. But even though there were more opportunities for women to take office within the trade unions than there had been in the First World War, many of them felt that they were not really welcome and that it was not considered very feminine to speak at meetings and engage in the necessary haggling over wages and conditions. Agnes says that she was always careful to dress in a very feminine way when she had a union meeting, presumably to offset this prejudice. Some of the craft unions, like the sheet-metal workers and the woodworkers, refused to admit women throughout the war, and the large and prestigious Amalgamated Engineering Union only recruited them after 1943, when it appeared to be losing ground in terms of numbers to the Transport and General Workers' Union, which was acting as a kind of catch-all for the vast influx of war workers. The AEU, however, issued its women members wtih special white cards

20 Agnes McLean (*2nd left, front row*) and workmates, Rolls Royce, Hillington. c.1943 (Courtesy of Thames TV/Channel 4, *A People's War*)

21 Agnes McLean and workmates, Rolls Royce, Hillington, c. 1943 *(Agnes is on right of frame)* (Courtesy of Thames TV/Channel 4, *A People's War*)

stating that they were temporary, and had a rule preventing women under 21 from becoming shop stewards, in order to preserve the dignity of trade union negotiations.[17]

Not all women felt like joining trade unions under such conditions. Doris White remembers the disapproving attitudes of the older male trade unionists, who were much in evidence in the workshops in view of the call up of younger men.

> One thing that really annoyed the men in our shop, especially Mr King, was the fact that us girls did not belong to a union. We could see no reason for us to do so as we were (as described on our cards) in temporary employment. What the men said was, 'Ye'll 'ave the rises though, won't yer?' Mr King, a lay preacher and union boss, his hands resting on his rotund stomach, covered by a white tie-around apron, would lean back and tell us of the folly of our ways.[18]

Doris felt they were being chastised as much for being young and carefree as for their failure to participate in the union. In some works, like the radiators section of Morris Motors, Cowley, men in the union were quite happy to recruit women in order to discipline those who were late or absent, rather than to take up their problems, which can hardly have endeared women to the concept of trade unionism.[19] All the same, women's trade union membership doubled during the war, from under 1 million in 1939 to 2.2 million in 1944, representing a quarter of all women workers.[20] They were able to put pressure on their unions to fight for a better deal for them. The general unions in particular were responsive to this pressure, and women's average weekly earnings in industry rose from £1 12s 6d to £3 3s 2d between October 1938 and July 1945. But the rises were negotiated within the framework of unequal pay. The differential between men and women's average earnings was narrowed by only 5 percentage points during the war: in 1945 women earned only 52 per cent of men's earnings.[21] Vera Douie, the author of a carefully researched attack on women's unequal position in wartime, wrote, 'They have not in fact fared so well in this respect as in the last war'.[22]

The only area in which equal pay did operate widely was transport. Women bus and tram conductors were granted equal pay with men by an industrial court award of April 1940 which was honoured by the local authorities. All the same the better-paid work of driving was jealously guarded by the men, and Zelma Katin who was a 'clippie' in Sheffield during the war, noticed that the employers economised where they could, for example by paying women 2d an hour less than men while they were training. But nevertheless equal pay in transport worked in women's favour. They were at the top of the women's pay league in 1945, with average weekly earnings of £4 1s 7d.[23]

In contrast, the familiar differential operated in civil defence and the forces. In ARP women were paid £2 15s a week compared with a man's £3 18s 6d, in 1943, and in the forces women received two-thirds of the pay and four-fifths of the food given to the men they worked alongside and replaced.[24]

Aline Whalley, a young Wren in the Fleet Air Arm, proud of her new skills as a Flight Mechanic, thought it most unjust that, officially, three women replaced two men.

> I always thought this was very wrong because the Wrens
> were not only better educated but they were better workers.
> They achieved promotion earlier than most of the boys. They
> were really very valuable indeed on the flights, took it
> seriously, didn't shirk, worked hard all day, and I think were
> much more efficient than most of the boys.[25]

Women in white-collar work, whose numbers expanded enormously during the war, did not fare much better. Women clerks and secretaries were accused of 'selling themselves cheap' because they agreed to work for employers at wages below the going rate. Elaine Burton explained that it was difficult for a woman clerical worker who had experienced unemployment in the first stages of the war to stand out for more, especially since rates were often not quoted in advance, and they were simply told what they would get when they were appointed. A woman running a college for shorthand-typists told her: 'I know one woman of thirty-four, capable, who was offered a job which was being done by another woman at £4 a week. The business was thriving and the employer said: "Offer her £2 10s".' Mrs Shipley, a wages clerk at a shipbuilders in South Shields, and Joy Brown, a bank clerk in Leeds, remember having to take on much more work than usual as the men disappeared into the Forces, for no extra pay.[26]

The civil service, experiencing a huge expansion of its

workload due to the growth of government activity during the war, decided to call back some of the women it had sacked on marriage. Their treatment can only be described as shabby. They were paid the rates of temporary staff, usually about half their previous earnings, and received no salary increments. All civil service women received a lower bonus than men.[27] Married women were also invited back into teaching and the 1944 Education Act made it illegal to sack women teachers on marriage in the future. But when women MPs tried to get equal pay written into the Act, Churchill in fury turned the issue into a vote of confidence in his leadership, the only one of the war. All but fifteen MPs were of course men, to whom the loss of Churchill was far too high a price to pay for the principle of equal pay, and the amendment was heavily defeated. The government then took the steam out of the equal pay movement by setting up a Royal Commission authorised only to 'examine', 'consider' and 'report' on the implications of equal pay. It did not complete its deliberations until 1946.

Women MPs did score one resounding victory for equality during the war, though not on a matter of pay, but that of compensation. Under the Personal Injuries Act of 1939 a woman incapacitated by a bomb received 7 shillings a week less than a man, even though, as Vera Douie put it, 'There is nothing chivalrous about bombs; they do not discriminate between men and women.' The women's parliamentary caucus built up considerable support in and out of parliament for equal compensation for to oppose it implied something more fundamental than opposition to equal pay. It suggested not that women were less competent than men, but that women's lives were less valuable than those of men. With the support of numerous women's organisations, Mavis Tate, MP, pressed the point in a parliamentary debate in November 1942, against government opposition based on the fear that this would open up the whole issue of equal pay and cause industrial unrest. But the government was cornered and from April 1943 men and women received the same compensation for war injuries. It was an important step for women, over 63,000 of whom were injured by enemy action between 1939 and 1945, 25,000 fatally.[28]

During 1943 a gush of praise for women similar to the astonished paeans of the First World War issued from the mouths of all sorts of officials. For example, an army colonel in charge of anti-aircraft batteries on the east coast said 'There is no question of having to allocate two women to do the job of one man . . . they are far more conscientious in their application to the job than men are,' and Ernest Bevin announced that 'The output of the women, instead of being that of three women to two men was slightly the other way.'[29] This praise struck some women, like Vera Douie, as somewhat insulting, based as it was on the rediscovery since the First World War that women were rather less incompetent than convention suggested. Needless to say, the acclaim was not accompanied by revised rates of pay.

CHAPTER 11

ON THE JOB

JOB SATISFACTION

When asked what they liked most about war work, women factory workers named the money first, and the company second.[1] Even though equal pay with men was achieved only in rare cases, war wages represented a substantial rise for most women compared with their pre-war average of only £1 10s a week. Earnings varied a lot, but in 1944 the average reached £3, and in a busy week with plenty of overtime and maximum bonuses, a woman in a royal ordnance factory might earn as much as £7 or £8.[2] To women who had worked as domestic servants, clothing workers or shop girls even average war wages seemed 'fabulous sums', just as they had in the First World War. Mona Marshall was earning only 10s a week as a nurse-maid in Lincoln in 1941, when she left for a job making shells for naval guns in a steelworks in Sheffield: 'I always remember the first wage that I earned . . . was two pounds, two shillings and two pence. That was my first week's wage and I thought I'd got the earth . . . two pounds two and tuppence all for myself. I thought it was wonderful.'[3]

These wages gave women a little more independence from their families and husbands than they had known before the war. Fares, meals at the factory and board and lodging swallowed up 70 per cent of a single woman's wage, but she still had a few shillings to spend on dances and the cinema, knitting patterns, cosmetics, cigarettes and magazines, or to save for a new pair of shoes or a visit home or to relatives.[4] Young women's sense of obligation towards their families was not necessarily weakened, however. Many Irish women work-

22 Mona Marshall and workmates at a Sheffield steel works. (*Mona is bottom right*) (Courtesy of Thames TV/Channel 4, *A People's War*)

ing in the Birmingham area regularly sent money home to hard-up families, and were particularly dismayed when a slack week made this difficult.[5] Married women with families to support were the least likely to have spending money left over, especially if their husbands were in the forces. The government allowed a private soldier's wife with two children the sum of £1 13s in 1940, and war work wages became essential to keep many wives out of debt. A survey in Leeds found that servicemen's wives living on their own with children owed on average 15s a week in 1942 and they were understandably unpopular with landlords and shopkeepers.[6]

In general women in the forces, civil defence and the Land Army were paid less than women factory workers. They were probably worst off in the Land Army which was not a government service in the same way as the others. Its members were employed directly by individual farmers who paid them what they thought they were worth. It rapidly became apparent that many farmers thought women were worth very little, and the County Agricultural Wages Board was forced to step in to make sure that their wages did not fall below £1 2s 6d for a 48-hour week, after deductions for board and lodgings.[7] Young women in a specialist branch of the Land Army run by the Ministry of Supply, the Women's Timber Corps, felt that they were considerably better off on £2 10s a week, from which they found their own keep.[8] Land Army girls were not allowed to forget that they were not part of a military army. They were forbidden the use of the canteens run for the armed forces at places like railway stations even though their wartime journeys were no less tortuous, and they were put behind the boy scouts in the parades celebrating victory at the end of the war in Europe, until they protested.

> The army was shattered; they didn't know what to do with this kind of insubordination, but we were quite determined. If they didn't put us somewhere else, we were going to go home. In the end they put us behind the ATS, so that was all right. We marched in step with them.[9]

Some Land Army women resented their low pay and status, especially in view of the importance of their work at a time when convoys bringing imported food were threatened by submarines in the Atlantic and shipping space was scarce. 'We were proud of being Land Girls, and we were fed up when we didn't get the recognition we thought we ought to have', writes Mrs Dorothy Barton. 'After all, we did a lot more than a lot of girls in the armed forces. If it hadn't been for us a lot of the people wouldn't have eaten.'[10]

In contrast to women in industry, the financial reward was not the thing which women in civil defence and the services liked most about their work. Army pay was not generous and there were complaints at the beginning of the war that a woman needed a private income in order to survive in the ATS, especially as an officer. Nina Masel thought that the WAAFs she was with in June 1941 were more patriotically motivated than other groups.

'The War' means something deeply personal to the WAAF. It's 'our' war. 'We're' fighting it, RAF successes are personal ones. And tragedies . . . are always from the personal angle of 'our boys'. We don't read the papers here as much as in civvy life, but we follow big moves, like Russia's entry into the war, with the keenness of a sportsman watching the Derby, having put all his money and goods on one horse – do or die.[11]

These feelings intensified as the bombing of Germany was stepped up. In 1942–3 the British organised night-time raids on German industrial towns, which gradually increased in intensity, leading in May 1943 to 'thousand bomber' raids on Cologne and other German cities. Patricia Graves trained to be a WAAF clerk on 'Special Duties' which involved her in equipping and briefing RAF pilots. 'We knew roughly where they were going, and we saw how many were going, and of course we were always watching and waiting for them to come back, hoping they'd all make it.' This kind of work was much-sought-after, but there were relatively few posts going, and shortly afterwards Patricia was 'remustered' as a pay clerk at a station called Gravely, which was far less exciting. 'It wasn't operational, so you felt out of touch with things. Well I did. When you're on an operational station you get much more into what's going on and how the war's going.'[12]

WAAFs themselves were not trained to fly planes. But a few women did have duties as women ferry pilots in a civilian organisation, the Air Transport Auxiliary. They formed something of an élite. The women involved, like Pauline Gower and Amy Johnson, who was killed flying a plane across the Thames Estuary in 1941, needed considerable personal determination as well as wealthy backgrounds to enable them to obtain their pilot's licences privately, since no training was given in the ATA. Their jobs were responsible. They had to fly new or repaired planes from the works to the airfields. The idea was to relieve airmen for other duty, but perhaps because of the high prestige of the job they were nevertheless accused of taking jobs from men.[13]

As this suggests, the amount of satisfaction which women got from their wartime jobs varied enormously. The same job might be intensely boring at times and extremely interesting at others. This was particularly so of some of the jobs in civil defence and the forces, where long periods of waiting for something to happen were punctuated by the frenetic excitement of hazardous activity. Theodora Benson joined an Air Raid Precautions (ARP) unit as a driver in 1939, in high expectation that devastating raids would start immediately. Instead there were nine months of 'Phoney War' to endure, and it was September 1940 before the Blitz turned civil defence workers into over-worked heroines and heroes who had to deal with the most grisly side of the war. In the meantime, wrote Theodora, 'We drank innumerable cups of tea, smoked endless cigarettes (there were plenty then) and got to know each other.' Even after the raids had begun, nights filled with the drama of driving through cratered and blacked-out streets to dig people, and parts of people, out of bombed buildings, were punctuated by 'nights of boredom and bickering, joking, grumbling and fun'. 'There couldn't be a service at once more important, more dangerous and more desperately boring than the ARP', wrote Theodora, 'life consists of waiting around for what are so gently described as incidents' which might vary from a direct hit on a packed air raid shelter to a few incendiary bombs which quietly extinguished themselves unaided.[14]

Servicewomen in jobs directly linked to the state of war operations experienced the same stop-go pace of work. Mary Lee Settle was a radio/telephone operator in the WAAFs, whose job was to sit in the flying control tower of an RAF station, 'earphones on, plugged into small Marconi transmitter-receiver crystal sets', issuing orders from the flying control officer and listening for pilots' responses, through the constant buzzing irritation of German jamming:

> Flying exercise kept us keyed to the sets and blotted out time with quick, concentrated work. Scrounging flips [i.e. begging plane rides] made me resurge afterwards as if I had gone to a well of action, and I found a reason for being there, tied to the earphones. In the vast periods of boredom between, when only jamming could be heard, it was hard for the hand not to reach forward to turn the set down, not to recede from it into the dead areas of animal waiting, waiting for the confinement of the closed signals room, the connection by wavelength, even the sense of floating displacement in the state of war itself to be over.[15]

The work of 'plotters', who were used in the WRNS and WAAF to plot the movements and routes of ships and aircraft on huge maps as a result of wireless messages, also came in stimulating bursts punctuated by long stretches of inactivity. Nina Masel sent reports from her RAF station in Preston, Lancashire, to Mass-Observation during 1941, during which she commented that if plotters did not read their way systematically through whatever there was to hand during the waiting periods, be it *Woman's Weekly*, Osbert Sitwell or Virginia Woolf, they became desperately bored with the job, even though it was extremely interesting when work came through and its confidential status lent it glamour and importance.[16]

Women making munitions were more likely to suffer from the monotony of industrial work than from these peaks and lulls, though some women joining up during 1942 were horrified to discover that their factories were not yet fully 'tooled up' for war production, so that there was a lot of hanging around before work began in earnest. Women who had been trained as welders, and who were proud of their skills, were understandably dismayed if they were not given any welding to do. The discipline which foremen and welfare officers attempted to impose on their new and often young recruits then began to jar, especially when a slack week was reflected in a thin wage packet. A young welder called Helena wrote angrily to her trainer early in 1942:

The times we've been in the offices since Christmas I wouldn't care to count, and after all our efforts, we get a five shilling rise. I wish they would rise me out of the firm for good. I drew for a week's wage £1 16s 0d last week. Of course stoppages off, but how do they expect a girl to live on that?

Agnes exploded a little later:

We are *not* welding, we are pushed from pillar to post, and today, after asking the foreman for a job, he said 'Just stand there in that corner'. That was at 7.45 at the latest, and at 3.15 in the afternoon, I was still standing in my corner. In desperation I walked over to where Ethel and Jenny were painting and very unconcerned sat down and started to paint. Hardly had I started when who should come pompously down, but Grandmother Marflitt [Welfare officer], 'What are you doing there?' said she 'who gave you permission to sit there?' I very steadily looked at her and said 'I gave it to myself'.[17]

Welding work was intricate, and women welders got great satisfaction from a neat weld, especially when they knew that their work was better than the next man's. Women like Doris White, employed as a 'Fitter, Grade Three' on aircraft repair and salvage work at Wolverton Works, also enjoyed their war jobs.

This was very interesting work. I learnt about castle nuts, and split pins, what a BSA spanner was, how to use an electric drill, what a five-eighth drill looked like, and most important, when my mate yelled, 'Cummon a five-sixteenth', to shove it through to him . . . I filed, I drilled, I screwed, I punched out old rivets. Bolts that someone had knobbled with a centre punch so that the nut did not come off, I filed feverishly until it was flat and off came the nut. Everything went into their respective boxes or bins for re-use. Sometimes I peered into the fuselages to see . . . middle-aged ladies bending or reaching, their plump bottoms straining the material of their boiler suits. They were hard at it, unscrewing controls and electrical systems.[18]

However, many processes in engineering had been broken

23   Mickie Hutton Storie, ATS Searchlight Regiment. (*Right of frame*)
(Courtesy of Thames TV/Channel 4, *A People's War*)

down to such an extent that the work had little intrinsic interest and was difficult to connect with the war effort. One woman could not bear the thought of spending the whole of the war flicking little nuts off a rod, others quickly became jaded pulling steel tube after steel tube through a vice, or drilling the same-shaped hole in innumerable metal discs for ten hours a day.[19] Some managements sought to remind women of the importance of their contribution to the war effort by showing films, bringing army captains, pilots, or naval officers to see them, or holding competitions between production lines, for which the prize would be a visit to one of the ships or planes they were helping to make. But many did nothing more than introduce 'Music While You Work' over the loud speakers, to encourage their workers, who were inclined to while away the hours with their own songs in any case. In fact singing, like going to the cinema, was a prominent feature of women's lives during the war. The most popular songs and films were the most romantic and sentimental. Songs like 'I'll Be Seeing You', 'Yours' and Vera Lynn's 'We'll Meet Again' echoed round many a factory. Mickie Hutton Storie was in the ATS, but her comment about what the songs and films of the day meant to her stands for those of many women in the Forces, the Land Army and the factories:

> We never stopped singing. We knew all the words. That played a very big part in our lives . . . We could lose ourselves. We could forget the horrors of the war. And it was marvellous that we could do that.[20]

However, there were still some managements which did not tolerate any spontaneous activity in their workforces, be it singing or swearing, like Peek Freans, where Helen Parker was soldering biscuit tins:

> They were a fussy firm you know. In the new building they listened to 'Music While You Work' but in the old building we had nothing. In fact you weren't even allowed to sing . . . If you swore, I know it sounds funny, but you'd be sent to the manager and you'd be suspended.[21]

Production grandually intensified in the build-up to the opening of the 'Second Front', as the allied invasion of Europe via the Normandy beaches was known, and some employers became worried about the indifference to work of many of their women workers, whose forte was supposed to be simple repetitive work 'which necessitated no acquired skill, but rather a capacity for doing the same job, day in, day out'.[22] Maurice Lipman, managing-director of Ekco Ltd, which was producing radar equipment at a 'greenfield' factory in Wiltshire, arranged for one of Mass-Observation's investigators, Celia Fremlin, to join the factory incognito, as a worker, to observe what was going on. Her report, which was published as *War Factory* in 1943, showed that women were doing all sorts of things to break up the monotony, from hanging around in the lavatory to making the most of a mechanical breakdown in order to have a rest and a joke with the chargehands. Men put it down to women's predictable incompetence, and some women played on this to gain longer breaks and easier discipline. But in more than one case women who had been 'slackers' on very simple work, became much more efficient when they were given something interesting to do, even if it was only the difference between drilling or stamping all day and assembly, where at least it was possible to see a product 'forming under your hands'.[23]

Theodora Benson thought that the Second World War gave women many more opportunities than the First World War. This is a debatable point. There was a wider variety of work for women, in the services and the Land Army, and of course Civil Defence was quite new, but some women in engineering thought their work was more limited, and with more men in reserved occupations there were fewer opportunities for women to do work that was recognised as skilled. But mobilisation was on a bigger scale, as it had to be to combat a 'total war' in which everyone was at risk from bombing and Theodora was glad to feel that women were sharing the dangers of this war: 'It is less grievous than agonizing in complete security while a whole generation of one sex offer their lives for us'.[24] Many women would have agreed with her, though such thoughts might not have occurred to working-class women for whom 'complete security' was an unfamiliar feeling even in peacetime. All the same, as in the First War, some women were worried by the thought that their work would contribute to killing people. Marie Maberley, who made shell cases at an ICI factory in Sutton, remembers 'You didn't let it get to you that it was going to kill women and children. You would go beserk if you

24 Nella Last and her son, c.1939. (Courtesy of The Tom Harrisson
Mass-Observation Archive)

did. You felt that it would fall over a military target.'[25] In fact under Air Chief Marshall Sir Arthur Harris, the allied strategy from 1942 was to bomb the German population 'out of house and home'.[26]

Other women were appalled by the prospect of thousands of young men dying in battle for the second time in the space of thirty years. Frances Partridge and her husband Ralph who refused to fight, decided that suicide in the event of invasion was the only rational outcome of an abhorrence of fascist rule coupled with a preference that no one should kill or risk death on their behalf. Of course the anticipated invasion did not materialise, but Frances spent a restless 'Pacifist's War' on their quiet Wiltshire farm, obsessed by the progress of the war, depressed by the growing militarism of erstwhile pacifist friends, and dismayed by the deaths of another quarter of a million young men.[27] Nella Last, who saw herself as an ordinary Barrow housewife and mother rather than an intellectual, had similar feelings of horror about the bombings and battles of the war. Early in the war she was suddenly struck by the sight of her 21-one-year-old son who had just received his call-up papers, reading the newspaper. 'It all came back with a rush – the boys who set off so gaily and lightly and did not come back – and I could have screamed aloud . . . We who remember the long drawn-out agony of the last war feel ourselves crumble somewhere inside at the thought of what lies ahead.'[28] Her personal solution was to throw herself into WVS work, even if it was only sewing, knitting and rolling bandages, to cast out the haunting images of death and destruction.

WORKMATES

After the money, the second most popular aspect of war work for factory workers was the company. For many women, young and old, one of the main contrasts with life before the war was the opportunity to mix with new people, especially other women. Older married women felt this in particular. One woman in her forties who had a part-time factory job told Mass-Observation:

I thoroughly enjoy my four hours working in the afternoon. I'm all agog to get here. After all, for a housewife who's been a cabbage for fifteen years – you feel you've got out of the cage and you're free. Quite a lot of the part-timers feel like that – to get out and see some fresh faces – it's all so different, such a change from dusting.[29]

When processes were organised so that women worked in groups or passed work from hand to hand along the bench they enjoyed it more than when they were isolated on a noisy machine. Being near enough to your fellow workers to sing and talk could be the saving grace of a boring industrial job. The same was true of agriculture. Valerie Moss, a student volunteer who worked on the land in the vacations, found that pea-picking was very tedious, 'but we chatted away like mad and gossiped and sang.'[30]

The idea that the daughters of dukes worked alongside the daughters of dustmen in the factories was as strongly canvassed in the Second War as in the First, as part of the 'national togetherness' campaign, but once again the evidence supports the idea of social segregation rather than the real mixing of classes. It is hard to find figures showing the social class of wartime factory workers, but surveys show that the vast majority had been in elementary school only, and a better-educated middle-class woman was an unusual and much-noticed phenomenon on the factory floor, like 'Feather ' in Inez Holden's documentary novel, *Night Shift*, who struck her fellow workers as 'the sort of girl who would have been "ladying it" at a First Aid Post attached to some auxiliary service.'[31] Whereas middle-class women had volunteered for munitions in the First World War, patriotism and glamour were associated with the services in the second. Managers tended to shrink from giving 'nicely brought up' girls shopfloor jobs in the factories. The Personnel Manager of a Birmingham engineering firm wrote in his diary in 1942:

January 16: See two more girls sent down from London. A striking blonde from a beauty parlour and a brunette from a gownshop, both in the West End. Capstan shop foreman afraid to put them on his machines; said they were too good a type. I was seriously concerned myself as our factory is an old shabby place and its sanitary arrangements of a very low standard . . . Local factory class girls are used to them. But to keep these things dark from the good type, comfortably brought-up girls who are now being conscripted and to tell them stories which so many of their employers can't even make come true, is cruel . . .

January 17: Started blonde and brunette on their job. Myself, W.M. [Works Manager] and Shop Superintendent all seriously bothered about them and always come back to our *bête noir* the sanitary accommodation . . . consultations during the day brought to light a way of fixing these girls up with clerical jobs and a staff status so that better amenities would be theirs.[32]

In parallel with the profound gulf between shopfloor and office jobs, there were well-recognised distinctions between the three women's services, the WRNS being seen as the most socially select and the ATS as the least. In addition there were divisions within each service. In the WAAFs, Nina Masel discovered that 'the trade division was almost identical with the social division – working-class were cooks, sparking plug testers, general duty hands, etc. – lower middle class were orderlies, teleprinters, clerks, etc. – middle middle class and above were administrative workers, radio operators, plotters, etc.'. She observed that new recruits' own behaviour fell into line with this formal division:

A month ago, 42 of us were called up and met together for the first time in a large room in Victory House, Kingsway. *Immediately*, cliques were formed. The moment you entered the room, you knew exactly which group to join, almost instinctively. The noisy group in the middle was the working-class one: barmaid, waitress, mill-girl, domestic servant and a few others. At the side, the Colonel's daughter was surrounded by an admiring semi-circle of actresses, a dress designer and 'ladies of leisure'. A hairdresser, accountant's clerk, school teacher and mannequin formed another group. Others paired off, skirting one or other of the main groups.[33]

At the same time, the war does stand out in many women's memories as a time when they mixed with people whom they would never normally have met. This was particularly the case for young women from the 'middle middle class and above'

25 Aline Whalley, fellow Wren trainees and two petty officers, Royal Naval Fleet Airarm, 1944. Aline is third from the right. (Courtesy of Aline Torday)

who had spent their teens in relatively restricted social circles marked out for them by their schools and families. Aline Whalley was the daughter of a bank manager, and had been sent to private boarding schools from the ages of 8 to 17. Wanting to do a job which made a direct contribution to the war effort, she chose the WRNS 'because quite honestly I wanted to be with people I would feel comfortable with, and from what I had seen of the other two services I knew that wouldn't be the case'. However, she was startled to find herself with tough, working-class Scottish girls on the flight mechanics' course which she insisted on joining (against the efforts of Wren officers to post her as a captain's secretary). She felt she learnt a lot from the experience. 'The War really did a lot of good to girls like me, who had been privately educated, it really did. It taught me that working-class people could have emotions, and that they could be bright, really bright, because my goodness some of those girls were clever. These were things I had simply never considered before.'[34]

Theodora Benson (who was higher still up the social scale, being the daughter of a Lord) reported a similar experience. In Civil Defence men and women worked alongside each other:

> The drivers were well-to-do people who could contribute their own cars before the Borough got round to providing any, the stretcher-bearers were all sorts, the officers were mostly tradesmen. We had all of course met and liked people like each other before, but had never mingled our lives so intimately, and it widened all our horizons . . . . There was something more than pleasant companionship: we learnt from the mixture of experiences and points of view, and our lives were made richer . . .[35]

The mixing of members of different social classes impressed those who experienced it, but was relatively rare, due to formal and informal methods of segregation. Wartime mobilisation was less respectful of the finer social distinctions operating within, rather than between, classes. To those sensitive to them they were clearly marked by occupation, language, dress and manners and crossing these subtle divides could be as much of an adventure as it was for Theodora Benson to mix with 'tradesmen' and 'all sorts'. Sadie McDougal was a miner's daughter living in Scotswood, Newcastle-upon-Tyne. As an exdomestic servant she had a low opinion of factory women when she started work at Vickers engineering works. 'I'd never met such people before ... We didn't speak the way they spoke. We couldn't understand the jokes they were telling ... But of course I finished my education there', she said, referring not to the industrial training but to the graffiti in the toilets.[36]

However, the opportunity to mix was as likely to reinforce social barriers as to break them down. Many women did not find it as easy to adapt as Sadie did, like a working-class woman who had been to secondary school and was drafted into a royal ordnance factory:

> They talk about the happy social life in the factories and how you all make friends ... I *can't* make friends with the girls. They have been in a factory of one sort or another since they left school at 14 years, and they resent me, and I just have absolutely no point of contact with them. We hardly speak the same language.[37]

All kinds of divisions and cliques were experienced by women war workers. Doris White, a Londoner exiled to Wolverton by the bombing, vividly remembers the criss-crossing tensions in her aircraft repair shop:

> We were now an eighty per cent girls' workroom, and how we rowed with each other. Country girls versus Londoners. In one corner the plain types with simple hair styles, in the other bleached blondes with lipsticked mouths. There were some who had been in the Works for years and years who had neither a smile nor a friendly word for us 'townies'. So we sat in our respective places for our tea-breaks and tolerated each other. A trip over someone's handbag, or the accidental knocking of someone's coat off its hook would result in, 'Bloody Londoner, go back where yer came from'. I kept quiet while my pals returned the fire with 'Bloody country swedes' or 'Bloody onion treaders'.[38]

Hostility in the factories between longer-serving women and newcomers, and local women and those from further afield, was sometimes based on fears of the availability of jobs after the war. Kay Jenner working at GEC in Coventry, wrote, 'Many of the Coventry women disliked the women from Wales and London. One of the worries was that they would stay in

Coventry after the war and so take jobs away from Coventry women.[39]

Divisions in the forces were based on far less rational grounds. As an American with a southern drawl, Mary Lee Settle was an outsider from the start, who could not be assimilated into any recognised WAAF groupings like those which Nina Masel identified. Instead she found herself in the 'odd man out' group, but even here she was not safe from disapproval of her language and habits. She alone undressed completely and washed every day, cleaned her teeth morning and evening, and said things like 'Are you all through with the salt?' Having come all the way across the Atlantic moved by a vague ideal of fighting against oppression, she found herself on the receiving end instead. It came to a head the night of her 'flight's' first day off. After a pleasant afternoon wandering alone round Hereford, Mary returned in the dark to her hut:

> I pushed open the curtain. Something fell against me like a dead weight, too quickly to frighten me or, fortunately, for me to tense my muscles. I felt myself grabbed by my arms and legs and flung out in an arc into the empty air like a sack of grain. I landed on my back in a large puddle in the soft mud. My letters flew out of sight; my sweets were gone. There was a roar of noise. In the door above me stood a mass of WAAFs, yelling. One, the leader, the little pinched-faced girl, kept calling over the others, 'That'll teach the fuckin' toffy-nose' . . . 'You think we're a dirty lot, with your baths and your bare body. Oo wants to look at it? A ten-bob tart's wot you are.'[40]

It was an initiation rite from which Mary learnt the rules of survival: to outswear her opponents and, like them, to keep her vest on at all times. She did not allow herself another proper wash until the occasion of an RAF dance: 'for three weeks, taking on the habits of the others, I had been warmer, healthier, more obscene, more relaxed', if considerably less hygienic.

Such cliquishness could cause isolation and distress, and may have contributed to the high rates of turnover in the WAAFs and ATS before they came under military law, in April 1941. After this it became possible to leave only if you could make a case on health or compassionate grounds, or by 'working your ticket', that is, as Mary's admin officer put it: 'In the event of pregnancy (fire, catastrophe, act of God) you are released from active duty at the termination of three months.'[41]

The formation of cliques had another side. Thrown together by the actions of powers way out of an individual's control, women in the services, the Land Army or the factory could become very close, especially if their backgrounds were similar. In contrast to the tensions in Mary Lee Settle's WAAF training camp, the group of eight WAAF plotters with whom Nina Masel shared a dormitory at Broughton House RAF Preston, became good friends, their layers of inhibition peeled away by the intimacy of service life, as her account of an evening together in their room illustrates. Readily acknowledging the boarding school atmosphere, Nina described how polishing buttons and squabbling over the bath, the iron and where to go on their next day off, was followed by a discussion of collective solutions for the horrors of 'decorating the walls' at dances:

'Let's put the gramophone on now.'
'And dance.'
Arm-in-arm together was put on, and we danced around the room, and into the bath-room, much to the annoyance of a girl from another room, who was in the bath. We always looked upon the bathroom as ours, because it adjoins our room – we use it as a gym, kitchen, etc., etc.
'Colonel Bogey' followed on the gramophone, and we marched in a row, and did drill. Florence, unable to resist the sight of bending trunks, stuck pins in our seats, and the keep-fit session ended in a general skirmish until we all lay panting on our beds.
'Now for the feast' said Ormond, and produced endlessly pieces of chicken and stuffing and bread. Florence provided crumpets cooked on Marjorie's stove in the bathroom (Mary was in the bath; she's not modest).
Mary: 'Call these crumpets?'
'Yes I do.'
Mary: 'Why, in Scotland if you called those crumpets, the real crumpets would get up and slap you in the face.'
Florence: 'You and your Scotland! If you don't like them, you needn't have them.'
'You know,' said Ormond, chewing contently on her bed, 'I'm quite happy, tonight.'[42]

Belonging to a small group of comrades could be an enriching experience, productive of life-long friendships. References have already been made to the women welders who wrote to their trainer during 1942. They were sent by their employment exchanges in Penistone and Huddersfield to train to be welders in Sheffield during 1941–2. The factory where the Huddersfield women were to return to weld Bailey Bridges was not ready for them, so their one month's training in Sheffield stretched to six, giving them plenty of time to get to know each other and their young trainer, Val Pearson, whose father ran the steelworks. She not only taught them the art of welding but also found them billets, negotiated their pay and helped with family and love-life problems, as well as sharing many a joke. After they had eventually started work at Hopkinson's the Huddersfield women wrote regularly and affectionately to Val, who saved their letters for Mass-Observation. The correspondence records the support they gave each other and the fun they had, through the ups and downs of work, play, courtship and marriage during the war. They are still friends today and two of them have continued to write regularly to 'Miss Pearson' (or 'Dear Vagrant' as they affectionately call her on account of her weekends in the country) ever since. One extract will give the flavour of their friendship:

> Well Miss Pearson WHEN you come to Huddersfield we shall have to visit Fanny it seems, because she is on the club. I bet Jack will be upset about her. If she does not alter he will find her in bed when he comes home next month. You will have to send her a catalogue now for Expectant mothers. I think you had better send me one too because I am 4 days late but I think there is a chance yet because I ache back and front. I wish I was coming to Sheffield tomorrow. Anyhow if you don't come to Hopkinsons before next month Emily and I are going to take a day off and visit you.[43]

CHAPTER 12

LOVE, SEX AND MARRIAGE

Nina Masel thought that a consequence of the intimate lives that young women led in the forces was that 'conventional barriers and restraints are torn down and conversation gets down to bedrock'. She and her fellow WAAF plotters were unusually candid with each other about their situation:

> We're all in the same boat and we're all after the same thing. So why kid each other? And what is this thing we're all after? Obviously, a man. Preferably an officer or a sergeant pilot. I should say that 85 per cent of our conversation is about men, dances (where we meet men), 15 per cent about domestic and shop matters and a negligible proportion on other matters.[1]

WAAFs who found themselves in a minority on a RAF station had no problems as far as supply was concerned. 'It's easy to get a man. In fact it's difficult not to.' What counted was the rank of the target. The middle-class plotters set their sights on 'commissions and wings', that is officers and pilots, and they would not sink lower than 'ground stripes', that is non-commissioned officers who did not have flying duties. Yet in spite of the abundance of attention and the freedom from home constraints, their moral code appears to have remained remarkably intact. 'The average Ops girl admittedly likes a man who can kiss well' but 'definitely abstains from actual immorality.' The 'accepted term for dealing with unwanted passion' was 'coping' in the WAAFs, as in 'I *like* Bill and he *is* a Squadron Leader and all that but I simply can't face all the coping I have to do every evening.' An over-ardent male was being 'difficult' in the Wrens. As a driver, Marjorie Wardle had to take Naval Officers where they wanted to go, but she certainly did not let them go as far as they wanted, when they

205

got 'difficult'. She found Americans particularly troublesome.[2] Possibly they did not pick up the more subtle British methods of saying 'No'. Possibly they did not expect their advances ever to be refused. After all, their entry to the war after the bombing of Pearl Harbor in September 1941 could be seen as saving Britain from military disaster, and the cigarettes, nylons and chocolates which they generously bestowed could be seen as relief from desperate privation.

Poles had no such claims to be the 'cavalry' coming to the rescue, but they could nevertheless be very pressing. Polish sailors, airmen and soldiers fled to Britain after the collapse of Polish resistance to the Nazi invasion of the autumn of 1939 and were attached to British units. Valerie Moss, student/land girl in Devon, remembers some scrapes which she and a friend got into when asked to 'make up a party' with servicemen from RAF Chiverton nearby. Americans were bad enough.

> The really dangerous ones, though, were the Poles! You didn't go anywhere by yourself with the Poles if you could help it. They were very pleasant and terribly chivalrous and glamorous, full of gold teeth and braid and all the rest of it, but all they wanted to do was get you behind a hedge. I remember going to Barnstaple on a Saturday off, and two Poles attached themselves to us. We really got fed up with them, and we proceeded to speak entirely in Welsh, which neither of us could really speak. We recited the whole of the Lord's Prayer in Welsh to each other, talking a line at a time, and various things like the national anthem, so that it sounded like conversation. They didn't know what nationality we were, and we made them keep guessing, but of course, they never guessed. In the end they gave up. They realised we were having them on and they went off.[3]

Unwanted sexual advances could not always be disposed of so easily, especially by a girl on her own, and stories abound of what would now be called sexual harassment, in the streets and at work. The blackout was particularly disliked by women for this reason, and some young women dreaded finding themselves alone in a railway carriage with a serviceman especially in view of the long hold-ups typical of wartime journeys. Women in isolated places also felt vulnerable. Dorothy Barton and the Land Girl she shared with were so afraid of the cowman living below them, who used to knock on their window late at night and get them out to attend to fictitious problems, that they not only turned the key in the lock, but had a bolt fitted to the inside of the bedroom door. However, the moment Dorothy went away for the weekend he 'tried it on' with her friend, and Dorothy returned to find that she had virtually barricaded herself in, and had locked the cowman right out of the house. They appealed to the farmer to dismiss the man, but instead he got rid of them: 'he didn't think we could run the farm by ourselves'.[4]

Teasing between men and women was rampant in the workshops. It was usually good-natured, but the sexual undertones were not far from the surface and it must sometimes have been hard for women to bear. Doris White remembers the 'caterwauling and whistling' that went up in all-male shops when girls walked through en route for the stores, and although she made light of it, she generally took a friend with her 'not wishing to go alone'.[5] Teasing could be a way of belittling new women workers towards whom men felt antagonistic. Mark Benney's aircraft fitters sat apart from their first dilutee at tea-breaks and spoke to her as little as possible on the job until she refused to be left on her own any longer:

> There followed for the next few weeks, an arduous clumsy attempt to assimilate Vera, as we came to call her, through the medium of badinage, horse-play, flirtation. Lofty, more direct than the rest of us, would put his arm round her waist and pretend to caress her breasts. Stan derived great fun from making fictitious dates with her – 'but I'll have to think up an excuse for the missus first'. She accepted all this amiably enough, but somehow she would not see herself exclusively as a joke, the way we did. She wanted to discuss the work, the factory, the war and the future as seriously as anyone else.[6]

Teasing and sexual badinage were not usually physically threatening to women, even when they were a veil for hostility. But some women working with the public found themselves exposed to male violence and they were not always prepared to be passive victims. Protests by Newcastle tram conductresses prompted Zelma Katin's fellow workers in Sheffield to compare experiences in their canteen:

26 Dorothy Barton (*second from left*) and fellow Land Girls. (Courtesy of Age Exchange Theatre Trust)

One girl was hurled from the platform into the roadway, sustained a broken jaw and was unconscious. As her assailant could not be seen in the darkness she was unable to obtain redress and actually lost wages. Another girl, of an Amazonian build, was struck in the chest by a soldier when she told him there was no room on the tram, but she immediately retaliated by felling him with a blow from the ticket-holder. Many of the girls had been hurt in some way, either by hooligans or by passengers trying to 'get fresh' and they blamed the magistrates for imposing fines that were too low.[7]

Sexual harassment was one thing, but flirting could be fun, and many women enjoyed the mix-up of war not only because it offered new relationships with other women, but also because of the contact with men. Huddersfield had its quota of American and British servicemen, and the seven women welders were often asked out, even those who were married, engaged or going steady. They enjoyed a drink and a party, and in the absence of husbands and lovers in the forces they recorded many a jolly evening in their letters to Val, no doubt embellished for her benefit. The fact that they were living at home, in familiar neighbourhoods, may have made even things like attempted pick-ups in the blackout less scaring than they might have been. For example Agnes, who was half-way through having her teeth out, reported going home one blustery night:

Last night I joined the paratroops, the wind lifted me completely up, and had it not been for a soldier who very obligingly was in the way of my so called flight, I might have landed in Coleridge Rd. I really thought my umbrella would have been inside out. He insisted he saw me home, to keep my feet on the ground. Outside our door he kissed me, and, etc., but I wasn't having any. He kept murmuring 'Gorgeous', in my ear, and I thought, 'It's a damn good job its blackout, if he only saw my fangs.' Anyhow I managed to get away saying I had my husband's and my chips, and they were going cold. Fan [lodger] does come in handy sometimes. Mother remarked about my hat being on one side, so I told them what had happened. We all had a good laugh.[8]

There were a lot of servicemen about. By 1944 52 per cent of all British men between the ages of 19 and 40 were in uniform. There were four and a half million British servicemen altogether, and in addition there were one and a half million Allied, Dominion and Colonial troops stationed in the United Kingdom in the run-up to 'D-Day', the start of the allied invasion of Europe on June 5/6 1944. Associated with the abundance of servicemen was an increase in venereal disease, repeating the First World War pattern. The number of men coming forward for VD treatment more than doubled in the first two years of the war, reaching a peak in 1942. After that it declined slightly, possibly because more servicemen were posted abroad, while the number of women seeking treatment continued to rise. Some young men believed that the war had lessened men's inclinations towards restraint. Near the end of the war, a male clerk in his thirties wrote:

> Sexual morality has decayed a great deal in recent years, and the war has spurred on a process already set in motion earlier. Promiscuity is no longer considered wicked, though failure to avail oneself of safeguards against either pregnancy or VD is considered to be not 'comme il faut'. No-one seems to see any value in fidelity to one and the same partner (once the glamour has passed) and indeed it doesn't seem to have any value by our present day standards. Men don't reckon to be obedient nowadays to any laws that can't be enforced upon them.[9]

For older women who had been home-bound before the war, mixing with men could be intoxicating, sometimes with disturbing effects on married life. Hetty Fowler and her husband had run a fish and chip shop in Hull before the war, but their supplies of customers, staff, fat, fish and paper all disappeared in the first panic-stricken weeks, so he joined the National Fire Service. After a stint in the 'National Kitchens' cooking meals that were delivered to places like schools, canteens and British Restaurants, famous in wartime for their cheap nourishing meals, she joined the Ambulance Service.

> We worked 24 hours on duty and 24 hours off. Strangely enough my husband in the National Fire Service worked 24 on and 24 off, but in the opposite shift to me. So of course

27 Hetty Fowler in her Ambulance Service Uniform
(Courtesy of Thames TV/Channel 4, *A People's War*)

we didn't see each other. I reported for duty at 9 o'clock in the morning at the station and we used to have a roll call outside the office and as we lined up for roll call he would just be leaving and he would walk past and look at me and say, 'good morning, Mrs Fowler', and I would say, 'good morning, Mr Fowler'. And that was our – that was what we saw of each other . . .

You had to be very careful not to drift because I made friends and I know he made friends . . . You see across the road from where our station was – was a soldiers' camp and we got to know quite a lot of the soldiers. And every week they had a dance and the officer in charge used to ring up to our station officer to borrow some females to dance with these soldiers. So we all used to go across to dance with the soldiers, in our heavy shoes with a thick sole and army boots, on a concrete floor. But it was very enjoyable . . . we were sort of thrown together in war and we all thought we hadn't much longer to live, so why not get what we can out of life . . . I was just an ordinary wife and mother. But when you come out of your house and get among people, you're dancing with men, he thinks you're rather nice and you think well perhaps I am, but nobody's told me for years and you rather like it, you see, and you begin to see in yourself a different person – whereas you were just humdrum you began to try to make yourself look nice again . . . . It was nice that someone thought you were attractive. So of course when you got back with your husband he didn't think I was any more attractive, we were just the same – and it's not easy to take. But you can't say to him, 'I know a man who thinks I'm nice.' You can't say that, can you, to your husband? Very strange, very difficult.[10]

Hetty's marriage continued, but others collapsed. The number of divorces increased from 6,092 in 1938 to 15,221 in 1945, the rate rising from 1.5 to 3.6 per 10,000 of the English population during the war, with further rises to follow.[11] The liberalisation of the divorce laws in 1937 would no doubt have caused the number of divorces to go up even if there had been no war, but women's own testimony attributes some of them to its disturbing effects. For example, it prompted Mrs Cheshire in Lancaster to confront the fact that she had made a 'bad choice'

28 Hetty Fowler and her husband. Her marriage survived though others did not (Courtesy of Thames TV/Channel 4, *A People's War*)

and she was relieved to terminate her pre-war marriage: 'Mind you if the war hadn't come along and we hadn't been separated I suppose it would have gelled out of custom.'[12] Some dissolutions were probably the result of 'marriage fever' which swept Britain in the early years of the war when the feeling that life was about to come to an end stimulated many young people to get hitched quickly. In 1940 22 people were married per thousand of the population, compared with 17 in 1938, the highest figure since records began in the early nineteenth century.[13] The long ensuing separations caused by the call up were inevitably a strain. A probation officer at the Thames Police Court commented:

> Many excellent young mothers have been unable to stand the loneliness at home, particularly when their husbands are abroad, with not even spasmodic leave to break the monotony . . . Hasty war marriages, on embarkation leave, sometimes between comparative strangers, with a few days or weeks of married life, have left both parties with little sense of responsibility towards one another.[14]

There was a four-fold increase in the number of divorce petitions filed for adultery between 1939 and 1945, and whereas before the war over half the petitions had been filed by wives, in 1945 58 per cent came from husbands. The Forces' Welfare Services, inundated with urgent appeals, made it possible for servicemen and women to obtain divorces more cheaply and expeditiously than civilians — morale was felt to depend on it.

Commentators tended to blame women for the rising divorce rate, and gloomy forecasts were made about the effects of 'broken homes' on the future generation by the Marriage Guidance Council, founded in 1938, and others.[15] The stigma of divorce was not swept away in the rising tide of 'decree nisi' granted. But wives who felt that they were 'let out of the cage' during the war and who, like Hetty Fowler, began to see themselves as different people from the 'ordinary wives and mothers' they had been before, were not all married to men willing or able to accommodate the change. The greater availability of divorce must have been welcomed by many couples.

Growing anxiety about divorce was coupled with worries

about the birth rate during the war. Marriages may have reached a record high in 1940, but births reached a record low in 1941. There were fears that parents were in 'revolt' against reproduction, and that there would be an increasing proportion of old people in the population supported by dwindling cohorts of young people.[16] As in the First World War, concern about the family tended to focus on mothers rather than fathers, and these anxieties stimulated a debate about how to make marriage and motherhood more attractive to women in the post-war world. All sorts of things were suggested, from baby-sitting services to streamlined kitchens and rest homes for tired housewives.[17] These ideas in themselves were far from unwelcome, though few were actually realised, but well before they had begun to be bandied about, the birthrate had in fact picked up. After its all-time low of 14.4 per 1000 of the UK population in 1941, it rose to 15.9 in 1942, its highest point since 1931, and continued to rise to 17.9 in 1944.[18] Admittedly, these figures included illegitimate births, and of course commentators much preferred the population to be augmented safely within the bounds of conventional marriage. Indeed, the rising proportion of illegitimate births added fuel to the fire of the family moralists.

Illegitimate babies formed 4.4 per cent of all live births in 1939, but their numbers more than doubled during the war years, and in 1945 they constituted 9.1 per cent. It was widely thought that the cause of the increase was the loosening of moral standards and spread of unrestrained sexual behaviour among young men and women, due to the war. However, careful scrutiny of the statistics shows that this was an alarmist view. Before the war, in 1938, one in three mothers conceived their first child out of wedlock but 70 per cent of these 'irregularly conceived maternities' were later made respectable by marriage. During the war the main change was not that more women conceived before marriage, but that fewer of them got married before the birth of the baby. The figure in 1945 was only 37 per cent. There is no doubt that this had a lot to do with the war. The call up had the effect not only of throwing couples together but also of separating them abruptly, and in many cases they were a long way from their families, who in peacetime would have both patrolled their daughters' courtships and insisted upon marriage if they 'got into trouble'.

After its peak of 22 per thousand in 1940, the marriage rate fell to only 14 in 1943–4.[19]

Another change related to the war was that more illegitimate children were born to women over thirty and to married women. Records were not kept nationally, but in Birmingham during 1944–5, one third of all illegitimate children were born to married women, half of them servicemen's wives. Such a woman was in a predicament, because a wife had to have her husband's consent before she could offer a baby for adoption, yet the family home which she ran and maintained was considered in law and social policy to belong to her husband. She was therefore powerless to decide whether her child should be adopted or should stay with her in 'his' home, but was at the mercy of her husband's decision.

Not many of the mothers of the 337,000 illegitimate babies of 1939–45 have left accounts of their experiences. Pauline Long is an exception. She was 18 when the war broke out, and had clear ideas on marriage, informed by her membership in the Communist Party and her reading of interwar 'free love' feminists like Dora Russell (who had two 'extra-marital' children as well as two fathered by Bertrand Russell).

> During the war I was conscripted in to the Services, first in the ATS and then changed when I became pregnant and had a child, to becoming a cook in the Land Army. In this way I was able to get a roof over our heads and earn a living for us both. There was no other relevant way: 'service' was still more than a memory, and it was the only thing a 'bad girl' could do. My 'badness' of the time was based on left wing politics, and I did not want to be dependent on a man, believed marriage was Bourgeois, and that women were equal (but different). We relied on the sheath as contraception since there was no way I knew then of getting, as an unmarried woman, anything different. The idea of abortion arose, but the backstreet stories were so horrific that I discounted the idea immediately. Anyhow even backstreet abortions required cash and I had none. The child's father was also a revolutionary and also believed in all my ideals so therefore he saw no reason to do anything for me, and indeed would not have known what he could have done.[20]

Pauline's CP friends urged her to get married, but she held to her resolve. Other women who did not have her intellectual conviction, may have shared her awareness of the practical possibilities opened up by war.

Suddenly it was possible to have a baby and to get a second ration book; to find quite easily a place in the nurseries, and to have lunch at the 'British Restaurants' for (I think) 1/6d.[21]

There was still plenty of disapproval, and the 'sinful' were expected to be penitent, but welfare organisations which made arrangements for unmarried mothers in the forces and in industry were surprised by the independent attitudes of some unmarried mothers, and the gagging effect of old taboos was going. A woman civil servant in her fifties gave Mass-Observation an example of this.

I know of one case of a girl having to resign from our office because she had 'got into trouble'. Other girls talked about her and the occasion quite freely, and the general attitude seemed to be that it was a great pity that she had been so foolish – but she always was a queer sort of girl – and there were sympathetic conjectures about how she would get another job. Years ago, when a similar thing happened, the girl concerned simply dropped out of office life – no-one even said openly why she left – she just went home on sick leave and never returned. I can remember one of her best office friends saying very seriously, 'Oh, she was a *bad* girl', but apart from that her name was never mentioned.[22]

Some women did attempt abortion, which was illegal unless a woman's life was in danger. Mary Lee Settle recounts how she had to deal with a five-month foetus hidden in a hat-box in a cupboard when she was 'duty officer' in the old country house where her WAAF unit was billeted. The abortee explained that she could not go to the Medical Officer: 'I'm married. My chap is stationed in Africa. We've not seen each other for a year', so the discovery was followed by a secret visit with her to a village GP. The Huddersfield welders referred in their letters to 'births in the lav' and 'black pills'.[23]

It seems impossible to discover whether there was an increase in abortions during the war, compared with the years before.[24] By its very nature it was not something that was reported unless it went disastrously wrong. But the declining likelihood of 'legitimising' a pre-marital conception, and particularly the increase in extra-marital pregnancies among married women with husbands serving abroad, suggest that abortion must often have been considered.

It is hard to compare the changes in marital and sexual behaviour during the two world wars in human rather than statistical terms, because of the lack of comparable information. In addition, what women were actually experiencing has to be disentangled from what they were said to be experiencing. Charges of immorality were flung at women in both wars but often as another way of saying that women should not be doing 'unfeminine' things like working on munitions or wearing a service uniform. The rise in illegitimacy and divorce was much smaller in the First World War than it was in the next. Possibly the absence of so many servicemen at the front during 1914–18, compared with the presence of so many in camps all over Britain throughout 1939–45, made the biggest difference to the patterns of illegitimacy, while divorce was of course much more difficult and expensive to obtain in the First War. In the Second War there was certainly pressure on women from men to make themselves sexually available. Women's responses were varied. Some found this frightening, while others enjoyed it. Some women were terribly distressed by consequences such as extra-marital pregnancy or the break-up of their marriages, while others took an independent line on both ending a marriage and keeping an illegitimate baby. The Second World War saw more social tolerance of divorce and a slightly less punitive attitude to unmarried mothers. But the images of smiling mothers and bouncing babies with which papers like *Picture Post* illustrated features about raising the birthrate from 1943 onwards, carried an unequivocal message. Married motherhood was still a girl's true destiny.

HOURS

The things women liked least about work in the Second World War related to the conditions under which they worked, especially the hours that were expected of them. A survey conducted in 1943 revealed that half of women workers dissatisfied with industrial conditions felt that their hours were too long.[1] It seemed that nothing had been learnt from the First World War experience that increasing a worker's hours did not usually result in higher productivity, but on the contrary contributed to numerous problems arising from fatigue.

In the first months after the fall of France and the evacuation from Dunkirk workers willingly put in 70 hours a week. Such a frenzied burst of activity could not be sustained, but employers were reluctant to reduce hours, and in some 'non-essential' industries like boot and shoe making they tried to lengthen them because they were losing workers to munitions. In 1941 most women in industry were required to work a 12-hour day for five and a half days a week and then shift work was introduced, so many women worked at night. Factory legislation passed in 1937 was suspended for the duration of the war to make this legal. But night work was particularly disliked, especially as the years of war mounted. Doris White, working in the aircraft repair shop at Wolverton, graphically describes the toll it took:

> Mornings I walked through the alley, sometimes in complete darkness, to our home in Victoria Street, cold and tired. The thought of food sickened me, my stomach feeling queasy as if my whole system was out of gear. Declining Mother's offer

ood I wearily climbed the stairs to the cold 'boxroom' and flopped into bed, the sheets still slightly warm from mother's body. Mother's contribution to the war effort was emptying the chamber-pot ready for me in the day. Sweet oblivion it was, until – rumble, rumble, Mrs B was having coal delivered, and into the barn it shot, bag after bag. A sigh, turning over, until – shouts and squeals told me the children had been released from Moon Street School, sounding like they had been shut up for weeks. Sleep was punctuated with all the sounds of life of people who slept at the proper time. But, when the time came to sleep at night, then I could not sleep in peace. My pet hate being spiders, I now dreamed of them . . .[2]

The nightmare could be even worse for married women, who tended to get up early after coming off nightshift, to shop, wash, cook, collect children from school and see to all the other demands of the home. With a blithe disregard for the damaging consequences of such pressure, employers claimed that shift work was the solution to the double burden, since it enabled women to get their domestic work done on their 'rest days'.[3]

The working week was lengthened still further by the time it took to get to many factories, particularly the royal ordnance factories hastily erected on 'greenfield' sites, to produce guns, bombs and bullets at a safe distance from the towns. Chorley, a filling factory in Lancashire, was notorious in this respect. In 1940–1 28,000 workers, most of them women, poured in each day from the neighbouring towns. Burnley was one of the nearest, but in order to work from 8 am to 7 pm a worker had to leave Burnley at 6.30 in the morning and did not get home till 8.50 at night, after a miserable journey braving air-raids and the habitual Lancashire rain without shelter.[4] Wartime transport was being run with depleted staffs and limited fuel allowances, so there was not much that transport workers could do unless the local authorities agreed to put on 'specials', as they did eventually at Chorley. The pressures of their own jobs did not make conductresses particularly sympathetic to the 'travelling public'. Jean Stoddart, a teenager growing up just outside Ayr in Scotland, worked at weekends and in the evenings as a volunteer in a Merchant Seamen's canteen.

I had to commute by bus to work in Ayr. Bus services were

drastically cut and the buses were cold, unlighted and prone to breakdowns. It was not uncommon for a bus to be late in arriving or not to turn up at all. To the grumbler who complained of standing for an hour in the rain the conductress offered only the cold consolation of 'Dae ye no ken there's a war on?'[5]

Not surprisingly in view of the transport problems, possession of a bicycle improved one's chances of selection for the Land Army, and hitch-hiking became the accepted form of transport for servicewomen, even those who would not have dreamt of doing such a thing before the war.

The long hours were particularly hard on women with homes to look after, who included not only married women but some single women too. Sixty-two per cent of married women and 45 per cent of single women told Mass-Observation investigators that the main reason they absented themselves from work was because they had domestic responsibilities to attend to, whereas only 1 per cent of men referred to such reasons for absence. Men more often cited illness, fatigue, frustration with work or the pursuit of pleasure as reasons for taking days off.[6] The long hours made some women feel as though the factory was robbing them of part of their lives, like one young woman working at Ekco, making radar, who said:

It's funny, when you're in there the time goes so slow you think it will never be eight o'clock; but somehow when you look back the weeks seem to fly by. I've been here two years, but I sometimes feel I've only been here a few weeks. It gives me a nasty feeling, like it's running away with my life.[7]

Women who bore the main brunt of shopping, cooking and caring for a family undoubtedly suffered the greatest strain, and we shall look more closely at how they coped in the next chapter. But young single women living at home experienced their own domestic difficulties on account of the long hours they spent at the factory, in spite of the advantages of having someone at home to look after them. Several of the Ekco workers described how everyone had either gone out or was ready for bed by the time they got home at about 9 o'clock and one 18-year-old recounted with some bitterness an incident which made her feel she had been displaced from normal domestic decision-making:

The billeting officer had been round, and they were talking about it when I got in. 'What's happening?' I asked; 'Are we to have some evacuees? I hope it's not children. Don't let them send us any children, Mum, we've enough of children in this house.' Quite nicely I said it, but Doreen (her sister) turned on me quite sharp. 'You leave it to Mum and me,' she said; 'it don't matter to you who we have and who we don't, you're never there.' Just as if it wasn't my home as much as hers.[8]

Following official concern about the possibility that fatigue might impair efficiency, hours were supposed to come down to 55 per week during 1942, though the semi-independent Industrial Health Research Board did not think this was a sufficient reduction and pressed the government to limit night work for women and increase the number of holidays.[9] However, as in the First War, the government's main objective was to increase war production, and it was not prepared to go any further. A 55-hour week still meant a 10-hour day for five and a half days, and from August 1942 any women aged 20 to 45 without household responsibilities who was lucky enough to be working less than 55 hours was required to do compulsory fire watching at her place of work, which further extended the time away from home. This was not so bad if nothing much was going on, but it could be an exhausting responsibility during raids. The mounting fatigue is expressed bluntly in some of the women welders' letters, like this one from Amy:

I am in a very poor way today Miss Pearson, I am sorry to say. I have had a hectic week what with the Ripplay one night and Sirens the next. I have had to get up 3 nights on ARP duty from 2.0 AM until about 3.30 each time so I am bugared up [sic] now. I wish Hitler was in bleeding Hell.[10]

Reduction of hours was not a popular issue among men, whose first consideration was to maximise earnings, particularly in view of the income tax bill to be paid on the previous year's earnings. The standard rate of income tax almost doubled in the first two years of the war, and the Pay As You Earn scheme was not introduced until 1944. But part-time work was in demand from married women like Zelma Katin in Sheffield who wrote to her employers explaining in strong terms how impossible it was to combine 48 hours exhausting work on the trams with maintaining her home and her son. Eventually she got a part-time arrangement on the buses, which she found much less taxing. However, when the government introduced direction into part-time work for women in 1943 the idea was not to relieve married women already in work of some of their hours of industrial work, but to give the government the opportunity to direct into work more of those outside who had so far been exempt from direction on account of their household responsibilities, and who could not be persuaded to volunteer. After their initial suspicions employers concluded that part-timers were good value for money. They tended to be more efficient and less absentee than full-timers, and cost less in terms of bonuses, holiday pay, insurance contributions and the like. It was also possible to give them some of the most unpleasant types of work, which it was difficult to get full-timers to do efficiently all day long.[11]

SICKNESS

Tiredness made women prey to sickness. A government enquiry listed numerous minor ailments which beset women during the war. As in the First World War, the most common were anaemia and nervous disorders, closely followed by colds and gastritis. Women's sickness rate was about half as much again as that of men,[12] which the Industrial Health Research Board attributed to the interaction of the low pre-war standards of health among women, with the excessive hours expected of them in war work, the strains imposed by domestic work and their relatively poor diet during the war. Even when they had access to a canteen, women tended to fill up quickly on milk, puddings, cakes and biscuits, whereas men ate more meat and cooked meals, many of which were of course prepared by their womenfolk.[13] However, dietary problems occurred mainly among women in industry and transport. Those in the services received regular and plentiful meals. Mary Lee Settle in the WAAFs was astonished to see the difference this made to most of the women in her 'flight' a few weeks after joining up. Her comment echoes similar observations made in the First World War:

> I noticed that the girls around me had begun to fill out and glow. Their skin was losing its thickness. They looked seventeen. In what seemed to me a life without joy which was imposed on most of them without their choice, they were beginning to thrive. The days that had stripped me of weight, well-being and habit so soon were acting on them in the opposite way. Air, exercise, regular meals and the very act for some of them of sleeping above ground for the first time in years were making the blood run better through their bodies.[14]

The fatigue felt by women in industry was conducive to accidents, though some workplace injuries seem to have been part and parcel of the job. Of course women did not have a monopoly of occupational health hazards, and men in heavy and dangerous work had for a long time been prone to horrible accidents and illnesses. But during the Second War, as during the First, the rapid expansion of production and the practice of putting women on to new types of work with minimum training at the lowest possible cost to the employer, exposed women war workers to all sorts of risks. Factory inspectors found that the accident rate was lower among women than among men, but it rose alarmingly during the war, as more women came on to heavy and dangerous work. Women suffered 71,000 accidents in 1942, nearly double the number in 1941 and five times as many as in 1938, and of course many accidents were never reported. War is often seen as promoting welfare. But as far as women in munitions were concerned, even the official historian concluded that it was amazing that peacetime standards of health and safety were maintained, let alone improved upon.[15]

At the insistence of Ernest Bevin, who as an ex-docker had first-hand experience of the health hazards confronting industrial workers, the government empowered factory inspectors to order employers on government contracts to improve safety at work and medical care. Some of the nastiest accidents to women occurred because there was no casing round machinery and moving belts in which hair or clothing could easily get caught. There were cases of women being scalped by the machinery, especially when flowing 'Veronica Lake' hairstyles came into vogue in 1943. Under pressure from the factory some improvements were made and automatic safety switches were introduced, to Lisa Hadden's good fortune:

> Sparks used to fly when you did the drilling, but we never had anything over our hair or eyes. We wore a hat, but it didn't really cover your head. I had a bit of hair in the front of my face, and that caught in the machine. I was sent to hospital, but I wasn't hurt, just frightened. My hair jammed the belt up and the machine stopped.[16]

Women like Lisa who worked with metal had to watch out for flying metal shavings as well as the dangers of getting caught in the machinery. Sadie MacDougal, turning brass shells at Vickers in Newcastle, remembers having 'shamrocks' all over her arms from the hot splinters, and Mona Marshall transforming steel 'billets' into shells in Sheffield, had a particularly unpleasant experience soon after arriving there.

> I got the machine going and it was going perfectly and I sat on the end of my machine, just sat there, and a piece of turning flew out, and you know wood shavings, well imagine that as red hot steel, and the force that it comes out and it hit me straight across the face, there, and it went straight through! Well I could have lifted my teeth out, it loosened my teeth, and blood just gushed out. Anyway they got the ambulance out, took me to the hospital, stitched me up, and I went back to work in the morning . . . I was in terrible pain because I stiffened up here, it wasn't the cut as much as the force that it had come and I was absolutely rigid for a week.[17]

The factory inspectors could direct an employer to take on a doctor and a nurse, and by 1944 there were about 1,000 works doctors dividing their time between 1,500 factories. This was a huge advance on the situation in 1939 when only 60 were available, and in view of the shortage of doctors in wartime it opened up new opportunities for women doctors outside their usual medical ghettoes of paediatrics and gynaecology. Between 7 and 10 per cent of the wartime works doctors were women. But all the same the figures need to be seen in perspective. By 1944 67,400 workplaces were covered by the Essential Work

Order, and there were in addition many others. Kay Jenner remembers that even a large factory like GEC in Coventry, turning out electrical components for aircraft, provided no more than 'a surgery with two nurses. The most they offered was an aspirin and a cup of tea. There was a works doctor who attended once a week but I never heard of anyone seeing him.'[18] Workers at smaller factories would be lucky if employers honoured their obligation under the 1937 Factory Act to provide a First Aid box and a seat.

Tess, a labour supply officer for the Ministry of Supply, remembers that the smaller firms tended to skimp generally when it came to health and safety.

> Towards the end of the war some private firms were doing some of the work in small filling factories, to get extra production and I sometimes discovered that these private firms were cutting corners on safety regulations. They'd say to me: 'We're not as fussy as they are' meaning the government factories, and I always said: 'This has been worked out on the experience of the First World War and it is a condition of your contract. We cannot afford to have accidents, people suffering from yellow skin disease, or dermatitis.'[19]

Once again it was mainly women who worked on toxic processes and once again many contracted dermatitis and suffered the toxic effects of work with TNT and other explosives in the filling factories.[20] In 1916 toxic jaundice had been 'discovered' and to this was added, in 1942, the 'discovery' of toxic anaemia. In spite of the greater awareness of the problem following the experiences of the First World War, there was still much uncertainty about the solution. Whereas in the First War experts had decided that toxic effects were caused by contact rather than inhalation, attention returned to the possibiity that the poison was airborne in the Second War. Particularly high concentrations of TNT dust were found during 'biscuit breaking' when solid TNT was being broken up, and when workers were sweeping up at the end of shifts, and suction ventilators and vacuum cleaners were introduced in some of the royal ordnance factories to remove the dust, though ventilation systems in many factories were not operated properly at night because of the blackout. In spite of the improvements Mrs Jones, who worked at Bridgend filling factory in South Wales, had memories of working with TNT which echo those of women of the First War:

> We worked with yellow powder, which made everything go yellow. Our overalls were supposed to be white, like drill. You had to cover your hair, otherwise you would be blonde. Even your hair went yellow. The powder used to get into everything. It was horrible. A lot of people couldn't stand it. They were ill, and they were removed then. You had to do your turn in the powder shop, and we used to try and get out of it. It used to be terrible, especially if it was at night, because everything was closed in at night. We would be in there dealing it out for people to use. We wore masks in there, because you didn't want it to go down your throat.[21]

To combat dermatitis new equipment for handling TNT and other powerful chemicals which lessened the amount of skin contact was introduced, and in some filling factories women were given 'make up time' when they could apply barrier creams to their hands and faces and tuck their hair into turbans. Managements were also urged to insist that women washed very thoroughly and to supervise their ablutions (which cannot have been liked).

The various steps taken did represent an advance on the protection offered to women in the First World War, which is reflected in the comparable figures. Whereas 403 cases of toxic jaundice were now believed to have occurred in the First War, of which 105 were fatal, 105 were reported in the Second War, of which 21 proved fatal. All the same, deadly chemicals remained dangerous to work with. In addition to toxic jaundice there were 15 cases of toxic anaemia of which 7 were fatal, and over 500 cases of aniline poisoning, and the less lethal hazard of dermatitis remained, in the words of the official historian, 'a cause of anxiety, sickness and loss of production', affecting an *average* of 829 women a month in 1942 and 500 a month in 1943.[22] Royal ordnance factories were supposed to rotate their workers as a preventive measure, but once somone had contracted any form of poisoning the only solution was to remove them completely from contact with the substances affecting them. Mary Lee Settle was struck by the weird appearance of Viv who was transferred from a filling factory to the WAAFs. Sitting in the depot cookhouse on their first evening, she looked 'as if she were spot-lit by her own color. She was yellow, a sort of inhuman, chemical shade of yellow which had dyed her skin and her hair . . . Even her eyeballs, as she too stole a glance around her at the others, were yellow.'[23]

Although chemical poisoning attracted the most attention, the rising number of cases of TB also worried the Industrial Health Research Board. The incidence of pulmonary tuberculosis among women increased by about 16 per cent between 1940 and 1944. Officials were relieved that there was not more of the disease among young women, who had suffered particularly badly in the First War, and noted that older men were now the group hardest hit. Nevertheless the problem was not negligible among women. The 'herd life' in industry and the forces, the poor ventilation and lighting due to blackout, and above all fatigue caused by the long hours of work, travel and nights broken by air raids on top of domestic chores, were said to lower women's resistance. But the rationing which was introduced early in this war at least acted as a breakwater against a drastic decline in women's nutrition, and although many billets were unsatisfactory, the hostels of 1939–45 were an improvement on those of the First World War. In 1943 approximately 1 million persons were living in billets and 60,000, most of them women, in hostels, where they were not now required to share beds![24] After a committee reported urgently in 1942 Mass Radiography Units started to tour the country to help with the early detection of TB in factories and in the forces.

As a preventive step, 'rest-breaks' were introduced for women working on munitions who showed signs of acute fatigue. The idea was that they should go to one of six centres for a 2-week holiday, with financial assistance if necessary. Officials discovered, however, that the women who most needed a break because of their responsibilities to homes, husbands, children and lodgers on top of war work, could not get away precisely because of those responsibilities. In 1944 local authorities were given the power to provide home helps, but a householder had already to be 'suffering hardship owing to sickness or emergency' before she was considered eligible, and in any case few authorities employed many.[25] Over 10 million adult men were not away in the services, but no steps were taken to train husbands to take on the domestic burden. Such a thing would have been much too disturbing even in wartime.

Every job seemed to have its hazards and many women felt inadequately protected. Women sewing gas-sensitive pads on to the cuffs of military uniforms found that the chemicals with which the pads were impregnated melted the ends of their fingers. 'They used to have buckets of liquid, so we could soak our fingers to try and heal them' explained Maria Tardos, a Cypriot immigrant who was put on this very low-paying work.[26] Women painting the dials of aircraft instruments with luminous paint were at risk of cancer due to the radio-active materials in the paint. However careful they were with their masks, the women welders suffered from 'arc eye', a painful condition which kept the sufferer awake at night with a feeling of soap in her eye. Flash from the welding torches also caused burns on the arms and sometimes on the feet, which itched unbearably when they got warm. Poor Amy had a nasty time with arc eye, and was eventually advised to give up welding because of it.

On Tuesday night about seven o'clock I had quite a shock, after I had washed myself, my left eye was rather troublesome so I used some Optrex, no response, Borasic Crystals, no response, golden eye ointment and still no better. After all this I put a tea-leaf poultice on, and tied a bandage round, this eased it a bit but oh what pain I had. I could not bear the light so we took a globe off. Believe me I was frantic. I got up Wednesday morning with an eye the size of two, but went to work. Mr Robinson sent me to the Ambulance Room and the Nurse said I had to watch it did not turn septic. I had a fit, she said it was burnt in the corner, NOT WITH SLAG. I must have had my mask on one side, anyway we have got the new ones now thank you. I had to go the Ambulance Room 5 times yesterday to have my eye seen to . . . I could not see to weld.[27]

OPTING OUT

Sickness, accidents, fatigue and boredom led inevitably to absenteeism. Married women were absent twice as much as men, losing 10 to 15 per cent of their working hours in this way, and the habit of taking time off occasionally was widespread. At one ordnance factory over 80 per cent of the women were absent at some time in a 6-week period.[28] Government officials were suspicious of the high rates of absenteeism among women, and some suggested that women were malingering. Those women whose work was excrutiatingly monotonous may well have been glad of a day off, like the Ekco machine-shop girls who felt that it was most unfair that they had to come into work on wintry days, when the women who lived in far-flung villages did not come because the bus could not get through the snow to pick them up.[29] But evidence from other factories suggests that women were anxious not to miss a day's pay if they could help it. Their wage packets were already thin enough. The exceptions to this were weekends, when married women tended to regard work as dispensable, even when it was paid at overtime rates of two or three times the weekday rate. The absence rate at ROF Aycliffe was 50 to 60 per cent of its 9,000 women workers on Saturdays and Sundays, days when the men made a point of coming to work.[30] It was as if married women made a calculation in which the demands of their homes were placed against their need for the wage and the factory's need of them, and that at the weekends the former outweighed the latter.

For some women factory conditions were a bitter disappointment. They had been led to expect brand new factories, light, clean and airy, with good canteen and medical facilities on the spot, and pleasant and hygienic cloakrooms. Very few factories lived up to this image, and some were much as they had been in the First World War. Sadie MacDougal remembered the oil and grease in her Tyneside engineering workshop, which somehow penetrated all the layers of clothing you were wearing and even fell into your tea if you did not drink it quickly enough; Margaret Kippin was dismayed to find herself inspecting aircraft components under a leaky corrugated iron roof at a hastily erected factory behind the owner's garage in Walton-on-

Thames; and many women were critical of managements which expected them to work with damp feet after a long walk to work, or to eat at break-times with dirty hands. Some women fought for basic amenities like tea-breaks, better ventilation (a constant problem with blacked-out windows), sanitary towel machines and hot water in the toilets and cupboards where they could leave things like handbags safely, rather than have them cluttering the workbench, and are proud to remember their successes in these respects.[31]

But when it all became too much women left, like the woman whom a Mass-Observer caught hurrying home from work at lunch-time one day.

When I arrived with her, the whole house was in a complete mess. Two days' washing up is piled high in the sink; a great bundle of washed but unironed clothes lie on the floor beside the sink; odd shoes and socks belonging to the children are scattered about on chairs; and the table is a mass of crumbs and dirty crockery . . . She says: 'It's no good, I can't keep up with it. I thought I'd like to do a bit and bring in some more money, but I can't keep up with it. If I could just have a couple of days to get it straight, then it would be alright, you could keep it under, but I can't manage like this.'[32]

The Essential Work Order introduced by Bevin in March 1941 to regulate conditions of work in war industries stated that a woman could leave munitions only with the permission of the National Service Officer. But if she was not in her twenties and therefore outside the conscripted age group, and gave family responsibilities as her reason for wanting to leave, NSOs found it difficult to refuse. The rate of women's 'turnover' was particularly high at some of the royal ordnance factories early in the war, like Chorley in Lancashire, where almost as many women were leaving each week as were joining. At other factories a turnover rate of 0.9 per week was not uncommon, meaning that the factory had to replace half its workforce annually.

Employers' responses to both absenteeism and high rates of turnover were to step up supervision. It was felt by some that young women unaccustomed to industrial life needed disciplining, but inevitably supervisors who approached their job in this spirit were most unpopular, just as they had been in the First

World War, and they were probably not very effective at raising morale and making women feel like doing their best for the war effort. Male supervisors were often condescending and undermining, particularly towards women in relatively skilled jobs, like Margaret Kippin, the components inspector, who said of one of her foremen,

> I've had about four people in my life who I couldn't get on with, and he was one of them. I think he resented women being able to say that's not right. His attitude was: 'You're a woman, you don't know.' After all I had the drawing, so I did know.[33]

Women factory supervisors had an authoritarian 'school ma'am' image. The same was true of many of the officers in the women's services, who were generally recruited from the well-spoken, better-educated ranks of the middle-class. A Mass-Observer commented on the supervisory styles she had encountered:

> The particular forewomen employed at the works are kindly and well tempered, but with very steady somewhat ascetic natures. They tend to assume a responsibility for the girls which exceeds the bounds of their job. There are many types of girls who resent the almost maternalistic attitude of the forewomen, and are irritated when judgements are passed on their private lives, their dress, their language and their boy friends. Irritation so roused seems to be cumulative till ultimately almost any utterance of the forewoman is regarded as an unwarranted interference, and deeply resented, so that permission to leave is at last the only solution to the tension roused.[34]

During the Second World War, however, a new style of supervision was advocated by the Ministry of Labour, known as 'human factor management'. Rather than being based on discipline and philanthropic but patronising concern about the worker's well-being, the new style was based on sympathetic understanding of the worker's physical and social needs, and attempts to meet them, albeit on the principle that such an approach was more likely to raise productivity than more officious methods. Mrs Dyer, a supervisor at a small arms factory in Birmingham, commented on the contrast between the

29 Margaret Kippin (*second from left*) with co-'viewers' Jean and Nesta and
chargehand Andy (who they did get on with)
(Courtesy of Age Exchange Theatre Trust)

approach expected in this war and that of the last.

> Mr Bevin wants labour handled with a velvet glove! It is so different to the last war when discipline meant so much. Then an order was given and it was obeyed: now, a reason has to be given for everything.[35]

Tess, the labour supply officer, remembered a woman working in a foundry who embodied the new style. 'She'd been in the Music Halls, and she was a welfare officer. She said "I've only got two qualifications for being a welfare officer. I've got a good bosom to cry on, and I can make a damned good cup of tea." '[36]

Works councils and joint production committees on which representatives of management and workers sat, were also the product of 'human factor management'. In general male-dominated unions cornered these new wartime organisations, and women's representation on them was small, but where women did get on to them they were often reported to fight energetically on behalf of the particular demands of the women who had elected them.[37] Women themselves noticed the difference between the old and new types of supervisor and in general appear to have appreciated not being treated like naughty children. But even good supervision could not change fundamental problems, like hours that were too long, work that was too boring and above all having 'too much to do all round'.

CHAPTER 14

DOUBLE BURDEN

It is sometimes thought that the government stepped in like a beneficent uncle during the Second World War to take over many of the domestic jobs traditionally ascribed to women, in order to release them for war work. In fact government records and women's own experiences suggest that state intervention into the domestic sphere was limited, even though it was, of necessity, greater than in the First World War. Some government departments like the Ministry of Labour, desperate to increase the labour supply, favoured more radical steps, but there was a stubborn reluctance at the heart of government to introduce any policy that would change the conventional role of women at home, even at the height of a total war. In addition, the government was actively encouraging women to enlarge their domestic role through the 'make do and mend' propaganda directed at the 'housewife'. Shortages were even more acute than in the First World War, and the state depended on women to make up deficiencies in diet, clothing and comfort, an extra load for already burdened women to bear. Women's accounts of how they coped with the double burden between 1939 and 1945 echo those of the inter-war years, the First War and the years before that. Good organisation and grim determination were the hallmarks. This quote from a 40-year-old Midlands woman, mother of six, four of whom were under 12, stands for many:

> I get up at 5 in the morning and get the worst of my housework done, and the children all washed and dressed, and I do the washing and get my dinner started so it'll only need a warm up in the evening. Then I go to work, and I come back at 9.30 in the evening and give them all their

supper and tidy up a bit. I seem to manage. Sometimes when the alarm goes on Sunday morning I say to myself 'I won't go today'; but then I think if everyone said that on Sunday mornings, then what would happen. And so I get up.'[1]

CHILDCARE

Childcare was the biggest headache for mothers of young children, closely followed by shopping, cooking and house-work. Experiences varied but there were many working mothers who could not find a nursery in their area though they would have welcomed one, like Clara Moore. She and her two little boys were bombed out twice in Southampton, which was such a harrowing experience that she decided that they must get out of the town. As a serviceman's wife she was getting only £1 7s a week, so there was no alternative but for her to get a job, and she worked in a factory making pistons and piston rings for aircraft engines at Lymington, 18 miles away. There was no nursery, even though there was a growing number of women workers at the factory, and Clara had to make do with a variety of expedients. At first she left the boys on a farm which the Southampton Council found for them as evacuees, but paying a surprise mid-week visit she was upset to find her 2-year-old tied down in a cot, and took him back to her bed-sitting room in Lymington where her landlady minded him while she worked. Obviously this could not be a permanent arrangement, so she advertised for a minder and found some one who lived near Bournemouth who took both children. Clara visited them and took them out every weekend, but remembers the whole episode as emotionally taxing:

> I missed them, terrible. It was a terrible wrench. I used to cry myself to sleep at night, you know, thinking about them, wondering if they're all right. When I used to leave them it used to be terrible, you know, to leave them there, but it was just one of those things . . . it was safer for them to be there than being in the bombing. I could never go through that bombing in Southampton again, never . . .

Instead of me advertising for somebody to mind mine
I would have preferred a day nursery for them to have gone
so that I could have gone and got them when I came out,
you know, attached to the factory where I could have taken
them and then I would have had them at night. Wouldn't
have seen much of them during the day but I would have
had them at night, you know, to come home to. I wouldn't
have lost that baby-childish feeling that you get because
after all they were young, one was two and one was four,
they were very young. I lost that little bit of them growing
up.[2]

Whether working or not, many mothers must have felt
anxious about evacuating their children to the countryside to
stay with strangers. Under the official schemes mothers were
supposed to accompany children under school-age, but this was
usually impractical if the mother, like Clara, needed to be doing
paid work. In any case living as a lodger in unfamiliar
countryside with no friends around was not popular with the
urban mothers who were persuaded to go at the beginning of
the war, and did not last long. Later, during the Blitz of
1940–1 on London and other major ports (like Southampton
and Liverpool) and large industrial cities (like Coventry,
Birmingham and Manchester), and the subsequent waves of
Baedeker, V1 and V2 bombing, mothers were again frightened
into sending away their children, and women in rural areas
were persuaded to add to their busy lives the task of looking
after them.

There were, however, some nurseries for the children of
working mothers. A very small number of firms set up their
own factory crêches on the spot, but these were frowned upon
by the government department responsible for the care of pre-
school children, the Ministry of Health. Ostensibly, the reason
for its disapproval was that factories were targets for German
bombers so children would be in danger there, but in most
industrial areas the risk from bombing was as great at home.
The reality was probably that nurseries set up independently
were outside its control, something which the Ministry of
Health took very seriously.[3]

Pre-war day nurseries had been rescue agencies for the
children of mothers seen as in some way inadequate, and

Ministry of Health officials continued to think in this way in spite of the changed conditions of war. The Ministry of Labour, responsible for increasing the supply of women workers, fought a running battle with them over enlarging the supply of nursery places during the war. But it was hard for the Ministry of Labour to insist on the provision of nurseries, since it had itself decided that mothers of children under 14 should be exempt from compulsory call up. Its anxieties about nursery places indicate how dependent wartime industry was on mothers volunteering for war work.

At the start of the war many nurseries were closed because they were in evacuation areas, and their buildings were requisitioned by the army or services like the ARP, for use as things like billets or rest centres for the bombed out. In October 1940 only 14 were functioning as day nurseries. Gradually the Ministry of Health and the local authorities, which shared the costs, established more nurseries, but the wheels of bureaucracy ground slowly. In the spring of 1941, local employment exchanges became aware that the recruitment of married women was being held up by the difficulties of finding somewhere for their little children to go during the day, as well as by the problem of caring for older children after school, and by the autumn of 1941 groups of women all over the country were campaigning for nurseries. For example, women in Hampstead in north London marched through the streets with toddlers in push-chairs holding placards saying things like 'Nurseries for Kids! War work for Mothers!'[4] The TUC Women's Advisory Conference and the Labour Party's Women's Sections threw their weight behind these campaigns. Leading Labour women like Mary Sutherland did not want mothers of young children to work, but if they had to because of personal need and the national emergency, it was up to the state to provide somewhere for them to leave their children.

Over and over again, however, such demands met the opposition of Medical Officers of Health, the local Ministry of Health officials. Their objections were various. Some said that mothers in their areas were not entering war work, so nurseries must be unnecessary, others that mothers were making their own childcare arrangements so they obviously did not want nurseries. Underlying these somewhat specious arguments was the view, which was also that of the Ministry they represented, that 'a mother's place is in the home, where she should look after her own children'.[5]

For Clara, a bombed-out serviceman's wife, such an arrangement was simply unattainable in wartime, and of course plenty of other women whose circumstances were less desperate felt they would like to contribute to war production if there was somewhere safe where they could leave their children. The economic imperative for women like Clara to do paid work, coupled with the insatiable demand of industry for labour power in the two years before the opening of the Second Front, did produce an increase in the number of day nurseries. By the time the allied invasion of Europe was under way, in the autumn of 1944, there were 71,806 places in about 1,500 wartime day nurseries, many of which were prefabricated huts. The Treasury paid the capital costs, and the running costs were shared between the Ministry of Health, the local authority and the mother, who paid about 1s per child per day. In addition there were a few thousand places for the 3- and 4-year-olds in nursery schools and nursery classes of ordinary elementary schools. These were open during school hours, which obviously was not very helpful for women working normal factory shifts, though a few ran after-school play centres. To be much use to working mothers day nurseries had to be open from about 7.30 in the morning to 8 at night.

The 1,500 nurseries taking nearly 72,000 children represented a huge increase on the mere 14 nurseries of October 1940, and is in sharp contrast to the 105 set up during the First World War for 4,000 children. But all the same they accommodated a remarkably small proportion of the children for whom they were intended. By one generous estimate, there was provision in 1944 for only a quarter of all the children under 5 of women war workers.[6] The rest were minded by whoever could be found, be she friend, neighbour, relative or stranger.

In fact the preference of the Ministry of Health for home-based forms of childcare led to minding overtaking nurseries as the official solution to the wartime problem. The Ministry's main official circular on the subject, issued in December 1941, stated that it was up to women themselves to make 'the greatest single contribution'. They 'must between them carry out the two tasks of looking after the children and working in the

30 Miriam Power before the War. (Courtesy of Thames TV/Channel 4, *A People's War*)

factories . . . in this way there will be real partnership in the war effort.'[7] Minding was presented as a wartime innovation, but of course it was the time-honoured way in which married women with children had organised childcare when they needed to work. Mothers or other close relatives or friends had traditionally been preferred as minders, and many women managed to make such arrangements in the war. But where families had been split up or where relatives were themselves working it was difficult, and in any case minding tended to be a stop-gap during periods when mothers had to work, rather than a long-term solution.

Miriam Power moved between homes and jobs making *ad hoc* arrangements for her two children throughout the war. Her husband was taken prisoner by the Italians and then went 'missing', her mother had a heart attack and died during the first bomb alert in Hull, and her own house was bombed, so she very much had to fend for herself. Her son had just started school and at first Miriam's sister minded her little girl, while Miriam worked at Armstrong's engineering works making 'shock hub absorbers', but the sister had taken in her sister-in-law's family as well as Miriam and her two children, so that did not last long. Miriam found a room elsewhere and for a while her landlady minded the little girl, until that arrangement fell through and Miriam gave up her job at Armstrong's. Once she had found somewhere else to live, Miriam took on a part-time job at Hodgson's Tan Yard making glue from animal remains, and it was with relief that she discovered that a new nursery had opened opposite her son's school, where her daughter, who was by then 3, could go every morning until she was school age. But to make ends meet, Miriam also worked in the evenings in a fish and chip shop, trundling the little girl along in her pram while her son played around the area or in the shop, sometimes till 1 in the morning, and at weekends and in the school holidays she went carrot-weeding and potato-picking while the children amused themselves in the fields. Life was not easy, financially or emotionally, and like Clara, Miriam missed her husband and worried about him, while putting a brave face on it all. 'You just did manage, and that was all.'[8]

31 Miriam Power and her two children c.1945 (Courtesy of Thames TV/Channel 4, *A People's War*)

SHOPPING

Shopping, washing, cooking and the rest of the housework also presented problems for women workers who were running homes. As with childcare, there were traditional ways of coping, mainly by relying heavily on relatives and friends, but life was difficult for women whose circumstances had been radically altered by the war. The poor state of working-class housing before 1939 was worsened by bombing. Zelma Katin's husband was called up into the army shortly after they had moved to Sheffield on account of his job, so she was alone in a new place far from her family, with a high rent to pay and a 14-year-old son to look after. She went to work as a conductress on the trams. Digestive problems due to inadequate time for eating had been the cause of pre-war strikes by trammen, and had resulted in re-adjustment of hours, but Zelma felt that women could not make as good use of the free time as the men could.

> Unlike them, we have to use our 'relief' and after-duty hours to buy in the shopping, cook for the family, and tidy up the house . . . I envied those conductresses who had mothers or other relatives at home to do at least some of the eternal household drudgery.[9]

Shopping was a particular problem in wartime. The hazards imposed on trade by the submarine blockade around British shores meant there was limited shipping space, and priority was given to items essential for munitions making, so there were shortages of all imported foodstuffs and some, like oranges, bananas and onions, virtually disappeared from the stores. Farmers and Land Girls were of course doing their best to make Britain self sufficient in food, and everyone with a garden or allotment was urged to 'Dig for Victory'. Rationing of basic foodstuffs like butter, bacon, sugar, meat, tea, preserves and cheese was introduced during 1940–1 in order to prevent the acute shortages which had arisen during the First World War. But the inevitable consequences for shoppers were long hours spent standing in queues. Nothing much remained in the shops by the time most people left work at the end of the day, so women workers either sacrificed their lunch-hours or lost pay by taking time off to get the shopping done.

Industrialists became increasingly concerned about married women's high rate of absenteeism in industry (about twice that of men) and blamed the difficulties of wartime shopping above all else. During 1941, when shortages were biting hardest, they petitioned the government to do something so that production would not suffer, but though various ideas were put forward, either the retailers or the factory owners made objections. For instance, it was suggested that factories should run their own stores, as one or two did, but local shopkeepers complained that this added to retailing competition to their detriment. On the other hand, the idea that everything should be rationed, and that women should register with a set of shops for all their needs, was rejected on the grounds that this would interfere with the free play of the market. An ordering and delivery service seemed a good idea, and a few shops like the Co-ops adopted it, but most retailers saw it as an added burden when they were already understaffed. Priority cards entitling women munition workers to go to the head of queues were tried in some places, but shopkeepers stopped honouring them when they saw the discontent they caused among their other customers. Almost all women were working hard during the war, and women in occupations like transport, and those who had lodgers or other people's children to look after, felt strongly that it was unfair for women who happened to be working on munitions to have this privilege.[10]

The government decided that there could be no official national solution to the problem, but came to the conclusion that shopping was something which women could sort out for themselves, in rather the same way that it threw childcare back on to women's own resources by adopting the minder policy. A Ministry of Food official argued 'It should not be beyond the ability of married women war workers to arrange for a neighbour or friend to purchase their food for them', and the Ministry issued a statement advocating 'neighbourhood shopping leagues'.[11] This was all very well, and no doubt neighbours did help each other when they could, but shopkeepers were often reluctant to sell scarce goods to anyone but the householder in person, and it was a big responsibility to impose on a neighbour who was almost certainly busy herself. As one woman worker put it, 'It's all problem all this shopping. You can't get anyone to do it, it's too big a thing to ask when it takes so long.'[12]

Older schoolchildren were frequently roped in to do the shopping, particularly girls. Celia Bannister, living in Fleetwood on the Lancashire coast, remembers:

> Because I was the only girl in the family, I was responsible for day-to-day shopping and each Saturday morning bought in for the weekend before receiving my Saturday sixpence pocket-money. I hated all the queueing it involved; the pushing and shoving, the bad-tempers and the inevitable queue-jumpers who could slip into the line in front of a child unchallenged. People changed with the frustration and pressure it caused and normally kind people, on both sides of the counter, became rude, abrupt and inconsiderate.[13]

All the same, Celia was an effective shopper, even at the age of 9 or 10. She lodged her own ration book at a vegetarian 'Health Centre'. 'I'd decided to become a vegetarian, not for ethical reasons, but because it entitled me to a big fruit tart each week, slabs of compressed fruit and nuts, dried banana and tasty breakfast cereals'.[14] More than one working mother must have wished she had the support of a daughter well on her way to maturity, like the Birmingham woman working at Tube Investments Ltd, who described the way she endeavoured to cope with the double burden to a Mass-Observer:

> I'm going home to do an evening's scrubbing. First, I've got to do my bit of shopping on the way home. I have to queue for it, because they make no allowances for me being in the factory all day. My two little boys are in school all day. They have their dinners there, and the teacher keeps them till 6 o'clock when I call for them. But I have to get a meal ready, and there's always some washing and mending to be done every night. I never get to bed before 12. I wish I had a daughter about 14 years old. My friend's got a girl of 14 and she is such a help.[15]

The most common 'solution' to the problems presented by shopping and the double burden generally was for employers to give women unpaid leave in which to shop. After forebodings about what it would do to production, employers decided that it was better for the smooth running of the factory than women

32 Celia Bannister at the outbreak of the war (Courtesy of Celia Bannister)

going off haphazardly, and Factory Inspectors said smugly that such arrangements for women workers 'relieve them of some of their domestic responsibilities'.[16] In fact all that shopping leave did was regularise the previous pattern of absenteeism, and it definitely did not *reduce* the amount of domestic work a woman had to do, though, like shift work and part-time arrangements, it may have made the balancing act rather less frantic.

MAKING DO

Once the shopping was done women faced other hard and time-consuming jobs, among which washing up and cooking loomed large. The poor state of working-class housing before 1939, worsened by bombing, did not make these tasks any easier. Half a million homes were seriously damaged during the war, and nearly half of all homes had no internal source of hot water in 1945, making the weekly wash a daunting chore.[17] Laundry work was designated an essential civilian service in 1941, which meant that laundry workers could not leave without permission (much to their resentment since they were still among the worst-paid women workers). An increasing number of working women used laundries at least when they were desperate, but many women found them expensive, and services like collection and delivery were hit by petrol rationing. Not surprisingly, the demands of women from many occupations and political groups who met under the umbrella of a 'Women's Parliament' in Glasgow in January 1942 to air their grievances as women workers, included 'cheap laundry and clothing repair facilities' in a list of measures which they agreed would ease the double burden, but neither this nor many of their other demands were met.[18]

Making nourishing meals out of wartime ingredients was another challenge. In 1943 the basic weekly ration per person was 4 ounces of bacon, 1s 2d worth of meat (this was about the price of a leg of mutton), 3 ounces of cheese, 2 ounces of tea, 8 ounces of sugar, 4 ounces of preserves, and a total of 8 ounces of fats (2oz cooking fat, 2oz butter and 4oz margarine).

Eggs and milk were 'controlled'. This meant that most people could get only 30 eggs a year and about two pints of milk a week, though 'priority classes' like children and expectant and nursing mothers could have three fresh eggs a week and a pint of milk a day. In addition many things in short supply which were not regarded as 'essentials', like canned and dried foods, soap, cereals, sweets and biscuits, were put 'on points' which meant that each item was given a 'points value'. Everyone was issued with a certain number of points per month and could choose which items to buy according to what was in stock and the quantitiy of both points and cash they had to spend.[19]

Innumerable dodges were possible, and women were encouraged to take them by 'Gert and Daisy' on the radio and by a press and poster campaign launched by Lord Woolton, the homely, potato-faced Minister of Food. Dried egg from America was available in the shops by the middle of 1941, and fresh eggs could be preserved in waterglass, fat could be saved from roast meat to fill out the meagre allowance of 2oz of cooking fat per person per week, sugar could be forgone in tea and saved up for making cakes and puddings, potatoes (of which there seemed to be plenty) could be used instead of pastry, saving flour for bread. But the cook's life was made more difficult by the absence of crockery and cutlery in the shops, by power cuts, and by the shortage of fuel. It took a lot of energy to make fire bricks from coal dust and sawdust to eke out supplies.

Not everyone had the patience of Nella Last, who cooked not only for her own family, but also for the WVS canteen in Barrow, and who took pride in 'making a lot out of a little'. In November 1941 she made a cake which earned her many compliments but had clearly taken much ingenuity to produce:

> When I tasted my cake I was really surprised – it was so good – when I recollected it had only ½lb sugar, ½lb lard and dripping (skimmed off good beef bones when making sandwich spread), 2 eggs out of my waterglass bucket and 2lb and a half of S.R. flour. The 'soul' of it was the peel of 2 oranges that had been stewed with my prunes – to flavour the prunes really but I'd put it in and added the sugar so as to sweeten the peel too. Cut in thin slices it looked so attractive.[20]

33   Nella Last towards the end of the war (Courtesy of The Tom Harrisson
Mass-Observation Archive)

Nella was something of an expert and was recognised as such at the WVS Centre where she did regular voluntary work. Her battered old recipe book full of her grandmother's 'economy' recipes was much in demand at the centre, for she came from a family which was no stranger to 'making do' even in wartime.

Better-off housewives who had employed domestic servants before the war suffered in a different way. Frances Partridge lived on a small farm with her husband and her young son, where they reared hens, ducks, rabbits and an annual pig, and cultivated fruit and vegetables, so they were never short of food, but by December 1941 Frances had lost her nannie and her cook, and by the middle of 1943 she no longer had any 'daily help', either. She did her best with the washing and cleaning, and taught herself to cook, but the house was large and she was inundated with visitors who arrived without their ration books and gorged themselves on the Partridges' home produce. Her husband clearly did not see it as part of his role to help her, telling her cheerfully, 'For a woman not to be able to cook is like impotence to a man.' Though realising she had much less to put up with than many people, Frances nevertheless loathed her submersion in mindless chores, and was infinitely grateful for the advent of any domestic help, however temporary:

February 10th, 1944
Slowly sinking into the bog, down and down. Dog-tired
every evening, I doze on the sofa. Up to bed and sleep lightly,
toss and turn, and have visions of dirty plates and vegetables
waiting to be peeled. Down in the morning bung-eyed, to see
the ancient red bricks of the kitchen floor getting blacker and
blacker.
However, yesterday, a miracle, a new figure turned up.
Honest brown eyes behind specs, strangely fitting false teeth.
What joy, what comfort![21]

The situation was very different for a bombed-out service-man's wife like Miriam Power. She was trying to juggle paid work and the care of little children in all kinds of temporary accommodation, including, at one stage, a pig-sty which she cleaned out, white-washed and lived in for about three months until the council moved her out. Meals for herself and her children were a constant compromise between the time there was for shopping and cooking and the money at her disposal.

> Used to go and buy everything you could that was cheap, or
> what you could get hold of, you see, and you'd have 'make
> do' meals ... I used to buy bones ... you could get hold of a
> lot of bones and make a big pan of broth, and all things like
> that – bread and jam if you got your bit of jam ration. We
> used to do condensed milk sandwiches with sugar on top.[22]

Her part-time job at the fish and chip shop had a very
important perk attached to it.

> I was very, very glad of that job, because when there was any
> fish and chips left I used to pile them all up and bring 'em
> home ... So the next day, or maybe a couple of days, we had
> a right good tuck in with fish and chips.[23]

Zelma Katin, on the trams in Sheffield, was scathing about
the fact that the woman's page in the tramworkers' magazine
was devoted to cookery, 'heedless of the bitter fact that female
war workers have little time for the culinary arts'.[24] Her biggest
worries after her wages were the low standard of the food she
managed to obtain for herself and her son, and the impossibi-
lity of keeping her home up to its pre-war standard of
cleanliness and good order. Like Frances Partridge, Zelma
began to hate the stultifying nature of 'petty housework' in a
way that she had not during the eighteen years of her marriage
before the war when she had not gone out to work, and she
resolved that when her husband returned from the army he was
going to help. For the time being she found ways of coping.
Since it was too exhausting to rush home to cook her son's
mid-day meal, he would have to do it himself,

> unless he overcame his repugnance to school dinners, which
> were too 'mushy' for him. I could hardly blame him for
> refusing the fivepenny over-boiled meals supplied by the
> Education Department, even though they would have rid me
> of the considerable worry of feeding him adequately in my
> absence.[25]

When children could be persuaded to eat them, school meals
were undoubtedly a relief to many hard-pressed mothers. The
service expanded enormously during the war. In 1938 school
meals had been provided for one in thirty schoolchildren

whereas in 1944 one in three received them. But even this impressive increase meant that two-thirds were fed in some other way, presumably mostly by their mothers.

Works canteens also grew in number from a mere handful before the war, to nearly 12,000, and every workplace over a certain size was supposed to have one. In addition, 'British Restaurants' were introduced by some local authorities, initially to overcome the cooking problems presented by air-raids, when bombing severed power supplies and smashed pots and crockery. They were retained to provide people with wholesome food 'off the ration' and there were demands for more of them. As Mrs Shipley of South Shields said, 'It wasn't a restaurant by any means, but it was a nourishing meal.'[26] Canteens varied greatly in popularity and were rapidly absorbed into workplace politics, the taste of the tea and the adequacy of the accommodation as well as the pay of the canteen workers (usually women) becoming new sources of tension between workers and management. But although many workers appreciated having hot food on the premises or near by, as they had in the First War, surveys showed that few took their main meal of the day in either a canteen or a British Restaurant partly because of the quality of the food, but also because it was generally cheaper for a family to eat altogether at home than separately at school and work, and men in particular wanted their wives to cook for them. It was an integral part of the domestic arrangements they were used to. Nella Last's husband, for instance, turned up like clockwork for every meal.

> He told a friend that his main thought and chief delight was his food, that he *liked* eating and, as soon as he had had one meal, started looking foward to the next! He added piously that he was always thankful that I was such a marvellous cook and manager! Sometimes I could YELL.[27]

On top of all the food shortages, clothing was also rationed from June 1941. Everyone was issued initially with a basic allowance of 166 coupons a year to spend as they wished on clothes, which all had a coupon value as well as their money value. Clothing prices rose alarmingly fast during the war, and the Ministry of Information issued booklets showing housewives how to 'Make Do and Mend'. Celia Bannister's mother took this very seriously.

My mother made me a cream coloured flannel suit out of her past summer coat. She unpicked woollen garments and re-knitted them into Fair Isle jumpers, gloves and berets. Her sewing machine worked over-time, turning collars and cuffs on shirts, producing short pants for Arthur out of frayed long ones, and making dresses and even a camel coat for me.[28]

For an expert needlewoman like Celia's mother, wartime austerity represented a challenge against which she enjoyed pitting her wits, and in any case 'making do' reached the status of a patriotic act in the Second World War. Knitting was quite a craze among factory women, and some got round the absence of silk stockings and the shortage of nylons (introduced from America in 1942) by getting their legs painted. Sadie Mac-Dougal of Vickers engineering works in Newcastle-upon-Tyne explained:

For a pair of stockings it was three coupons, out of twenty what had you left? So that's why we got our legs painted. Got a straight line up the back, like a pair of fully fashioned stockings, only in paint. We used to sweet-heart some of the boys from the drawing office who could draw nice straight lines and put the dots on.[29]

But there were undoubtedly many women for whom austerity was no fun at all, especially the hard-pressed wives of absent husbands. Mrs Muriel Windle was the mother of four children one of whom was suffering from polio, and her husband, called up into the army in 1941, was sent to the Far East and did not return until 1945. Muriel writes that she had very little leisure and virtually no ambitions during the war, apart from wanting her husband back in one piece.

At the time one just did not have time to think, life had to go on, each day brought its routine and problems and often it was a case of pushing yourself to the next job. The worst time was when Barbara and the boys were in bed and I eventually sat down to the mending, sewing and knitting, often to hours of unpicking cast-offs from friends to make clothes for the children.
Still it ended, and we survived![30]

34 Celia Bannister (née Shepherd), c.1943, with her parents and brothers. The children are supposed to be showing off gifts sent by the wife of an American colonel-surgeon whom the family had entertained. Celia is posing with a skipping rope, Arthur is hiding a yo-yo (which he considered beneath his years) in his lap, and Peter is holding a bowl of soap suds for a bubble pipe. Celia explained that gifts of food or clothing would have been more welcome than these toys, especially to her mother who went 'thinner and thinner as she gave us most of her rations. You can see by the portrait taken of her at the beginning of the war how much she aged in a few years.' The children's jumpers and the boys' trousers are examples of Mrs Shepherd's ability to 'make do and mend'
(Courtesy of Celia Bannister)

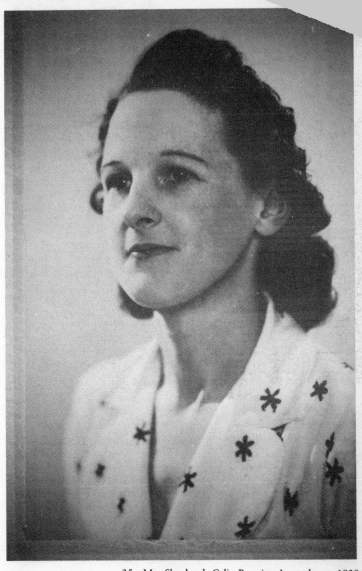

35 Mrs Shepherd, Celia Bannister's mother, c.1939
(Courtesy of Celia Bannister)

CHAPTER 15

DEMOBILISATION
1945–50

The last part of the Second World War was more long-drawn-out than that of the First. From the allied invasion of Europe in June 1944 to Hitler's suicide on 30 April 1945 and the final surrender of the Nazi forces in May, victory was anticipated any day, with mounting impatience. Hitler's 'secret weapons', the terrifying V1 and V2 flying bombs and rockets, which pursued their pilotless flight to arbitrary destinations by day or night from June 1944 till the end of March 1945, made the end all the more urgently desired. But there were set-backs, at Arnhem in Belgium, where strong Nazi resistance turned back the allied advance in September 1944 and in the Ardennes, where a Nazi counter-offensive was launched in December. The devastation in France, Belgium, Holland and Germany caused by saturation bombing and the malnutrition and hardships suffered by the civilian populations under Nazi rule, especially the inmates of Nazi concentration camps, did not make progress any easier, and deeply moved many of the British servicemen and women who witnessed them. But the Allies made better progress in the spring of 1945, the Russians broke through the Nazi defences in the east in February and March, and in Italy the dictator Mussolini was shot on 28 April. By now the end of the war in Europe was imminent.

When victory in Europe was finally announced there was the same flood of relief that there had been in November 1918. It exploded in a burst of euphoria on the evening of 8 May 1945, which was particularly warm and summery. In London crowds surged round Nelson's column and up the Mall to Buckingham Palace, as if clapping eyes on the Royal Family would seal the fact that the war was really over. Lights blazed into the night for the first time for nearly six years, drink was consumed in

257

large quantities, kissing and dancing were rampant and servicemen, titillated by the *Daily Mirror*'s full disrobing of its cartoon character Jane for the first time, were more than ever inclined to take advantage of any woman in the crowds.

Celebrations took place in relative backwaters, too, and usually it was the women who provided the necessaries. In Fleetwood on the Lancashire coast, Celia Bannister remembers that:

> Trestle tables were set up outdoors and weighed down with food, the like of which we children had not seen in years, and in some cases, never . . . Each family gave to the party what they could in the way of food and money. We children watched round eyed as the tables were set with meat and fish paste sandwiches, meat pies, sausage rolls, cakes, trifles, blancmange, tinned fruit, tinned salmon, buns, jam tarts and bottles of pop.[1]

Frances Partridge recorded that 'the news of peace actually brought a *sense* of peace, very refreshing like a good drink of water to a thirsty person' and she was relieved to discover that pacifists were not turned against in the VE celebrations as they had been in 1918 on the grounds that they had done nothing to help to win the war.[2] It was as if peace rather than victory was being celebrated.

Yet in a sense VE day was a false end. The war in the Far East looked as if it would continue indefinitely, and servicemen and women were still being posted out to India and Burma in the summer of 1945. Then saturation bombing was taken to its zenith, with the dropping of atomic bombs on Hiroshima and Nagasaki in August 1945, bringing sudden death to at least 110,000 people, almost all civilians, and lingering death to many more. The Japanese surrendered on 14 August 1945. VJ day meant the release and gradual homeward trek of thousands of British, American and Australian prisoners of war, a small number of them women. But the new destructive force which world leaders could now command also planted the seeds of fear in some hearts and eventually led to a bigger peace movement than any that the twentieth century had yet seen. The First World War had manifestly failed to be the war to end war, and the Second had led to the invention of weaponry which could end the world.

JOB PROSPECTS

Some women feared that the end of the Second World War would be a repeat of the end of the First as far as their job prospects were concerned. As early as 1942 a woman told Mass-Observation that she did not expect to get fair treatment after the war:

> Look at the last war. Those hundreds of women ran our trams and did a wonderfully good job. When the war was over the Transport Department snarled at them, 'You're doing a man out of a job' and they were flung into the streets without a word of thanks.[3]

In fact demobilisation was not as abrupt for most women workers in 1945–6 as it had been in 1918–19 when some women had been told to down tools and go home the minute the armistice was announced and most others had been displaced within a few months.

In the Second World War lay-offs started earlier and went on longer. Some engineering factories started making redundancies during the war, as soon as targets of munitions and equipment needed for D-Day landings had been reached, though there were some unexpected hiccups. For example, the numbers employed in the filling factories (mostly women) were reduced from 133,400 in December 1942 to 77,100 in June 1945, even though the demand for ammunition after D-Day meant that those who were left had to work even harder.[4] At this stage the women laid off were not supposed to abandon the war effort, but were directed by the Ministry of Labour to other work, for instance in aircraft factories, where production was still being stepped up. However, by 1945 they were being encouraged to return to pre-war women's trades and, as at the end of the First World War, they were not always happy to do so. Conditions in some of the royal ordnance factories had been very poor early in the war, but improvements had been made and women were reluctant to leave places like Chorley in Lancashire to return to the old textile mills from which many had come, where wages and conditions were inferior and there was no guarantee that they would be reinstated in what they considered suitably skilled work.[5]

Women protested against redundancy at several engineering factories during 1945, but far from securing the support of their own unions, they found that the male shop stewards were urging their employers to lay them off first. The craft unions had not bothered much with the clauses of the dilution agreements relating to equal pay, but they became assiduous in insisting that the clause stating that women 'shall be regarded as temporarily employed' should be honoured. Barbara Davies, an ex-weaver from the little village of Mytholmroyd in West Yorkshire wanted to stay in her war job at Armstrong Whitworth's aircraft factory in Coventry but remembers:

> At the end of the war, it was traumatic really, because as the jobs slowed down we were told that our services would be no longer needed. I went in on night shift one night and was told that I was made redundant and that my services were no longer needed. And, as you can imagine, this displeased me very much, so straight round to the union representative we went and we discussed the matter with him. And he said that the jobs were for the men coming out of the forces and that we had to leave the job for them. And I understood it perfectly, but I didn't approve. But not matter how we tried to pressure him, there was nothing that we could do at all. In fact I think really we were quite an embarrassment to him. It was all decided, and so we just had to leave the premises and that was that.[6]

Some women remember the personal pressure that was applied. Eileen Smith needed her job in the stock records department of a cable company after the war, because her husband's pay was so poor.

> I was talking to the men one day. They said to me, 'When we came out of the forces there were women here doing our jobs.' One man told me that the way he got his job back was by an elderly man who worked there saying to one of the women: 'You know you're married and ought not to need a job, and all the time you're staying here the bloke who used to do your job before the war is out of work.' The woman only worked another month and handed her notice in. The firm hadn't asked her to leave, the men did.[7]

In some works and offices the women were not ousted

altogether, but were forced to move back into the segregated slots which women had occupied before the war. In many banks in peacetime only men over 30 were appointed as cashiers working on the counter, but due to the call up young women in their twenties took over these jobs. Often they were expected to continue to do their 'machine jobs', adding up and making the books balance, in addition to the new responsibilities. Joy Brown on the counter in a Leeds bank at the age of 23 recalls that 'it was jolly hard work'. She was paid £1 8s to start with, rising by 5s a year. 'It never went up by anymore than if I'd been doing ordinary tapping out on the machine or adding up. The bank never paid the ladies any more for doing men's work.' But insult was added to injury when men returned after the war. Not only were women removed from the counter, but they had first to teach the men the job.

> I had a lieutenant commander for about a fortnight. He was really as dim as you could make him, when it came to totting up money and all the rest of it. He'd say: 'Joy, I'm never going to do it.' I said: 'I'm sorry, you've just got to learn, Brian, you've got to do it.' After that a lieutenant colonel had to learn. He was a bit quicker on the uptake. They took over on the counter and we watched them for a week and stood by them for a week and watched them do the work, and then we went back to the jolly old machines, the ledger machines, and the statement machines, and the shorthand and typing.[8]

But although many women in shops and offices were forced to take second place to men at the end of the Second War, they were not dismissed en masse. All the regulations and controls of wartime and the subsequent development of the 'welfare state', generated an immense amount of paper work, and there was an astonishing increase in the number of women clerks and typists in national and local government during and after the war. In 1939 these sectors employed 123,200 women and in 1946 518,990. The rising birth-rate and the reform of the health and education services meant there was a growing demand for teachers and nurses too. Numbers of women in the male-dominated professions were also creeping up. There were 7,198 women doctors and 549 women dentists at the end of the war, compared with 2,580 and 82 respectively in 1928. The numbers of women solicitors, barristers, accountants and architects also grew during the war, from a mere handful to a few hundreds.[9] All the same women professionals remained overwhelmingly a minority in a male world in the 1940s. But it was, at last, possible for women to stay in white blouse and professional occupations after marriage.

In general, even though there was pressure on women to make way for men, there was not the same wholesale dismissal of women that there had been at the end of the First World War, when half a million women workers were thrown on to the dole within six moths of the armistice. The economic and political circumstances of 1945–50 were different from those which had followed the First War. The economy had again been severely battered by the war and the government was again saddled by huge debts. But the new Labour government had a much more interventionist approach to these problems than that of the Liberal government of 1918. The withdrawal a few weeks after the Japanese surrender of the American Lend-Lease agreement, under which payments for American goods imported during the war were to have been spread over a long period, plunged the country into worsening currency crises which led eventually to the devaluation of the pound in September 1949. But before this the government decided that the over-riding priority was to boost exports in order to redress the floundering balance of payments and to this end it hung on to many of the wartime controls over manpower, industry and consumption.

Men continued to be called up into the armed forces until 1950 and for ten years after this two years' National Service was obligatory for boys on leaving school. Women were also still 'controlled'. Call up under the National Service Number 2 Act was suspended as early as September 1944, but women were urged to volunteer for the forces during 1945–6 so long as they were not in one of the occupations where there were now acute shortages of women workers. These included jobs in the cotton, rayon and nylon industries, nursing and midwifery and the Women's Land Army. Until December 1945 the only way a woman aged 18 to 40 could get a job was through the employment exchange, unless she had a child at home, the idea being that the Ministry of Labour would be able to direct her to work of 'national importance'. Until industries which had come under the Essential Work Orders were 'descheduled' gradually during 1946, women as well as men still had to get permission from a Ministry of Labour official before they could leave their jobs; the official policy was to direct young women to take the place of older ones waiting to be released from industry.[10]

However, women were treated differently from men: the assumptions which guided demobilisation, like those which had informed mobilisation, were based on conventional views of women's role in marriage and the home. Officials assumed that women who had been directed to work far from home should go back, and that others should give up work when their husbands were released from the forces or when they married. Consequently little was done about women who simply vanished from work, like Doris White who had so much enjoyed her job in aircraft repair at Wolverton:

> No-one asked us to leave work, and we dared not ask to leave, so in awe were we of the Works. But, as the men filtered home there were weddings and homes to set up. There were weddings, such as my own, where the man had to return afterwards, back to base to finish his service time. We had managed to find a house to rent, although in a run-down condition, and with my man away, it was left to me to get it in shape. Although I had not been given my cards, I asked for a week off – but I never did go back, I'd had enough, and in any case now I had my Navy's wife's pay book, which gave me £2 5s 0d a week.[11]

Above all mothers of young children were no longer expected to work and it became harder for them to do so. In spite of the continuing labour shortage in many industries, there was no reversal of the wartime policy that nurseries were a temporary expedient, and after 1945 the Treasury halved its subsidy. The main responsibility for funding a full-time nursery now lay with the local authorities, and since they were bound under the 1944 Education Act to provide nursery schools (operating during school hours for 3- to 5-year-olds only) where there was local demand, many local authorities simply closed their day nurseries. If mothers of small children wanted or needed to go out to work they would now, even more than during the war, have to resort to minders.

An image of wives and mothers longing to return home was

created by policy-makers and in the press, but, in spite of the difficulties of coping with the wartime double burden, Doris White noted that plenty of the other married women at her aircraft repair shop did not want to leave. 'A lot of women were glad of the war work money, as they were buying their homes, and service allowances did not stretch far.' An AEU survey conducted in 1944–5 revealed that 66 per cent of women in engineering wanted to stay on after the war.[12]

Their hopes were not altogether unrealistic. Some war industries such as aircraft repair at De Havillands near Oxford and at Wolverton, and a number of the royal ordnance factories like those in Staffordshire, carried on for several years after the war, and continued to employ women. Industries like shipbuilding and repairing were busy because of the destruction of so much shipping, and women welders and riveters stayed on. They were regarded as a rump, however, and as they left it was men, not other women, who took their places. The same was true on the railways and in the post office. Other war industries, like the aircraft and engineering factories around Bristol, Coventry and London, ordnance factories like Aycliffe near Darlington, and the Rolls Royce factory at Hillington, where the celebrated strike for equal pay had taken place in 1943, adapted to peacetime production. Some became the nucleus of new industrial estates where all sorts of engineering and light manufacturing firms took root. The resistance to equal pay during the war ensured that women were still cheaper to employ than men, and since much of the new work was simple and repetitive it was automatically stereotyped as women's work. Even though the number of women in engineering fell after the Second World War it did not return to the pre-1939 levels. In 1951 women formed 22 per cent of the engineering work force, compared with 34 per cent in 1943 and only 10 per cent in 1939. Food processing, tobacco, synthetic fibres and a host of service industries including transport and distribution also took on larger numbers of women after the war, than they had in the 1930s.[13]

Women did not disappear from the land straight away, either. The Women's Land Army was not disbanded until 1950, such was the importance of continuing the struggle for self-sufficiency. Nevertheless some farmers got rid of their Land Girls as soon as they could, to the lasting regret of those who had enjoyed their work. Dorothy Barton remembers coming out of the Land Army as a 'terrible wrench. I felt as if I'd lost something . . . Part of me was still in the country.' A job in a typing pool was 'sheer hell' and she and a friend escaped on 'farming holidays' with the Forestry Commission whenever they could.[14]

There was enough industrial work available in the 1940s for the government to become concerned about a shortage of labour in some areas. Even though it would not re-open the nurseries, a propaganda campaign was launched in 1947 to entice more women back into industry, and in this climate there was no repetition of the pressure on women seeking jobs to take only domestic work, as there had been after 1918. Institutional cleaning was expanding with the post-war creation of new schools, hospitals and office blocks, and such jobs were preferred to personal service, but shortages of institutional cleaners led to recruitment campaigns in Europe and the British Caribbean.[15] The demand for domestic servants was largely unsatisfied and remained so. The middle class had to make do with daily helps and later au pair girls.

Women in the armed services were in a rather different position from women in industry. For most of the half million in the ATS, WAAF and WRNS there was no prospect of staying on. Some of those who did were posted out East, an opportunity which Marjorie Wardle, who had become a Fleet Mail Officer, seized as preferable to going back home to be 'the daughter of the house'.[16]

Marjorie spent the months after VJ Day in Ceylon receiving ex-prisoners of the Japanese and helping with arrangements for their return to Britain. Some servicewomen were sent to occupied Europe to assist with rehabilitation and reconstruction, words which stood for the task of wrestling with untold depths of human misery. But for most the prospect of the end of the war and demobilisation stimulated feelings of intense personal uncertainty.

Age and length of service determined the order in which women were released, so in general the older you were and the longer you had been in the services, the speedier would be your release, though married women were given priority over everyone else. A servicewoman received four weeks' paid leave and some clothing coupons in exchange for her uniform when she was demobbed, and she also took with her grave doubts about whether the skills learned in the forces would be considered useful by civilian employers. Who would want women who could operate kinetheodolites, radio transmitters or searchlights, or for that matter who were skilled flight mechanics? Women in industry seemed to have a more secure future. Nina Masel recorded the confused fears and aspirations of her fellow WAAF plotters as early as 1941.

> Dorothy H: There'll be a lot of unemployment after the War.
> Bunty: Yes and you know who'll cause it – the munition workers. These girls who are earning fabulous sums, now, they won't be content to go back to ordinary wages, and they'll collar all the best jobs, and there'll be nothing left for us to do.
> NM: But you didn't work before the war.
> Bunty: No, but I jolly well won't want to sit about at home, after the war. Until I was 21 I'd never been away from Mother. It's bad for you. I'm learning things now. I just couldn't stay at home.[17]

The official assumption was that servicewomen could not expect to use their special technical skills in civilian jobs and should think in terms of entering university or training for one of the women's occupations, like teaching, nursing or clerical work. Marjorie Wardle had to dole out such advice to Wrens in the process of demobilisation, when she worked as a Resettlement Officer during the spring and summer of 1946.

> They had been trained to do high technical jobs in the Fleet Air Arm especially and they were servicing planes and they were doing jobs that women hadn't done before and haven't done since. And these jobs came to an end, you see . . . those skills that they'd developed during the war were not required, by and large, when they got out. They wouldn't be required to use skills servicing aircraft. Those jobs went back to men.[18]

Aline Whalley, herself a flight mechanic, was well aware of this, and devoted her efforts during her last months in the Wrens to obtaining a Ministry of Education grant to attend the London School of Economics:

I didn't think about doing a technical job, partly because I knew that at that time there would have been no way that one could have had a technical job that wasn't manual work. And I did not want to just do manual work . . . it wouldn't have been demanding. And although I suppose there must have been a few girls going to university and training to be engineers, I didn't know any. I liked my job, I loved it, but I couldn't really see myself going on learning about engineering.[19]

In view of the treatment meted out to the first woman member of the Institute of Mechanical Engineers in 1944 in the pages of *The Engineer* (see chapter 10), it is hardly surprising that women wishing to be professional engineers were thin on the ground.

Of the servicewomen who passed through Marjorie's hands 'Some went back to clerical jobs, some went back to offices, some went back to factories', but above all, 'a lot of them got married'. Nina Masel reported throughout the war that among her fellow WAAFs marriage was 'the average woman's stand-by, the way out, the final security'.[20]

HOMELIFE

Marriage was certainly popular at the end of the war. Although the rate did not top the 1940 figure of 22 per thousand of the population, at 19 per thousand in 1945 it represented a marked recovery on the slump to 14 in 1943, and remained well above the pre-war rate. The wartime trend had been towards younger marriages and this continued too. In 1938 one bride in six had been under 21, whereas in 1945 the figure had risen above one in four. Many wartime romances with allied servicemen led to marriage. Such liaisons accounted for 5 per cent of all marriages in Scotland and in 1945–6 80,000 GI brides set sail from Britain for the USA.[21] The youthful marriages of the Second World War and the pattern of emigration following it were new developments, but in both wars there was a similar cycle of boom, slump and recovery, as though both the advent

36 Leading Wren Air Mechanic Aline Whalley, Hinstock, 1944
(Courtesy of Aline Torday)

37 Marjorie Wardle on the occasion of her marriage to Victor Smith, Colombo, Ceylon, July 1945. They are both wearing tropical naval uniform
(Courtesy of Marjorie Easterby-Smith)

of war and the advent of peace stimulated marriage, whereas war itself limited nuptial opportunities.

The desire to get together and to set up home was strong after the disruption of the war. Marjorie Wardle married while on her posting to Ceylon in 1945, though ironically she and her husband were then separated for fourteen months since she was posted to Yeovilton in Somerset and he to Singapore. Ruth Moore's husband was called up four months after their marriage at the beginning of the war, and he was then away for six years. She wrote: 'I stayed in a strange part of the country so that our home together should be our anchor ... My life goals were to have my husband alive at the end of the war, to survive myself, and to have a normal peaceful life.'[22] However, the strains of getting back to normal were considerable. The reconciliation problems of wives who had given birth to illegitimate children in their husbands' absence must have been acute, but even a husband returning to a family of children he had fathered came home as something of a stranger both to them and to his wife. Miriam Power spent the war wondering whether her husband, who had escaped into Switzerland from an Italian prisoner of war camp, was alive or dead, and was naturally pleased when he reappeared:

> Mind you it was a bit difficult getting back to married life, you know, as things was, because it was strange you see. He had been away such a long time, everything was strange. The little girl said one day to me, she said, 'Who's that nice man, mummy?' 'Why' I said 'it's your daddy, love.' She didn't recognise him at all. It was difficult really to get her to sort of realise who he was. And yet you felt a bit strange yourselves when they came home. You felt as though you was starting all over again, somehow.[23]

Women were warned that men returning from active campaigns or from prisoner of war camps might show all sorts of signs of stress, from silence and depression to tears, violence and compulsive drinking. The published advice which circulated gave women the task of penetrating the barriers of brutalisation with patience, tact and gentleness.[24] But it must have been hard for wives to act like this when they were themselves worn down by six years of bombing, blackout, long hours of work, and single-handed responsibility for homes and children. Lisa Hadden, mother of a small boy, worked in engineering for four years during the war. When her husband came out of the army she found herself suddenly isolated with a new set of problems:

> When my husband came home we'd have parties and everything, but when he got into bed of a night, you'd find him waking up screaming, and you'd have to calm him down. This is what the family don't know. I expect there's a lot of wives like me. You had it on your own, and you'd tell it to the family, and they'd think you were kidding.[25]

Servicemen were told that it might take them years to settle down into family life again. But even though the ex-serviceman was warned that his wife was likely to have 'managed pretty well during his absence' and to 'have a pleasant feeling of independence and self-confidence', there were no suggestions that roles might have to change radically. He was expected to want 'to resume his rightful place as the breadwinner of the household' as soon as he could.[26] Certainly some returning soldiers were adamant that their wives should not work once they were back. Clara Moore was probably one of many wives who accepted this conventional attitude:

> I didn't want to go on working after the war. I only did it to keep them safe and for the extra money to help me, you know, because my husband had very low money, low pay in the army, and when he came out the army he didn't want me to work anyway. He said 'Your place is in the home', and I wanted to stay with the children anyway, look after the children, look after him. I didn't want to go to work . . . I don't think he would have tolerated it anyway.[27]

But even among women keen to return to conventional married life, there was a new spirit of determination to resist its more oppressive aspects. Zelma Katin wrote that she and many of her fellow clippies looked forward to coming off the Sheffield buses when their husbands came out of the army. 'But on the other hand we all want more interesting lives than we used to lead.' She was convinced that this would depend on husbands and wives doing 'the washing up of the dinner plates' together:

> When you work together with your husband you do not have
> that gnawing little ache in your brain telling you that
> something is missing, that you are not quite complete.
> Wherever I move I see husbands and wives caged up
> separately in their specialist spheres . . . But there is now in
> marriage enough leisure for friendship as well as
> matrimony.[28]

The basic structure of marriage did not change, and in many individual cases and occupational groups marriages remained as segregated as they had ever been, but the Second World War probably hastened the trend towards the companionable marriage that had begun between the wars. Even if women found in the post-war decades that maintaining a sharing relationship between a breadwinner husband and domestic wife was hard, it was a style of marriage which was markedly different from that which most women's mothers and grand-mothers had experienced, and women like Zelma Katin and Nella Last were glad that their role in the war had helped them to the discovery that it was not necessary to be dominated by a man and his needs.

However, for some couples being reunited was more than they could cope with, and the divorce rate continued to rise. In 1938 there were 6,092 divorces in England, in 1945 there were 15,221 and in 1947 they peaked at 58,444, a rate of 13.6 per ten thousand of the population compared with 3.6 in 1945 and 1.5 in 1938. Husbands continued to file more petitions than wives, and adultery continued to be the main cause cited.[29] This was seen at the time as indicative of an increase in women's extra-marital sexual activity during the war. How-ever, it could also be the cheapest way of arranging a divorce, since the cost of proceedings brought by servicemen against their wives was met under the army welfare scheme. Kitty Murphy was glad to feign an affair with an American master sergeant in order to give her husband grounds for divorce, so that they could end a marriage which she had been pushed into by her parents.

> I knew that my husband had got somebody else and I got
> grounds for divorce but it would have cost me three or four
> hundred pound to foot divorce proceedings. And I'd heard
> that he could divorce me if he had grounds through the army

and it would cost nothing. So we, him [the GI] and I
arranged whereby we gave my husband and his wife grounds
for divorce. I wrote to his wife pleading with her to give him
his freedom so that we could get married and he wrote to my
husband asking him to do the same . . . I had no intention of
marrying him, none whatsoever . . . I got my divorce and
after the war it became Absolute.[30]

Home life was not made any easier by the other strains of the
post-war years. Rationing of most major foodstuffs did not end
until 1954 and meat rationing continued until 1956. Bread had
not been rationed during the war itself, but shortages of grain
were so acute immediately afterwards that it was introduced
from July 1946 to July 1948. In that year the basic weekly
ration for an adult consisted of 13oz meat, 1½oz cheese, 6oz
butter and margarine, 1oz cooking fat, 8oz sugar, 2 pints of
milk and 1 egg.[31] Anyone going shoping still had to contend
with long queues and the delays associated with cancelling
coupons and clipping points. Aline Whalley, by now married,
remembers the struggle she had to keep house in a tiny
basement flat just after the war, at the same time as studying
for a degree:

In those days you had to queue for food still you see. You'd
hear there'd be sausages somewhere and you'd join the queue
and if you were having guests that weekend to come and
stay, as we always were, then it meant going round and
joining the queue again. It was all very difficult and I found it
extremely difficult to cope with all these different subjects,
but I did struggle through and I got my degree.[32]

Clothes were still rationed too until March 1949 and
furniture and household goods were in short supply, even
though the government continued its 'Utility' scheme, introduced in 1941, until 1951. Under the 'Utility' scheme the
designs manufacturers were permitted to use for clothes,
furniture, crockery and other domestic goods were standardised
so that there would be enough simple and serviceable articles at
fixed prices to meet essential needs. Women continued to be
urged in the press to be resourceful and to develop skills with
the needle and the saucepan. Though spared the bombing, the

pressure on many housewives' resources may have been even greater than in wartime, since they now had to provide for nearly five million ex-servicemen who were no longer being fed and equipped under the auspices of His Majesty.

Perhaps the most basic domestic problem of the post-war years was the housing shortage. Opinion polls showed that most people regarded housing as the biggest issue in the 1945 General Election[33] and memories of the disillusioning consequences of Lloyd George's promise of 'Homes fit for Heroes' after the First World War were very much alive. Cast as principal home-makers, women were intimately concerned with the task of getting somewhere to live after the war, but the prospects were not good. In 1939 472,000 dwellings had been officially designated as slums, and during the war half a million had been destroyed or made permanently uninhabitable, and a further quarter of a million had been badly damaged.[34] By the end of the war there were two million new married couples looking for homes, and with them came the baby bulge. The rising number of births in the second half of the war was checked in 1945, and then rose to a new maximum of 20.7 births per thousand of the population in 1947, echoing the less dramatic baby boom of 1919–20.[35] Even though the birth-rate dropped a little between 1947 and 1951, it remained higher than the pre-war rate. All these new people could not be squeezed into the existing dilapidated housing stock.

Unlike the situation after the First World War, the Labour government's intervention was fairly effective, and 900,000 new houses were built under the government schemes of 1946–51. This was a considerable achievement when compared with the one and a half million houses which inter-war governments had managed to provide in twenty years, but it fell short of Labour's target and left long waiting lists in many areas. Most local authorities operated some sort of points system to decide who had priority, and Mary Sweeney, who had been full of optimism for the 'fantastic world' which Labour would build after the war, remembers how it worked in Liverpool:

> Eventually we had two children and one room. We must have gone to the housing place every day. . . . There was once, the queue was a mile long, and I'd been there about

four hours, and he said, The Man we used to call him, 'There's no point in your coming here when you've only got two children. Come back when you've got six.' And I said, 'I don't intend to have another six.' And he said, 'Well you've got no chance then have you. I mean you haven't got enough points so there's no point you coming here. So go and have another six kids and come back and you might get a house.' I said, 'Oh yeah'. Well I was that upset that I just stood and cried anyway. And I went back and I said, 'If we don't get a house I'm going to put the kids in a Home and I don't know, I'm going to join something or other, because I'm not going to put up with this no longer.' And eventually, which was about another 12 month, me mother's landlord had a house on a back tenement and he gave us that.[36]

Fearing that the post-war building programmes would inevitably proceed slowly, the government had begun preparations for rehousing people in 1944, with the production of prefabricated houses in ex-aircraft factories. By 1948 125,000 'prefabs' were assembled, ostensibly as a short-term solution, though people were still living in them in the 1960s and beyond. Some couples took things into their own hands and during the summer of 1946 46,335 women and men moved into 1181 ex-army camps.[37] The movement was tolerated while it confined itself to such 'surplus' accommodation, and some councils stepped in to regularise and sanitise the squats, but the government was quick to suppress the occupation of private property.

Like Mary Sweeney in Liverpool, Kitty Murphy in London felt disillusioned about the post-war environment. She had spent her first eleven years in one room in north Woolwich and then during the war she and her family were bombed out of the house they had eventually found to share with her crippled grandfather.

It seemed a long while before anything really got done . . . there was still bad housing a long time after the war, prefabs were going up, prefabricated houses, they were only supposed to be up for 10 years and they was up for 25, 30 years, and them tower blocks started getting built, and I thought oh God you know have we gotta live in them, them kinds of places. Everywhere seemed to be cramped . . . what I

38 Kitty Murphy before the war, aged 16 (Courtesy of Thames TV/
Channel 4, *A People's War*)

expected was houses to have nice gardens, front gardens, back gardens, I expected it to be . . . trees and a bit of green . . . but it wasn't, it was all bricks and mortar again.[38]

THE POST-WAR YEARS

Life was hard and somewhat cheerless for women in the second half of the 1940s. The winter of 1946–7 was the coldest on record and it was followed by floods and a wet summer. Not only was food short and the environment desolate, with almost every town pock-marked by bomb sites on which weeds flourished but building began only very slowly, but women's expectations of rewards for their hard work during the war were fulfilled only in a most limited way, in spite of the fact that a record number of women, 24, was elected to Parliament in the 1945 General Election.

The 'Welfare State' did bring women some gains. Family Allowances introduced in August 1946 under legislation passed while the wartime coalition government was still in office, were, at feminists' insistence, paid to the mother, even though they did not 'endow' her as Eleanor Rathbone would have liked, but contributed just a few shillings towards the maintenance of second and subsequent children. Under Beveridge's proposals for social insurance, formulated in 1942 and introduced in legislation of 1946, housewives who were not working or who opted not to pay contributions were considered to be covered by their husbands' National Insurance contributions and a 'joint benefit' was paid to a couple when the man fell ill or became unemployed. This replaced a complex system of allowances, though of course it still treated the married woman as a dependant. In addition pregnant women who were earning were at last entitled to thirteen weeks' maternity benefit to enable them to give up working before and after the birth of the child. The National Health Service was established in 1948, on the principle of access to medical consultation and hospital treatment without charge, a real boon for the many women for whom medical help had been beyond reach pre-war because they were not in an insured occupation.

However, when it came to direct economic rewards women were less fortunate. The Royal Commission on Equal Pay, set up after parliamentary feminists succeeded in getting equal pay for teachers written into the 1944 Education Act, reported in 1946. The majority report supported equal pay only for the common classes of the civil service, and even this did not have the power of a recommendation. Thus the Labour government was not bound to introduce equal pay for men and women in the public services, and in practice opposed it on the grounds that it would have inflationary tendencies. In 1948 the Trades Union Congress and its Women's Advisory Committee (which had been fighting hard for the implementation of equal pay) were persuaded to drop the demand and support the government's wage freeze. The Report of the Royal Commission subscribed to the same old notion that women in industry were inherently less efficient than men that the War Cabinet Committee on Women in Industry in 1919 had expressed.[39]

Three of the four women who sat on the Commission wrote a Memorandum of Dissent which advanced the view that the 'efficiency gap' was being closed by modern technology, and was in any case much smaller than the average pay differential. They also said that it was unfair to penalise all women for the bad time-keeping and absenteeism of a few. It seems that they had the long-term single woman worker in mind, rather than the newer phenomenon of the married woman worker, who during the war had been the worst offender as far as time-keeping went. They did not make suggestions about how the married women's 'disabilities' might be removed (through, for instance, improved childcare, laundries, shopping facilities or re-allocation of household responsibilities).[40] In this they were in line with the views of women in the labour movement generally after the war. The Women's Advisory Committee of the TUC was emphatic, as the Working Women's Organisations had been before the war, that married women should not *need* to work, and that mothers of small children in particular should not work.

However, the views of labour movement women were now moving out of step with social trends, for, as we have seen, the proportion of married women in the labourforce did not fall off after the war, but was as great in 1951 as it had been in 1943. The Women's Advisory Committee proposed in 1942 that married women should be encouraged to leave work at the end of the war by the offer of a lump sum made up of their wartime National Insurance contributions, echoing the idea of 'mother's pensions' put forward at the end of the First World War. But women trade unionists objected so strongly that the Committee had to withdraw its proposal and issue a reassuring statement to the effect that it supported the right of all women to work after the war.[41] The job prospects of older, married women had improved by the late 1940s compared with the 1930s and before. Whereas in 1931 10 per cent of married women went out to work, 22 per cent did so in 1951, and while in 1931 nearly half of all women workers were under 25 and very few were aged 35 to 59, in 1951 the under-25s represented only one third of women workers, and the other two thirds were made up of roughly equal proportions of women in their thirties, forties and fifties.

The belief that mothers of young children should not work was the prevailing view of the time. Medical opinion had since the nineteenth century held that a woman's place was in the home where she should look after her own children, for the sake of their physical and emotional well-being. The demand for women's labour in the two world wars had done little to shake this. Increasingly in the 1940s psychologists contributed the authority of their view that children who were not mothered intensively during their first five years and possibly throughout their schooldays, would grow up suffering from all sorts of neurotic and psychopathological ills. This view became something of an orthodoxy among those in positions of power over women, like doctors and members of the educational and social services. With, in addition, the panic about the birthrate in the 1940s, women were confronted with a powerful cluster of ideas urging them to give up work and go home. 'Rearing babies through happy healthy childhood to independent maturity is even more important than wiring aeroplanes, and is a very much more absorbing and exacting task', wrote Gertrude Williams in *Women and Work* in 1945, sounding a typical note.[42]

How much women actually took this prescription to heart must have varied enormously. Clearly it did not have much effect on Mary Sweeney, who went to work on the Liverpool buses when her youngest child was six months old, in order to 'maybe bring them up better or buy a house or something'. But Pauline Long was more susceptible to the orthodoxy. She recorded with bitter hyperbole the effect of the post-war changes on her life:

Come 1945: a letter in the post one Friday morning: 'This nursery shuts today (for good) at 6 pm. Please remove all your belongings with your child this evening'. And I was a single parent; no more nurseries. The Government needed jobs for the returning heroes; women had to make their homes and beautify them with feminine charm (up the birthrate). Came Macmillan and we'd never had it so good. Came Bowlby who told us that it was all our fault if anything went wrong with our children's lives if we left them for any time at all. Came demand feeding, babies inseparable from mothers on slings around our backs and fronts; came television, washing machines, and durable goods to make us feel wanted in the home. Came Do It Yourself. Came Guilt – never think of yourself as a person, never have sex outside marriage, never never never leave your child, be content with Uncle Government's lovely domestic hardware; never breathe a word of the orgiastic nights on the gun site (or the warmth of the all-women's residential Nissen huts and officers' buildings, not a man for miles).
Just remember, everything is always your fault. You don't have rights. The children have rights. The children are always right. You are always wrong. Just get on and do the washing and bake a cake. Don't speak. Be silent. You are no-one (except a machine to spend money).[43]

Such feelings were a far cry from the confident independence which she and many other women had felt during the war.

CHAPTER 16

CONCLUSION

In our introduction we asked whether the experience of participation in industry and the armed services in the two world wars led to lasting changes for women. Our review of women's experiences from before 1914 to after 1945 does not suggest that the wars led to steady advances towards the 'emancipation' of women, nor that there were spectacular gains followed by crashing losses. Although there were many changes, there was an undertow pulling women back during both world wars, by emphasising that change was temporary, that women were 'really' wives and mothers and their place was at home, and that they were doing skilled, important jobs and earning relatively high wages on sufferance.

In spite of this, women in both wars got a great deal of out their participation personally, in terms of new and lasting friendships, and the satisfaction of difficult work well done. There were many differences between the two wars as far as women's employment was concerned but in both women were drawn into industrial and military positions which they did not usually occupy. As well as taking the munitions jobs which abounded on both occasions, women were suddenly publicly visible in the First War, as porters or bus conductresses, for example, and in the Second War half a million were in uniform in the women's services and the Land Army. Women discovered their hidden depths, earned their own money (generally more than they had earned pre-war) and enjoyed the company in war work. Some left home for the first time, and felt the satisfaction of being independent of their families. Many women interviewed about what they got out of the First War made comments similar to Elsie Farlow's: 'it allowed women to stand on their own feet. It was the turning point for women'.[1]

It is a reflection of how transient that 'turning point' was that many women asked about the effects that the Second War had on them echo her remark almost word for word. 'It made a great deal of difference to me' said Mona Marshall, nursemaid turned steelworker, 'it made me stand on my own feet, gave me more self-confidence', and Joan Shakesheff, a factory girl who joined the Land Army, said 'it changed the whole of life really for women'.[2]

During each war all sorts of observers saw signs of women's new sense of self-esteem and thought that it heralded a radical shake-up in women's position. An employer in the First World War prophesied that 'women will not want to return to their domestic duties after the war'[3] and a woman interviewed by M-O in 1943 said 'I think the war has made a lot of difference to housewives. I don't think they'll want to go back to the old narrow life.'[4] Nella Last, the Barrow housewife, wrote in her diary on 5 December 1942 after a day at the WVS Centre:

I thought of a stack of dirty crocks to tackle after tea, of pictures and furniture that were once polished every week, and now got done when I had the time. I wondered if people would *ever* go back to the old ways. I cannot see women settling to trivial ways – women who have done worthwhile things.[5]

At another level publicists in both wars warned of all sorts of dire consequences arising from women's new identity. In the First World War it was feared that women would put the future of the nation at risk by not settling down to being wives and mothers again, and insisting on holding on to their relatively well-paid jobs. In the event they were bullied back home or into domestic work, the idea being that they should learn to be better mothers and homemakers, and keep their returning servicemen husbands from turning to drink. Many women had to work for economic reasons, and nothing was done to improve their pay and conditions in laundries, sweat shops, domestic service and so on. Little was done to improve their lot as mothers either, particularly as far as housing and incomes were concerned. The Maternity and Child Welfare Act of 1918 did introduce some welcome ante- and post-natal care, but with greater emphasis on the health of the child than the mother: infant mortality declined, while maternal mortality rose between the wars.

In the Second World War there was less fear of women deserting the home altogether. All sorts of social surveys claimed confidently that 'women *want* to return to, or start on, domestic life when the war is over', choosing to ignore the hesitant and conditional answers which large proportions of women gave to their questions.[6] But it was argued that if women were to be persuaded to halt the falling birthrate they would have to be offered a greatly improved deal as wives and mothers, and during and after the war all sorts of ideas were discussed, from Family Allowances which arrived in a small way in 1946, to better housing, which was slower to come, and local authority babysitters, who did not materialise.

After the First World War single women had been attacked for 'taking men's jobs' even when they were in sex-stereotyped work like secretarial and routine factory jobs, but by 1945 it was considered normal, even desirable, for young women to work in such roles, and during and after the Second World War little distinction was made between young single and young married women. Both groups could help to fill the 800,000 jobs which needed workers in industry, distribution, offices, shops and schools. But there was a lot of ambiguity about prescriptions for other women. It was advocated with increasing authority that mothers of children under school age should not go out to work. Possibly there was something of a class divide as far as mothers of older children were concerned. On the whole middle-class women were expected to devote themselves to their homes and husbands and see their offspring all the way up the competitive educational ladder created in 1944, though the desperate shortage of teachers in the late 1940s and 1950s led to a campaign to recruit mothers back into teaching, and primary school teachers were now usually Mrs Somebody, instead of Miss. Similarly, working-class wives who lived in areas where there was a demand for (relatively cheap) women workers were expected to come back to the factory. After all, they had coped with the double burden during the war without either their homes or their employers suffering too much, whatever the personal consequences, and shift and part-time work which made it more possible for one person to do the two jobs had come to stay.

What attracted women back into paid work after the rigours of wartime coping? During both wars, women with family responsibilities found the experience something of a test of endurance, especially if their menfolk were in the forces. It was particularly hard in the Second War because women were having to put up with bombing at home and were being urged to 'make do and mend' as well as to keep their war jobs going. The surveys of the 1940s may have exaggerated the evidence, but many women did voice the opinion that homelife was all they wanted at the end of both wars, like the Lancashire woman who said she and her friends were not bothered about losing their jobs in 1918 because they expected to get married: 'That's the only thing we girls had to look forward to, if you understand, getting married and sort of being on our own.'[7] In 1944 Zelma Katin wrote with pleasure of giving up her job as a clippie to return home:

> I want to lie in bed until eight o'clock, to eat a meal slowly, to sweep the floors when they are dirty, to sit in front of the fire, to walk on the hills, to go shopping of an afternoon, to gossip at odd minutes.[8]

But in view of the pressures of post-war life on both occasions, one wonders how long this kind of feeling lasted. Nella Last was the non-earning wife of a joiner who devoted herself to his welfare and that of their sons throughout the inter-war years, but by the end of the 1930s she was at breaking point, desperate to put an end to her 'harem' existence and to get out of the house and do alternative, worthwhile work. For her the WVS was a life-line. For many women after the Second World War the main motivating factor was the inevitable, though unacknowledged, need for a wife as well as a husband to be a 'breadwinner'. But also the desire to escape from the isolation of the home, to mix with other women and see more of life, and to do work that was more satisfying than dusting, appear in later surveys of married women workers as important reasons for going out to work.[9]

Was it easier to work after marriage in the 1940s than it had been before either the Second or the First World War? Shifts and part-time work, and the reduction of the standard working week to 47 and later 40 hours, did remove the crippling burden of impossibly long hours. But crêches were not available in the

1940s, and there were no more places in full-time nurseries after the Second World War than there had been between the wars. Working mothers had to rely on relatives and minders still. The greater availability of contraception and gradual increase in the number of Family Planning Clinics meant that women could limit their families more easily (even though contraceptive advice did not become generally available for single women until the 1970s). The practice of having a couple of children close together was a big contrast to the large, spread-out families of the early part of the century. It made a difference to women's opportunities to go out to work, and to their health, which was less likely to be undermined for life when they were still in their twenties and thirties, especially with the advent of paid maternity leave for working women in 1946 and free health care after 1948.

Toilets and rest rooms at work were more standard, though there was still much abuse in smaller firms and workshops, which during the 1950s and 1960s began to be filled with immigrant women recruited by employers because they were seen as 'docile', 'unambitious' and 'cheap' just like previous generations of women workers. The wars may have contributed to the improvement of workplace facilities, though the energy which women in the Second World War had to put into seeing that clauses in the 1937 Factory Act relating to the worker's health and comfort were honoured suggests that there was nothing inevitable about this. Homework and other low paid and exploitative jobs for women, like night-time cleaning and all kinds of packaging and processing jobs, still abounded, even though personal domestic service was no longer one of them. State pensions were now available for women at 60, and wives who were not in paid work were at least recognised under the social insurance legislation of 1946, even if only as dependants.

Domestic technology certainly advanced in the inter-war years and after the Second World War. Vacuum cleaners, gas or electric stoves and irons, and an internal water supply together with some sort of boiler to heat water, were by the 1950s a standard part of most homes. But refrigerators and washing machines were confined to the better off in the 1950s, and clothes driers and dish-washing machines were things of the future even for them. In spite of the much-acclaimed rise of the 'property-owning democracy', there was still a great deal of sub-standard rented accommodation and local authorities' practice of housing people in tower blocks was particularly inconvenient for women with children. Did men take on more domestic work in the 1950s and 1960s? Surveys suggest that husbands played with children, and did jobs like washing up and cleaning windows occasionally, but very rarely took an equal share of managing the household.[10] It was still seen as a woman's problem to work out how the home and children could be taken care of in her absence, and a woman still required good organisation and considerable determination if she was going to cope with the double burden.

Employers were still not keen to train women or give them skilled or responsible work after the Second World War, because they regarded all women, whether single or married, as temporary, since it was still the prevailing view that her home made the first call on a woman's life. Trade unionists still defended better pay and higher status work against the entry of women. The 1940s and 1950s were years of intense segregation of work along sex lines, and of the establishment of grading schemes which effectively debarred women from the top grades. Even within the professions, where there were gradually increasing numbers of women, there were 'no go' areas. For example, the number of women solicitors crept up in these years, but the numbers of barristers remained very small.

Men and women still did not participate equally in other activities. Women may have won the vote in 1918, but they were not widely recognised as having their own political interests and their representation in Parliament was still very small. In 1945 the *Daily Mirror* urged women to 'Vote for Him', that is on behalf of their absent servicemen husbands, rather than for themselves, and the 24 women elected to the Commons formed a small proportion of the total of 640 MPs. As far as leisure was concerned women were still not accepted everywhere. For example, they were more welcome in pubs after the Second World War than before, but only if they kept off male territory: 'If I go to a pub with a young lady I take her to the saloon bar', explained a young man in 1944, 'That's all right. But if I go myself I go to the public bar – there's better conversation there, and I think the women should keep out and let the men have it to themselves.'[11]

All in all, even though there were many changes, above all in the practice of married and older women going out to work, the continuity in women's position at work and in the home between 1914 and 1945 is very striking. After 1945 what was important in life was still emphatically male, whether one was looking at work, leisure, politics, language or for that matter the way that historical accounts were written. The resurgence of the women's movement in the late 1960s heralded a new assault on the many ways in which successive generations of women have been confined within the 'cage' of domesticity and low esteem at home and at work. The rediscovery of women's history has played a major part in this attack, and this book is part of that process.

NOTES

CHAPTER 1 INTRODUCTION

1 We are both authors of separate detailed studies of attitudes and policies towards women workers in the First and Second World Wars respectively; Gail Braybon, *Women Workers in the First World War*, London, Croom Helm, 1981, and Penny Summerfield, *Women Workers in the Second World War*, London, Croom Helm, 1984. This joint enterprise has given us a chance both to concentrate on women's own experiences and to put the two wars together.
2 W.N. Medlicott, *Contemporary England 1914–1964*, London, Longman, 1967, and W. Franklin Mellor (ed.) *The History of the Second World War UK Medical Series, Casualties and Medical Statistics*, London, HMSO, 1972.
3 Mrs C.S. Peel, *How We Lived Then 1914–1918*, London, John Lane, 1929, p. 21.

CHAPTER 2 WOMEN BEFORE 1914

1 Jane Lewis, *Women in England*, 1870–1950, Brighton, Wheatsheaf, 1984.
2 Census, 1911.
3 See Angela John, *By the Sweat of Their Brow*, London, Croom Helm, 1980, p. 45 for information on women miners, and Barbara Drake, *Women in Trade Unions*, London, Virago reprint, 1984, for textile wages.
4 Gail Braybon's great-grandmother.
5 Andrew Mearnes, *The Bitter Cry of Outcast London*, quoted in David Rubinstein, *Victorian Homes*, London, David & Charles, 1974, p. 132.

6   C.S. Davies, quoted by Jill Liddington and Jill Norris, *One Hand Tied Behind Us*, London, Virago, 1978, p. 103.
7   Clara Collet, in the Royal Commission on Labour, Reports on the Employment of Women, 'Conditions of Work in London', 1893.
8   C.V. Butler, *Domestic Service*, London, Bell & Sons, 1916.
9   Ibid., p. 103.
10 E. Cadbury, M.C. Matheson, G. Shann, *Women's Work and Wages*, 2nd edn, London. T. Fisher Unwin, 1909, p. 115.
11 Ibid., p. 115.
12 Ibid.
13 Quoted by Elizabeth Roberts, *A Woman's Place – An Oral History of Working-Class Women 1890–1914*, Oxford, Basil Blackwell, 1984, pp. 58–9.
14 Ed. Margaret Llewelyn Davis, *Life as We Have Known It*, original edition 1931, reprinted by Virago, 1977, Mrs. Burrows.
15 Clementina Black, *Married Women's Work*, London, Bell & Sons, 1915, p. 7.
16 Helen Pease, Imperial War Museum, the Anti-War Movement tapes, 821/20.
17 Maud Pember Reeves, *Round About a Pound a Week*, original edition 1913, reprinted by Virago, 1979.
18 Sheila Ferguson and Hilde Fitzgerald, *Studies in the Social Services*, London, HMSO, 1954, ch. II.
19 Ed. Margaret Llewelyn Davis, *Maternity: Letters from Working Women*, original edition 1915, reprinted by Virago, 1978.
20 Liddington and Norris, op. cit. p. 18
21 Davies, *Maternity*, op. cit. p. 18
22 Ibid., p. 20.
23 E. Cadbury, M.C. Matheson, G. Shann, op. cit.
24 Helen Pease, IWM, op. cit.
25 Carol Dyhouse, *Girls growing up in Late Victorian and Edwardian England*, London, Routledge & Kegan Paul, 1981, p. 26.
26 Liddington and Norris, op. cit. p. 239.

CHAPTER 3 DILUTION: WOMEN IN 'MEN'S JOBS'

1   John Terraine, *Impacts of War 1914 and 1918*, London, Hutchinson, 1970, ch. IV.
2   See I.O. Andrews, *The Economic Effects of World War Upon Women and Children in Great Britain*, 2nd edn, New York, Oxford University Press, 1921, for full discussion of unemployment.

3   Ray Strachey, *The Cause*, London, Bell & Sons, 1928, p. 338.
4   John Stevenson, *British Society 1914–45*, London, Allen Lane, 1984.
5   I.O. Andrews, op cit., ch. V.
6   G.D.H. Cole, *Labour in Wartime*, London, Bell & Sons, 1915, ch. V.
7   Cole, quoted by B. Pribicevik, *The Shop Stewards' Movement and Workers' Control*, Oxford, Blackwell, 1959, p. 48.
8   G.D.H. Cole, op. cit, ch. III.
9   John Stevenson, op. cit.
10 See Gail Braybon, *Women Workers in the First World War*, London, Croom Helm, 1981, ch. II.
11 See, for example, S.J. Chapman, *Labour and Capital after the War*, London, Murray, 1918.
12 A.W. Kirkaldy, *Industry and Finance*, vol. II, London, Isaac Pitman, 1920.
13 Ibid.
14 Imperial War Museum, Women's Collection, EMP 36.
15 IWM, Wom. Coll., MUN 24/16.
16 *Common Cause*, 28/4/16.
17 Pribicevik, op. cit., and IWM, Wom. Coll., op. cit, MUN 29.
18 James Hinton, *Labour & Socialism*, Brighton, Wheatsheaf, 1983.
19 Ed. Basil Worsfold, *The War and Social Reform*, London, Murray, 1916, ch. 6.
20 British Association, *Draft Interim Report of the Conference to Investigate into Outlets for Labour After the War*, London, British Association, 1915.
21 IWM, Wom. Coll. EMP 33.
22 IWM, Wom. Coll. EMP 40.
23 Mrs C.S. Peel, *How We Lived Then*, London, John Lane, 1929.
24 W.E Shewell-Cooper, *Landgirl*, London, English University Press, 1941.
25 IWM, Wom. Coll. EMP 43.
26 IWM, Wom. Coll. EMP 43.
27 *Manchester Guardian*, 22/11/15.
28 I.O. Andrews, op. cit., ch. IV.
29 Braybon, op. cit., p. 160.
30 A.W. Kirkaldy, op. cit., p. 41.
31 Gail Braybon, op. cit. is largely about men's attitudes to women workers.
32 *ASE Monthly Journal and Report*, March 1917.
33 British Association Report, op. cit.
34 *Common Cause*, 30/6/16.
35 *Everyman*, 24/3/16, and *Yorkshire Evening Post*, 15/1/16.
36 Braybon, op. cit., p. 73.

37 IWM, Wom. Coll. MUN 29/15.
38 Braybon, op. cit., p. 85.
39 Wages are discussed in I.O. Andrews, op. cit., and Sarah Boston, *Women Workers and the Trade Union Movement*, London, Davis Poynter, 1980.
40 *Northern Whig*, 14/12/15. *Daily Chronicle*, 16/3/16.
41 Sylvia Pankhurst, *The Home Front*, London, Hutchinson, 1932, ch. XI.
42 Ministry of Reconstruction, Report of the War Cabinet Committee on *Women in Industry*, 1919.
43 Barbara Drake, *Women in the Engineering Trades*, London, Fabian Research Department, 1917.
44 A.W. Kirkaldy, vol. II, op. cit, p. 13.
45 A.W. Kirkaldy, *Industry & Finance*, vol. I, London, Isaac Pitman, 1917, ch. II.
46 A.W. Kirkaldy, vol. II, op. cit., p. 38.
47 Ibid., p. 54.
48 IWM, Wom. Coll, MUN 29/24.
49 Braybon, op. cit., p. 86.

CHAPTER 4 WAR WORK

1 Lilian Miles, Imperial War Museum, War Work tapes, 000854/04.
2 Isabella Clarke, IWM, W W tapes, 000774/04.
3 Monica Cosens, *Lloyd George's Munition Girls*, London, Hutchinson, 1916, pp. 43–4.
4 Mrs Mullins, Southampton Museum Oral History Project.
5 Lily Truphet 000693/07, Amy May 000684/05 and Annie Edwards 000740/15, IWM, W W tapes.
6 Florence Thompson 000722/05, Lilian Miles, op. cit., IWM, W W tapes.
7 Mrs Hunt, SM.
8 Dorothy Haigh 000734/07. See also Elsie Farlow 000773/, OWM, W W tapes.
9 Caroline Rennles, 000566/07, IWM, W W tapes.
10 L.K. Yates, *The Woman's Part*, London, Hodder & Stoughton, 1918, ch. I.
11 Caroline Playne, *Society at War*, London, Allen & Unwin, 1930, p. 137.
12 Naomi Loughnan, in Gilbert Stone, *Women War Workers*, London, Harrap, 1917, p. 38.
13 *Weekly Welcomes*, 3/3/17.
14 *Daily News*, 3/2/17.

15 *The Lady*, 3/8/16.
16 Monica Cosens, op. cit., p. 7, and A.K. Foxwell, *Munition Lasses*, London, Hodder & Stoughton, 1917.
17 Naomi Loughnan in Stone, op. cit., p. 25.
18 Mrs Emmerson, IWM Documents collection.
19 Joan Williams, *A Munition Worker's Career*, IWM, typescript in Documents collection.
20 Sybil Morrison, IWM, the Anti-War Movement tapes, 331/6.
21 E. Royston Pike, *Human Documents of the Lloyd George Era*, London, Allen & Unwin, 1972, p. 171.
22 Mrs C.S. Peel, *How We Lived Then*, London, John Lane, 1928, p. 132.
23 Mrs. C.S. Peel, op. cit., p. 21.
24 Peggy Hamilton, *Three Years or the Duration*, London, Peter Owen, 1978, ch. II.
25 IWM, Wom. Coll., MUN 24/16.
26 Sybil Morrison, IWM, op. cit.
27 Mairi Chisholm, 000771/04, IWM, W W tapes.
28 Mrs C.S. Peel, op. cit., p. 129.
29 Mrs Nightingale, SM.
30 Isabella Clarke, 000774/04, IWM, W W tapes.
31 Mrs Bell, Mrs Mullins, and others, SM. Annie Edwards, Lily Truphet, Amy May, op. cit., IWM.
32 Jerry White, *Rothschild Buildings*, London, Routledge & Kegan Paul, 1980, for the effect on one area of London.
33 Dorothy Haigh, op. cit., IWM.
34 Peggy Hamilton, op. cit., p. 37.
35 Monica Cosens, and A.K. Foxwell, op. cit.
36 Jane Cox 000705/06, Beatrice Lee 000724/06, Florence Thompson, op. cit., IWM, W W tapes.
37 *Common Cause*, 1/10/15. See also Mrs Bell, SM.
38 Mrs Marsh, SM.
39 Annie Edwards, op. cit., IWM.
40 Mrs C.S. Peel, op. cit., p. 133.
41 L.K. Yates, op. cit., p. 11.
42 Elsa Thomas, 000676/08, IWM, W W tapes.
43 Monica Cosens, op. cit., pp. 23–4.
44 Dorothy Poole, typescript, IWM, Wom. Coll, MUN 17.
45 Peggy Hamilton, op. cit.
46 Mrs Bryant, SM.
47 Isabella Clarke, op. cit., IWM.
48 Sarah Pidgeon, 000706/04, IWM, W W tapes.
49 Mrs Gregory and others, SM. Isabella Clarke, Lilian Miles, op. cit., IWM.
50 Elsie Farlow, op.cit., IWM.

51 A.K. Foxwell, op. cit.
52 Ibid., p. 132.
53 Monica Cosens, op. cit., p. 122.
54 Sarah Pidgeon, op. cit., Elsie McIntyre 000673/09, IWM, W W tapes.
55 Margaret Adams, IWM Documents Collection.
56 Mrs Stephens, Mrs Castle, Mrs Airey, IWM Documents Collection.
57 Amy May, op. cit., IWM. See also, Mrs Fry, who worked on the trams, SM.
58 Mrs Stephens, IWM Documents Collection.
59 Mrs Mullins, SM.
60 Naomi Loughnan in Stone, op. cit.
61 Mrs Airey, IWM Document Collection.
62 Mrs Nightingale, SM.
63 Elsa Thomas, op. cit., IWM.
64 Peggy Hamilton, op. cit. pp. 92–3.
65 Dorothy Poole, typescript, op. cit.
66 Isabella Clarke, op. cit., IWM.
67 *Trade Union Worker*, letter, Jan 1917.
68 Deborah Thom, in Angela John, *Unequal Opportunities*, Oxford, Blackwell, 1985.
69 Annie Edwards, op. cit., IWM.
70 Mary Lees, 000506/07, IWM.
71 L.K. Yates, op. cit., p. 9.
72 I.O. Andrews, *The Economic Effects of the World War upon Women and Children in Great Britain*, 2nd edn, New York, OUP, 1921, ch. 6. Also, Monica Cosens, op. cit.
73 Caroline Rennles, op. cit., IWM.
74 Monica Cosens, op. cit., p. 113.
75 A.K. Foxwell, op. cit., pp. 131–2.
76 Joan Williams, typescript, IWM, p. 42.
77 Ibid., p. 47.
78 Barbara Drake, *Women in the Engineering Trades*, London, Fabian Research Department, 1917, p. 77.
79 *Solidarity*, Jan. 1918.
80 IWM, Wom. Coll., MUN 29.
81 A.K. Foxwell, op. cit., p. 20.
82 Elsie McIntyre and Elsa Thomas, op. cit., IWM.
83 Frank Bradbury, 000675/06, IWM, W W tapes.
84 Laura Verity, 000864/08, IWM, W W tapes.

CHAPTER 5 HEALTH AND WELFARE

1   Mrs Mullins, Southampton Museum, Oral History Project.
2   Mrs Kilford, SM.
3   Mrs Ottaway, SM.
4   Jane Cox, 000705/06, Imperial War Museum, War Work tapes.
5   D.J. Collier & B.L. Hutchins, *The Girl in Industry*, London, Bell & Sons, p. 13.
6   Monica Cosens, *Lloyd George's Munition Girls*, London, Hutchinson, 1916, p. 49.
7   Ministry of Munitions, Health of Munition Workers, *Final Report*.
8   Barbara Drake, *Women in the Engineering Trades*, London, Fabian Research Department, 1917.
9   Joan Williams, typescript, IWM.
10 In John Burnett, *Useful Toil*, London, Allen Lane, 1974.
11 Dorothy Poole, typescript, IWM, Wom. Coll., MUN 17.
12 Peggy Hamilton, *Three Years or the Duration*, London, Peter Owen, 1978.
13 Elsie McIntyre, 000673/09, IWM, W W tapes.
14 Ed. A.S. McNalth, *The Civilian Health and Medical Services*, London, HMSO, 1953.
15 Monica Cosens, op. cit., pp. 154–5.
16 *Sheffield Independent*, 18/6/16.
17 T.A. Lamb, *TNT Tales*, Oxford, Blackwell, 1918.
18 Lilian Miles, 000854/04, IWM, W W tapes.
19 Mrs Mullins, SM.
20 Elsie Farlow, 000773/, IWM, W W tapes.
21 Mrs Mullins and Mrs Mortimer, SM.
22 P. Schweitzer et al. (eds.), *What Did You Do in the War, Mum?'* London, Age Exchange Theatre Company, 1985, p. 64.
23 *The Lancet*, 12/8/16, 'Observations on the Effect of TNT on Women Workers'.
24 Antonia Ineson, 'Science, Technology, Medicine, Welfare and the Labour Process: Women Munition Workers in the First World War', M.Phil thesis, University of Sussex, 1981, p. 167.
25 Ibid., p. 168.
26 *Weekly Welcome*, 3/3/17, 'My first day as a Munition Girl'.
27 A.K. Foxwell, *Munition Lasses*, London, Hodder & Stoughton, 1917, p. 22.
28 Health of Munition Workers Committee, Final Report, p. 13.
29 A.W. Kirkaldy, *Industry & Finance*, Vol II, London, Isaac Pitman, 1920.
30 M.C. Matheson, in *The Women's Industrial News*, July 1917.

31 Laura Verity, 000864/08, IWM, W W tapes.
32 Dorothea Proud, *Welfare Work*, London, Bell & Sons, 1916.
33 Helen Pease, IWM, Anti-War Movement tapes, 821/20.
34 Quoted in Gail Braybon, *Women Workers in the First World War*, London, Croom Helm, 1981, p. 146.
35 IWM, Wom. Coll. MUN 14/11.
36 IWM, Wom. Coll. MUN 29/18.
37 IWM, Wom. Coll. MUN 24/16.
38 IWM, Wom. Coll. MUN 29/14.
39 Dorothea Proud, op. cit., p. 266.
40 Monica Cosens, op. cit., p. 57.
41 Ibid., pp. 58–9.
42 A number of women, SM, and IWM.
43 Elsa Thomas, 000676/08, IWM, W W tapes.
44 Dorothy Poole, typescript, IWM, op. cit.
45 Antonia Ineson's thesis, op. cit., gives a full and interesting picture of this.

CHAPTER 6 DOMESTIC LIFE

1 Mrs C.S. Peel, *How We Lived Then*, London, John Lane, 1929, ch. X.
2 Caroline Playne, *Britain Holds On 1917, 18*, London, Allen & Unwin, 1933, p. 45.
3 A.K. Foxwell, *Munition Lasses*, London, Hodder & Stoughton, 1917, p. 30.
4 Mrs C.S. Peel, op. cit., pp. 128–9.
5 John Burnett, *A Social History of Housing*, London, David & Charles, 1978, ch. 8.
6 Sarah Pidgeon, Imperial War Museum War Work tapes, 000706/04.
7 *Labour Woman*, April 1916.
8 Mrs Peel, op. cit., pp. 96–7.
9 Caroline Playne, op. cit., pp. 67–8.
10 Elsie McIntyre, 000673/09, IWM, W W tapes.
11 Mrs C.S. Peel, op. cit., p. 98.
12 Dorothy Haigh, 000734/07, IWM, W W tapes.
13 Antonia Ineson, 'Science, Technology, Medicine, Welfare and the Labour Process: Women Munition Workers in the First World War', University of Sussex, M. Phil. thesis, 1981, p. 147.
14 Mark Swenarton, *Homes Fit for Heroes*, London, Heinemann, 1981, ch. III.
15 Lilian Miles, 000854/04, IWM, W W tapes.

16 Isabella Clarke, 000774/04, IWM, W W tapes.
17 Sarah Boston, *Women Workers and the Trade Union Movement*, London, Davis Poynter, 1980, ch. 4.
18 D. Thom, 'The Ideology of Women's Work 1914–1920', Ph. D. thesis, Thames Polytechnic, 1982, and Mrs C.S. Peel, op. cit.
19 Articles complaining about this appeared in a number of papers, for example, *Morning Post* 26/2/17.
20 Mrs Peel, op. cit., ch. VI.
21 Ministry of Reconstruction, *Report of the Women's Employment Committee*, 1919, Cd 9239.
22 Ministry of Munitions, Health of Munition Workers Committee, *Final Report*, p. 3.
23 Carol Ring, in *Common Cause*, 21/07/16.
24 *The Times*, 24/6/16.
25 Quoted in Gail Braybon, *Women Workers in the First World War*, London, Croom Helm, 1981, p. 89.
26 Elsa Thomas, 000676/08, IWM, W W tapes.
27 Interview, quoted by Antonia Ineson, op. cit., p. 67.
28 Ruth Granville in P. Schweitzer et al. (eds.), *What did you do in the War, Mum?*, London, Age Exchange Theatre Company, 1985, p. 66.
29 M. Kosak, 'Women Munition Workers During the First World War, with special reference to Engineering', University of Hull, Ph. D. thesis.
30 Sylvia Pankhurst, *The Home Front*, London, Hutchinson, 1932, p. 98.
31 Ibid., p. 99.
32 *Reynolds Newspaper*, 6/12/15.
33 Quoted by E. Royston Pike, *Human Documents of the Lloyd George Era*, London, Allen & Unwin, 1971, p. 174.
34 Sylvia Pankhurst, op. cit., ch. XIII.
35 From the *Police Chronicle*, 1918, quoted by Pike, op. cit., p. 180.
36 Royal Commission on Marriage and Divorce, London, HMSO, 1956.
37 Sheila Ferguson and Hilde Fitzgerald, *Studies in the Social Services*, London, HMSO, 1954, ch. III.
38 Quoted by Arthur Marwick, *Women at War, 1914–1918*, London, Fontana, 1977, p. 114.
39 Caroline Rennles, 000566/07, IWM, W W tapes.
40 Lily Lane, in P. Schweitzer, op. cit., p. 32.
41 Mrs C.S. Peel, op. cit., p. 121.
42 Mary Lees, 000506/07, IWM, W W tapes.
43 Laura Verity, 000864/08, IWM, W W tapes.
44 Sylvia Pankhurst, op. cit., p. 182.
45 Beverley, in P. Schweitzer, op. cit.

46 Mrs C.S. Peel, op. cit., p. 172.
47 Quoted in Arthur Marwick, op. cit., p. 95.
48 Ibid., p. 125.

CHAPTER 7 DEMOBILISATION 1918–20

1 Vera Brittain, *Testament of Youth*, reprinted by Virago, 1978, p. 460.
2 Helen Pease, IWM, Anti-war Movement tapes, 821/20.
3 Mary Lees, 000506/07, IWM.
4 Mary Macarthur, writing in Marion Phillips, *Women and the Labour Party*, 1918, quoted in Gail Braybon, *Women Workers in the First World War*, Croom Helm, 1981, and A.G. Gardiner, *The Warlords*, quoted in David Englander, 'Demobilisation in England After the First World War', unpublished paper.
5 A.W. Kirkaldy, *Industry & Finance*, vol. I, London, Isaac Pitman, 1917.
6 Draft Interim Report of the Civil War Workers' Committee, Beveridge Papers, London School of Economics.
7 Beveridge Papers, op. cit., BEV 26.
8 Vera Brittain, op. cit., pp. 467–8.
9 A.C. Pigou, *Aspects of British Economic History*, London, Cass, 1947, p. 35.
10 M.A. Hamilton, *Mary Macarthur*, London, Parsons, 1925, ch. XV.
11 I.O. Andrews, *The Economic Effects of the World War upon Women and Children in Great Britain*, New York, OUP, 1921.
12 IWM, Wom. Coll. MUN 29/25.
13 *Daily Chronicle*, 7/12/18.
14 *The Democrat*, 10/4/19.
15 *Woman Worker*, Feb. 1919.
16 *Manchester Evening Chronicle*, 25/3/19.
17 *Manchester Dispatch*, 27/3/19.
18 *Aberdeen Free Press*, 4/2/19.
19 *Evening Standard*, 9/1/19.
20 *Daily Express*, 19/2/19.
21 *Hull Daily Mail*, 14/2/19.
22 *Hull Daily Mail*, April 1919.
23 *Liverpool Daily Post*, 21/1/19.
24 *Morning Post*, 7/14/19.
25 *Labour Woman*, March 1919.
26 Deborah Thom, 'Women Munition Workers at Woolwich

Arsenal in the 1914–18 War', MA Thesis, University of Warwick.

27 Chief Inspector of Factories, Report, 1919, p. 9.

28 Letter from J.E. Price, *Woman Worker*, March 1919.

29 *Woman Worker*, June 1919.

30 *Woman Worker*, Feb 1920.

31 *Woman Worker*, March 1920, and Sarah Boston, *Women Workers in the Trade Union Movement*, London, Davis Poynter, 1980.

32 Deborah Thom, MA, op. cit.

33 SM.

34 All these women were interviewed by Southampton Museum.

35 Mrs Mortimer, SM.

36 National Federation of Women Workers Conference, 1920, Miss Stephen of Bermondsey.

37 Monica Cosens, *Lloyd George's Munition Girls*, London, Hutchinson, 1916, p. 160.

38 *Evening News*, 4/1/19.

CHAPTER 8 WOMEN BETWEEN THE WARS

1 Mary Lee Settle, *All the Brave Promises, Memories of Aircraft Woman 2nd Class 2146391*, London, Pandora, 1984, p. 19.

2 Board of Education Consultative Committee, *Secondary Education*, London, HMSO, 1938; A. Little and J. Westergaard, 'The Trend of Class Differentials in Educational Opportunity', *British Journal of Sociology*, 1964.

3 Vera Brittain, *Women's Work in Modern England*, London, Noel Douglas, 1928, p. 14; Charlotte Haldane, *Motherhood and its Enemies*, New York, Doubleday, 1928, p. 61; Royal Commission on Equal Pay, *Report*, London, HMSO, 1945, Cmd 6937.

4 Census of England and Wales, Occupational Tables, London, HMSO, 1911 and 1931.

5 Helen Forrester, *Liverpool Miss*, Glasgow, Fontana 1982.

6 Cicely Hamilton, *The Englishwoman*, London, Longmans Green, 1940, p. 23; Winifred Holtby, *Women and a Changing Civilisation*, London, Lane, 1934, p. 100; Census 1911 and 1931.

7 Parliamentary Papers, *Distribution of Women in Industry*, Appendix 2, London, HMSO, 1929, Cmd. 3508.

8 Parliamentary Papers, *Twenty-second Abstract of Labour Statistics, 1922–1936*, London, HMSO, 1937, Cmd 5556.

9 Edith Hall, *Canary Girls and Stockpots*, Luton, WEA, 1977, p. 37.

10 Glyn Hughes, *Millstone Grit*, London, Gollancz, 1975, p. 91.
11 Betty Ferry, Boot and Shoe Maker, in *Working Lives*, vol. 1, 1905–45, London, Hackney WEA/centreprise, n.d., p. 108.
12 Quoted by Charmian Kenner, *No Time for Women. Exploring Women's Health in the 1930s and Today*, London, Pandora, 1985, p. 2.
13 Hall, op. cit., p. 29.
14 Brittain, op. cit., p. 31; Pam Taylor, 'Daughters and Mothers – Maids and Mistresses' in J. Clarke, C. Critcher and R. Johnson (eds), *Working Class Culture: Studies in History and Theory*, London, Hutchinson, 1979; Pilgrim Trust, *Men Without Work*, Cambridge, Cambridge University Press, 1938, pp. 254 and 258.
15 M. Spring Rice, *Working Class Wives*, London, Virago, 1981, p. 98.
16 E. Roberts, *A Woman's Place*, Oxford, Blackwell, 1984; D. Gittins, *Fair Sex*, London, Hutchinson, 1982.
17 Roberts, op. cit.; P. Ayers and J. Lambertz, 'Marriage Relations, Money and Domestic Violence in Liverpool 1919–1939', in J. Lewis (ed.), *Labour and Love*, Oxford, Blackwell, 1986.
18 Katharine Chorley, *Manchester Made Them*, London, Faber, 1950, pp. 272–3 and 268.
19 Royal Commission on Marriage and Divorce, *Report*, 1951–1955, London, HMSO, 1956, Cmd. 9678, Appx. 2, Table 5.
20 G.D.H. Cole et al. *Victory or Vested Interest*, London, Routledge, 1942, p. 68.
21 Spring Rice, op. cit., p. 94.
22 N.A. Ferguson, 'Women's Work: Employment Opportunities and Economic Roles 1918–1939', *Albion*, 1963.
23 Thanks to Jenny Thompson for this information from her research into domestic technology between the wars.
24 J. Burnett, *A Social History of Housing*, London, Methuen, pp. 242–3.
25 Roberts, op. cit., p. 144.
26 Royal Commission on Population, *Report*, London, HMSO, 1949, Cmd 7695; Holtby, op. cit., p. 131.
27 Hall, op. cit., p. 35.
28 Hamilton, op. cit., p. 27.
29 Ruth Hall, *Marie Stopes*, London, Virago, 1978.
30 Gittins, op. cit.
31 Betty D. Vernon, *Ellen Wilkinson 1891–1947*, London, Croom Helm, 1982; Jill Liddington, *The Life and Times of a Respectable Rebel: Selina Cooper 1864–1942*, London, Virago, 1985; Kate Harding and Caroline Gibbs, *Tough Annie: From Suffragette to Stepney Councillor*, London, Stepney Books, 1980; Geoffrey

Mitchell (ed.), *The Hard Way Up, the Autobiography of Hannah Mitchell, Suffragette and Rebel*, London, Virago, 1977.

32 P. Brookes, *Women at Westminster*, London, Peter Davies, 1967, Part Two.

33 D. Russell, *The Tamarisk Tree*, London, Virago, 1981, vol 2, p. 206.

34 V. Brittain, *England's Hour*, London, Futura, 1981; Frances Partridge, *A Pacifist's War*, London, Robin Clark, 1983.

35 N. Longmate, *How We Lived Then*, London, Arrow, 1973, p. 364.

36 P. Scott, *British Women in War*, London, Hutchinson, 1940, p. 56.

CHAPTER 9 CALL UP

1 J. Hooks, *British Policies and Methods of Employing Women in Wartime*, Washington, U.S. Government, 1944, p. 16.

2 PRO Cab 67/9, Memorandum by Minister of Supply, 20 October 1941.

3 E. Burton, *What of the Women?*, London, Frederick Muller, 1941, p. 55; V. Sackville West, *The Women's Land Army*, London, Michael Joseph, 1944, p. 7; T. Benson, *Sweethearts and Wives*, London, Faber, 1942, p. 81.

4 Burton, op. cit., p. 178.

5 *The Engineer*, 28 March 1941.

6 H.M.O. Parker, *British War Production*, London, HMSO, 1957, p. 280.

7 Mass-Observation (hereafter M-O), *People in Production*, London, John Murray, 1942, pp. 94–5.

8 Hooks, op. cit., p. 16.

9 M. Allen, 'The Domestic Ideal and the Mobilisation of Woman Power in World War II', *Women's Studies International Forum*, 1983, vol. 6, no. 4.

10 PRO Lab 26/130, Meetings of the Women's Consultative Committee (WCC), 1941.

11 M-O, op. cit., p. 177; Penny Summerfield, *Women Workers in the Second World War*, London, Croom Helm, 1984, p. 142 and Table B4, p. 196.

12 PRO Cab 65/20, 10 November 1941.

13 Mass-Observation Archive (hereafter M-OA), TC 19, Cardiff, 9 February 1942; TC 32, Debate at an Air-Raid Warden's Post, 16 December 1941, and 'overheards' 25 November 1941; M-O, op. cit., p. 152.

14 M-O, op. cit., p. 143.
15 M-OA, TC 19, Coventry, November 1941; File Report 952, November 1941; TC 66/4/C-H, War Work Coventry 1941.
16 Angus Calder, *The People's War*, London, Panther, 1971, p. 385.
17 *Hansard*, v.382, c.1296, Mr Kirkwood, and v.382, c.1300, Mr Sloan. Thanks to Celia Briar for this reference.
18 M-O, op. cit., pp. 97, 166.
19 Wartime Social Survey (WSS), 'An Investigation of the Attitudes of Women, the General Public and ATS Personnel to the Auxiliary Territorial Service', New Series, No.5, October 1941 (hereafter WSS, ATS Survey).
20 P. Schweitzer, L. Hilton, J. Moss (eds), *What Did You Do in the War, Mum?*, London, Age Exchange, 1985, p. 17.
21 S. Joseph, *If Their Mothers Only Knew*, London, Faber, 1946, p. 9; Schweitzer et al., op. cit., p. 14; Thames Television/Channel 4, 'A People's War' Interview Transcript (hereafter Thames TV Transcript), Mickie Hutton Storie.
22 Aline Whalley, Interview with the author, March 1986; PRO Lab, 26/63, Women's Services (Welfare and Amenities) Committee.
23 WSS, ATS Survey, pp. 48 and 47.
24 M-O, op. cit., p. 152; M-OA, TC 66/4/C-H, War Work Coventry, 1941.
25 PRO Lab 26/130; A. Williams Ellis, *Women in War Factories*, London, Gollancz, 1943.
26 See the boxes of material in the Mass-Observation Archive Topic Collections 'Women in Wartime' (TC 32) and 'Industry', and Mass-Observation publications such as *People in Production*, London, John Murray, 1942.
27 Central Statistical Office, *Statistical Digest of the War*, London, HMSO, p. 11; WSS, ATS Survey, p. 14.
28 Hooks, op. cit., p. 24.

CHAPTER 10 DILUTION AGAIN

1 Thames Television/Channel 4, 'A People's War' Interview Transcript (hereafter Thames TV Transcript), Vi Maxwell; Mass-Observation Archive (hereafter M-OA), TC Industry 1941–7, Box 140, Tube Report.
2 M. Benney, *Over to Bombers*, London, Allen & Unwin, 1943, pp. 105–6.
3 P. Inman, *Labour in the Munitions Industries*, London, HMSO, 1957, p. 61.

4   Royal Commission on Equal Pay, Appendices to the *Minutes of Evidence*, London, HMSO, 1945, Cmd 6937, viii, Memorandum by AEU, para 33.

5   P. Schweitzer, L. Hilton, J. Moss (eds), *What Did You Do in the War, Mum?*, London, Age Exchange, 1985, p. 59.

6   Thames TV Transcript, Therese Roberts.

7   M-OA, TC 32, Women in Wartime, Box, 3, File F, Letters from Women Welders, 1942.

8   *The Engineer*, 14 July 1944.

9   Penny Summerfield, *Women Workers in the Second World War*, London, Croom Helm, 1984, p. 175.

10 J.T. Murphy, *Victory Production*, London, John Lane, 1942, p. 93.

11 B.I.L. Holden, *Night Shift*, London, Bodley Head, 1941, p. 97.

12 Summerfield, op. cit., pp. 172–3.

13 Thames TV Transcript, Agnes McLean.

14 Ibid.

15 Inman, op. cit., p. 365.

16 Thames TV Transcript, Agnes McLean.

17 Summerfield, op. cit., p. 157.

18 Doris White, *D for Doris, V for Victory*, Milton Keynes, Oakleaf Books, 1981, pp. 70–2

19 Summerfield, op. cit., p. 127.

20 Sheila Lewenhak, 'Trade Union Membership among Women and Girls in the United Kingdom 1920–1965', Unpublished Ph.D. thesis, University of London, 1971, p. 14.

21 H.M.D. Parker, *Manpower*, London, HMSO, 1957, p. 503.

22 Vera Douie, *The Lesser Half*, London, Women's Publicity Planning Association, 1943, p. 64.

23 Zelma Katin, *Clippie*, London, John Gifford, 1944, p. 48; Central Statistical Office, *Statistical Digest of the War*, London, HMSO, 1951, p. 205.

24 Douie, op. cit., pp. 47 and 36.

25 Aline Whalley, Interview with Penny Summerfield, March 1986.

26 Elaine Burton, *What of the Women?*, London, Frederick Muller, 1941, p. 100; Mrs Shipley, Interview with Penny Summerfield, November 1977; P. Schweitzer et al., op. cit., p. 27.

27 Douie, op. cit., pp. 73–4.

28 Douie, op. cit., p. 49; H. Smith, 'The Problem of "Equal Pay for Equal Work" in Great Britain during World War II', *Journal of Modern History*, 1981.

29 Douie, op. cit., pp. 39 and 52.

CHAPTER 11 ON THE JOB

1   Wartime Social Survey, *Women at Work*, by Geoffrey Thomas, June 1944 (hereafter WSS, Women at Work), p. 20.

2   Thames Television/Channel 4, 'A People's War' Interview Transcript (hereafter Thames TV Transcript), Kitty Murphy.

3   Thames TV Transcript, Mona Marshall.

4   Mass-Observation (hereafter M-O), *War Factory*, London, Gollancz, 1943, p. 79.

5   Mass-Observation Archive (hereafter M-OA), TC v/6/3 Industry 1941–47, Box 140, Tube Investments 1942.

6   Charles Madge, *Wartime Patterns of Saving and Spending*, Cambridge, Cambridge University Press, 1943, pp. 17 and 39.

7   Vita Sackville West, *The Women's Land Army*, London, Michael Joseph, 1944, p. 105; Elaine Burton, *What of the Women?*, London, Frederick Muller, 1941, p. 56.

8   P. Schweitzer, L. Hilton, J. Moss (eds), *What Did You Do in the War, Mum?*, London, Age Exchange, 1985, p. 9.

9   Ibid., p. 7.

10 Ibid.

11 M-OA, File Report 757, June 1941.

12 Schweitzer, et al., op. cit., p. 19.

13 P. Scott, *British Women in War*, London, Hutchinson, 1940, pp. 62–6.

14 Theodora Benson, *Sweethearts and Wives*, London, Faber, 1942, pp. 54 and 44.

15 Mary Lee Settle, *All the Brave Promises*, London, Pandora, 1984, p. 60.

16 M-OA, File Report 757, June 1941.

17 M-OA, TC 32, Women in Wartime, Box 3, File F, Letters from Women Welders, 1942.

18 Doris White, *D for Doris, V for Victory*, Milton Keynes, Oakleaf Books, 1981, pp. 11 and 25.

19 M-O, *People in Production*, London, John Murray, 1942, p. 156; M-OA, TC v/6/3 Industry 1941–47, Box 140, Tube Investments 1942; M-O, *War Factory*, pp. 26 ff.

20 Thames TV Transcript, Mickie Hutton Storie. Some of the most popular wartime songs can be found in Michael Leitch (ed.), *Great Songs of World War II*, London, Wise, 1975, e.g. 'Yours';

> *Yours* till the stars lose their glory!
> *Yours* till the birds fail to sing!
> *Yours* to the end of life's story.
> This pledge to you, dear, I bring.

21 Schweitzer et al., op. cit., p. 55.
22 *The Engineer*, 7 July 1944.
23 M-O, *War Factory*, pp. 26 and 56; M-OA, TC v/6/3 Industry, 1941–47, Box 140, Tube Investments 1942.
24 Benson, op. cit., p. 12.
25 Schweitzer et al., op. cit., p. 69.
26 Henry Pelling, *Britain and the Second World War*, Glasgow, Fontana, 1970, p. 153. Tom Harrisson, *Living Through the Blitz*, London, Collins, 1976, pp. 306–7.
27 Frances Partridge, *A Pacifist's War*, London, Robin Clark, 1983.
28 Richard Broad and Suzie Fleming (eds), *Nella Last's War, A Mother's Diary*, Bristol, Falling Wall Press, 1981, pp. 13 and 15.
29 M-O, *The Journey Home*, London, John Murray, 1944, p. 58.
30 Schweitzer et al., op. cit., p. 8.
31 B.I.L. Holden, *Night Shift*, London, Bodley Head, 1941, p. 13.
32 M-O, *People in Production*, pp. 164–5.
33 M-OA, TC 32, Women in Wartime, Box 3, File E, 25 April 1941.
34 Aline Whalley, Interview with Penny Summerfield, March 1986.
35 Benson, op. cit., p. 50.
36 Sadie McDougal, Interview with Penny Summerfield, July 1977.
37 M-O, *People in Production*, p. 156.
38 White, op. cit., p. 70.
39 Kay Jenner, Letter to Penny Summerfield, October 1977.
40 Settle, op. cit., pp. 36–7.
41 Ibid., p. 41.
42 M-OA, TC 32, Women in Wartime, Box 3, File E, June 1941.
43 Ibid., Box 3, File F, Letters from Women Welders, 1942.

CHAPTER 12 LOVE, SEX AND MARRIAGE

1 Mass-Observation Archive, TC 32, Women in Wartime, Box 3, File E, December 1941.
2 Ibid., p. 134, and Marjorie Wardle, Interview with Mark Easterby-Smith, April 1986.
3 P. Schweitzer, L. Hilton, J. Moss (eds), *What Did You Do in the War, Mum?*, London, Age Exchange, 1985, p. 8.
4 Ibid., p. 6.
5 D. White, *D for Doris, V for Victory*, Milton Keynes, Oakleaf Books, 1981, p. 16.
6 M. Benney, *Over to Bombers*, London, Allen & Unwin, 1943, p. 106.
7 Zelma Katin, *Clippie*, London, John Gifford, 1944, pp. 56–7.

8   Mass-Observation Archive, (hereafter M-OA), Women in Wartime, Box 3, File F, Letters from Women Welders, 1942.

9   M-OA, File Report 2205, January 1945, p. 2.

10 Thames Television/Channel 4 'A People's War' Interview Transcript, Hetty Fowler.

11 Royal Commission on Marriage and Divorce, *Report*, 1951–55, London, HMSO, 1956, Cmd 9678.

12 Transcript of Mrs M. Cheshire, Oral History of Girlhood Project, University of Lancaster, 1986.

13 S.M. Ferguson and H. Fitzgerald, *Studies in the Social Services*, London, HMSO, 1954, p. 18.

14 Ibid., p. 99.

15 M-OA, File Report 2495, June 1947.

16 R.M. Titmuss, *Parents' Revolt: a study of the declining birth-rate in acquisitive societies*, London, 1942.

17 D. Riley, *War in the Nursery. Theories of the Child and Mother*, London, Virago, 1983, pp. 167–8.

18 Central Statistical Office, *Statistical Digest of the War*, London, HMSO, 1951, Table 4.

19 Ibid., Table 8 and Ferguson, op. cit., pp. 90–4.

20 P. Long, 'Speaking Out on Age', *Spare Rib*, No. 82, May 1979, pp. 14–15.

21 Ibid., p. 15.

22 M-OA, File Report 2205, January 1945.

23 Mary Lee Settle, *All the Brave Promises*, London, Pandora, 1984, p. 108; M-OA, TC 32, Women in Wartime, Box 3, File F, Letters from Women Welders, 1942.

24 Royal Commission on Population, *Report*, London, HMSO, 1949, Cmd 7695, p. 33.

CHAPTER 13 HEALTH AND WELFARE

1   Wartime Social Survey, *Women at Work*, by Geoffrey Thomas, June 1944 (hereafter WSS, Women at Work), p. 22.

2   D. White, *D for Doris, V for Victory*, Milton Keynes, Oakleaf Books, 1981, p. 51.

3   PRO Lab 26/61, Reports from Inspectors of Factories, 18 September 1942.

4   P. Inman, *Labour in the Munitions Industries*, London, HMSO, 1957, p. 184.

5   Ruth Windle, 'War and Social Change', unpublished paper, Durham University Extra Mural Department, 1975, p. 32.

6   Mass Observation (M-O), *People in Production*, London, John Murray, 1942, pp. 167, 241, 244–7.

7   M-O, *War Factory*, London, Gollancz, 1943, pp. 42–3.

8   Ibid., p. 86.

9   P. Summerfield, *Women Workers in the Second World War*, London, Croom Helm, 1984, p. 132; Sir Arthur MacNalty (ed.), *The Civilian Health and Medical Services, Medical History of the Second World War*, London, HMSO, 1953, pp. 391–2.

10 Mass-Observation Archive, TC 32, Women in Wartime, Box 3, File F, Letters from Women Welders, 1942.

11 Summerfield, op. cit., pp. 143–5.

12 PRO Lab 26/131, 10 November 1943.

13 Wartime Social Survey, *Food*, April-July 1942 and June 1943, pp. 34, 14, 11; Select Committee on National Expenditure, Third Report 1942–3, Health and Welfare of Women in War Factories, 1942.

14 Mary Lee Settle, *All the Brave Promises*, London, Pandora, 1984, p. 39.

15 J.M. Hooks, *British Policies and Methods of Employing Women in Wartime*, Washington, US Government, 1944, p. 6; Inman, op. cit., p. 233.

16 P. Schweitzer, L. Hilton, J. Moss (eds), *What Did You Do in the War, Mum?*, London, Age Exchange, 1985, p. 16.

17 Thames Television/Channel 4, 'A People's War' Interview Transcript (hereafter Thames TV Transcript), Mona Marshall, p. 6.

18 Kay Jenner, Letter to Penny Summerfield, October 1977.

19 Schweitzer et al., op. cit., p. 29.

20 MacNalty, op. cit., p. 377.

21 Schweitzer et al., op. cit., p. 71.

22 MacNalty, op. cit., pp. 381, 385–6.

23 Settle, op. cit., p. 23.

24 Hooks, op. cit., pp. 13–14.

25 Ministry of Labour and National Service, *Report for the Years 1939–1946*, London, HMSO, 1947, Cmd 7225, p. 99.

26 Schweitzer et al., op. cit., p. 21.

27 M-OA, TC 32, Women in Wartime, Box 3, File F, Letters from Women Welders 1942.

28 Summerfield, op. cit., pp. 125 and 128.

29 M-O, *War Factory*, p. 78.

30 Select Committee on National Expenditure, 'Royal Ordnance Factories', Eleventh Report 1941–2, 1942.

31 M-O, *People in Production*, pp. 164–65; Sadie MacDougal, Interview with Penny Summerfield, July 1977; Schweitzer, p. 61, pp. 66–7; Thames TV Transcript, Agnes McLean.

32 M-O, *People in Production*, p. 232.
33 Schweitzer, op. cit., p. 61.
34 M-O, *People in Production*, pp. 129–30.
35 Peggy Scott, *They Made Invasion Possible*, London, Hutchinson, 1944, p. 108.
36 Schweitzer, op. cit., p. 30.
37 Summerfield, op. cit., p. 182.

CHAPTER 14 DOUBLE BURDEN

1   Mass-Observation Archive (M-OA), File Report 1631, March 1943.
2   Thames Television/Channel 4 'A People's War' Interview Transcript (hereafter Thames TV Transcript), Clara Moore.
3   S.M. Ferguson and H. Fitzgerald, *Studies in the Social Services*, London, HMSO, 1954, p. 190.
4   Penny Summerfield, *Women Workers in the Second World War*, London, Croom Helm, 1984, p. 77 and Chapter 4 generally.
5   PRO Lab 26/57, February 1941.
6   Ferguson, op. cit., pp. 190–1; Wartime Social Survey, *Women at Work*, by Geoffrey Thomas, 1944, p. 5; Summerfield, op.cit., p. 84.
7   PRO Lab 26/58, ML Circular 128/74 9 December 1941, covering MH 2535, 5 December 1941.
8   Thames TV Transcript, Miriam Power.
9   Zelma Katin, *Clippie*, London, John Gifford, p. 48.
10 Summerfield, op. cit., p. 108 and Chapter 5 generally.
11 PRO Lab 26/61, ML Circular 128/70, 'Workers' Welfare: Shopping Problems', 19 November 1941.
12 Mass-Observation (M-OA), *People in Production*, John Murray, London, 1942, p. 228.
13 Celia Bannister, *A Wartime Childhood*, Fleetwood, Celia Bannister, 1984, pp. 20–1.
14 Ibid., p. 22.
15 M-OA, TC v/6/3/, Industry 1941–7, Box 140, Tube Investments.
16 Summerfield, op. cit., p. 116.
17 M-OA, File Report 2315, December 1945.
18 M-OA, Diary No. 5390, Foreign Correspondent, Shipping Firm, Glasgow, 25 January 1942.
19 Summerfield, op. cit., pp. 104–5; A. Calder, *The People's War*, London, Panther, 1971, pp. 439–40.
20 M-OA, Diary No. 5353, Housewife, Barrow-in-Furness, 22 November 1941.

21 Frances Partridge, *A Pacifist's War*, London, Robin Clark, 1983, pp. 146 and 179–80.
22 Thames TV Transcript, Miriam Power.
23 Ibid.
24 Katin, op. cit., p. 71.
25 Ibid., pp. 17–18.
26 Mrs Shipley, Interview with Penny Summerfield, November 1977.
27 R. Broad and S. Fleming (eds) *Nella Last's War, A Mother's Diary 1939–45*, Bristol, Falling Wall Press, 1981, p. 222.
28 Bannister, op. cit., p. 13.
29 Sadie MacDougal, Interview with Penny Summerfield, July 1977.
30 Ruth Windle, 'War and Social Change', Unpublished Paper, Durham University Extra Mural Department, 1975, p. 20.

CHAPTER 15 DEMOBILISATION 1945–50

1   Celia Bannister, *A Wartime Childhood*, Fleetwood, Celia Bannister, 1984, p. 104.
2   Frances Partridge, *A Pacifist's War*, London, Robin Clark, 1983, p. 213.
3   Mass-Observation (M-O), *People in Production*, London, John Murray, 1942, p. 125.
4   P. Inman, *Labour in the Munitions Industries*, London, HMSO, 1957, p. 200.
5   Ibid., p. 201.
6   Thames Television/Channel 4, 'A People's War' Interview Transcript (Thames TV Transcript), Barbara Davies.
7   P. Schweitzer, L. Hilton, J. Moss (eds), *What Did You Do in the War, Mum?*, London, Age Exchange, 1985, p. 31.
8   Ibid., p. 27.
9   Ministry of Labour and National Service (MOLNS), *Report for the Years 1939–1945*, London, HMSO, 1947, Cmd 7225; Royal Commission on Equal Pay, *Report 1945–46*, London, HMSO, 1946, Cmd 6937.
10 MOLNS, *Report*, p. 139 and Chapter XVIII.
11 D. White, *D for Doris and V for Victory*, Milton Keynes, Oakleaf, 1981, p. 81.
12 Ibid.; Penny Summerfield, *Women Workers in the Second World War*, London, Croom Helm, 1984, p. 160.
13 Summerfield, op. cit., Table B.7, p. 199; MOLNS, *Report*, Appx XVIII.
14 Schweitzer et al., op cit., p. 7.

15 S. Patterson, *Dark Strangers*, Harmondsworth, Penguin, 1965, p. 62.
16 Marjorie Wardle, Interview with Mark Easterby-Smith, April 1986.
17 Mass-Observation Archive (M-OA), TC 32, Women in Wartime, Box 3, File E, 29 September 1941.
18 Marjorie Wardle, Interview.
19 Aline Whalley, Interview with Penny Summerfield, March 1986.
20 Marjorie Wardle, Interview; M-OA, File Report 1620, March 1943.
21 Central Statistical Office, *Statistical Digest of the War*, London, HMSO, 1951, Table 8; S.M. Ferguson and H. Fitzgerald, *Studies in the Social Services*, London, HMSO, 1954, p. 18; A. Calder, *The People's War, Britain 1939–45*, London, Panther, 1971, p. 360.
22 Ruth Windle, 'War and Social Change', Unpublished Paper, University of Durham Extra Mural Department, 1975, pp. 27–8.
23 Thames TV Transcript, Miriam Power.
24 P. and L. Bendit, *Living Together Again*, Gramol, 1946, quoted by Raynes Minns, *Bombers and Mash*, London, Virago, 1979, pp. 194–5.
25 Schweitzer et al., op. cit., p. 52.
26 Kenneth Howards, *Sex Problems of the Returning Soldier*, Manchester, Sydney Pemberton, n.d. [1945], pp. 62–3.
27 Thames TV Transcript, Clara Moore.
28 Zelma Katin, *Clippie*, London, John Gifford, 1944, pp. 49 and 123.
29 Royal Commission on Marriage and Divorce, *Report*, 1951–55, London, HMSO, 1956, Cmd 9678; Ferguson, op. cit., p. 20.
30 Thames TV Transcript, Kitty Murphy.
31 A. Marwick, *British Society Since 1945*, Harmondsworth, Penguin, 1982, pp. 74–5.
32 Aline Whalley, Interview with Penny Summerfield, March 1986.
33 P. Addison, *The Road to 1945*, London, Jonathan Cape, 1975, p. 267.
34 J.R. Short, *Housing in Britain, The Post-War Experience*, London, Methuen, 1982, p. 42.
35 Ferguson, op. cit., p. 19.
36 Mary Sweeney, BBC Radio 4 Broadcast, 2 April 1986.
37 P. Addison, *Now the War is Over*, BBC/Cape, 1985, ch. 3.
38 Thames TV Transcript, Kitty Murphy.
39 Summerfield, op. cit., pp. 174–7.
40 Royal Commission on Equal Pay, *Report*, Memorandum of Dissent.

41 Trade Union Congress, Pamphlets and Leaflets, 1942/7, Appx 1, and 1943/16, Appx. 1.
42 G. Williams, *Women and Work*, London, Nicholson & Watson, 1945, p. 126. See Denise Riley, *War in the Nursery*, London, Virago, 1983, for a fascinating discussion of post-war 'pronatalism'.
43 P. Long, 'Speaking Out on Age', *Spare Rib*, No. 82, May 1979.

CHAPTER 16 CONCLUSION

1   Elsie Farlow, 00773/03, Imperial War Museum.
2   Thames Television/Channel 4, 'A People's War' Interview Transcripts: Mona Marshall, Joan Shakesheff.
3   A.W. Kirkaldy, *Industry and Finance*, vol. 1, London, Isaac Pitman, 1917.
4   Mass-Observation, *The Journey Home*, John Murray, 1944, p. 58.
5   R. Broad and S. Fleming, *Nella Last's War*, Bristol, Falling Wall Press, 1981, p. 229.
6   M-O, *Journey Home*, p. 55; see also Penny Summerfield, *Women Workers in the Second World War*, London, Croom Helm, 1984, pp. 189–90 for other examples.
7   E. Roberts, 'Working-class women in the North-West', *Oral History* v, Autumn 1977, pp. 9–10.
8   Z. Katin, *Clippie*, London, John Gifford, 1944, p. 124.
9   E.g. Viola Klein, *Britain's Married Women Workers*, London, Routledge & Kegan Paul, 1965.
10 J. and E. Newsome, *Patterns of Infant Care in an Urban Community*, London, Allen & Unwin, 1963.
11 Mass-Observation Archive, File Report 1970, January 1944.

BIBLIOGRAPHY

PART 1 THE FIRST WORLD WAR

(i) PRINTED BOOKS

Andrews, I.O., *The Economic Effects of the World War Upon Women and Children in Great Britain*, 2nd edn, New York, Oxford University Press, 1921.

Black, C. (ed.), *Married Women's Work*, London, Bell & Sons, 1915.

Boston, S., *Women Workers and the Trade Union Movement*, London, Davis Poynter, 1980.

Braybon, G., *Women Workers in the First World War*, London, Croom Helm, 1981.

British Association, *Draft Interim Report of the Conference to Investigate into Outlets for Labour After the War*, London, British Association, 1915.

Brittain, V., *Testament of Youth*, reprinted London, Virago, 1978.

Burke, K. (ed.), *War and the State*, London, Allen & Unwin, 1982.

Burnett, J., *Useful Toil*, London, Allen Lane, 1974.

Burnett, J., *A Social History of Housing*, London, David & Charles, 1978.

Butler, C.V., *Domestic Service*, London, Bell & Sons, 1916.

Cadbury, E., Matheson, M.C., and Shann, G., *Women's Work and Wages*, London, T. Fisher Unwin, 2nd edn, 1909.

Chapman, S.J., *Labour and Capital After the War*, London, Murray, 1918.

Cole, G.D.H., *Labour in Wartime*, London, Bell & Sons, 1915.

Collier, D.J. and Hutchins, B.L., *The Girl in Industry*, London, Bell & Sons, 1918.

Cosens, M., *Lloyd George's Munition Girls*, London, Hutchinson, 1916.

Davies, M.L. (ed.), *Life As We Have Known It*, reprinted London, Virago, 1977.

Davies, M.L. (ed.), *Maternity: Letters from Working Women*, reprinted, London, Virago, 1978.

Drake, B., *Women in the Engineering Trades*, London, Fabian Research Department, 1917.

Drake, B., *Women in Trade Unions*, reprinted London, Virago, 1984.

Dyhouse, C., *Girls Growing Up in Late Victorian and Edwardian England*, London, Routledge & Kegan Paul, 1981

Ferguson, S. and Fitzgerald, H., *Studies in the Social Services*, London, HMSO, 1954.

Foxwell, A.K., *Munition Lasses*, London, Hodder & Stoughton, 1917.

Halsey, A.H., *Trends in British Society since 1900*, London, Macmillan, 1972.

Hamilton, M.A., *Mary Macarthur*, London, Parsons, 1925.

Hamilton, P., *Three Years or the Duration*, London, Peter Owen, 1978.

Hinton, J., *Labour and Socialism*, Brighton, Wheatsheaf, 1983.

John, A., *By the Sweat of Their Brow*, London, Croom Helm, 1980.

John, A., *Unequal Opportunities*, Oxford, Basil Blackwell, 1986.

Kirkaldy, A.W., *Industry & Finance*, Vol. I, London, Isaac Pitman, 1917, Vol. II, 1920.

Lamb, T.A., *TNT Tales*, Oxford, Blackwell, 1918.

Lewis, J., *Women in England 1870–1950*, Brighton, Wheatsheaf, 1984.

Liddington, J. and Norris, J., *One Hand Tied Behind Us*, London, Virago, 1978.

MacNalty, Sir A. (ed.), *The Civilian Health and Medical Services*, London, HMSO, 1953.

Marwick, A., *Women at War 1914–1918*, London, Fontana, 1977.

Medlicott, W.N., *Contemporary England 1914–64*, London, Longman, 1967.

Pankhurst, E.S., *The Home Front*, London, Hutchinson, 1932.

Peel, Mrs C.S., *How We Lived Then*, London, John Lane, 1929.

Pigou, A.C., *Aspects of British Economic History*, London, Cass, 1947.

Pike, E.R., *Human Documents of the Lloyd George Era*, London, Allen & Unwin, 1972.

Playne, C., *Society at War 1914–16*, London, Allen & Unwin, 1930.

Playne, C., *Britain Holds On, 1917, 18*, London, Allen & Unwin, 1933.

Pribicevik, B., *The Shop Stewards' Movement and Workers' Control*, Oxford, Blackwell, 1959.

Proud, D., *Welfare Work*, London, Bell & Sons, 1916.

Reeves, M.P., *Round About a Pound a Week*, reprinted by London, Virago, 1979.

Roberts, E., *A Woman's Place – An Oral History of Working-Class Women, 1890–1914*, Oxford, Blackwell, 1984.

Rubinstein, D., *Victorian Homes*, London, David & Charles, 1974.

Shewell-Cooper, W.E., *Landgirl*, London, English University Press, 1941.

Stevenson, J., *British Society 1914–45*, London, Allen Lane, 1984.

Stone, G., *Women War Workers*, London, Harrap, 1917.

Strachey, R., *The Cause*, London, Bell & Sons, 1928.

Swenarton, M., *Homes Fit for Heroes*, London, Heinemann, 1981.

Terraine, J., *Impacts of War 1914 & 1918*, London, Hutchinson, 1970.

White, J., *Rothschild Buildings*, London, Routledge & Kegan Paul, 1980.

Worsfold, B., *War and Social Reform*, London, Murray, 1916.

Yates, L.K., *The Woman's Part*, London, Hodder & Stoughton, 1918.

(ii) UNPUBLISHED SOURCES

Collections

The Imperial War Museum: the Women's Collection.

The Imperial War Museum: material from the Department of Documents.

The Imperial War Museum: tapes on Women War Workers held by the Department of Sound Records.

The Imperial War Museum: tapes on the Anti-War Movement held by the Department of Sound Records.

Southampton City Museum, Education Service, the oral history project on Women's Work in the First World War.

London School of Economics, Beveridge Collection.

Papers

Englander, D., 'Demobilisation in England after the First World War', unpublished paper.

Ineson, A., 'Science, Technology, Medicine, Welfare and the Labour Process: Women Munition Workers in the First World War', M.Phil thesis, University of Sussex 1981.

Kosack, M., 'Women Munition Workers During the First World War, with special reference to Engineering', Ph.D thesis, University of Hull, 1976.

Thom, D., 'Women Munition Workers at Woolwich Arsenal in the 1914–18 War', MA thesis, University of Warwick.

Thom, D., 'The Ideology of Women's Work, 1914–1920, Ph D thesis, Thames Polytechnic, 1982.

(iii) GOVERNMENT PAPERS

Chief Inspector of Factories, Reports.

Ministry of Munitions, Reports and Memoranda of the Health of Munition Workers Committee. Final Report, 1918, Cd 9065.

Ministry of Reconstruction, *Report of the Women's Employment Committee*, 1919, Cd 9239.

Ministry of Reconstruction, *Report of the Civil War Workers Committee on Substitute Labour*, 1918, Cd 9228.

Ministry of Reconstruction, Reports from the War Cabinet Comittee on *Women in Industry*, 1919, Cmd 135 and Cmd 167.

Royal Commission on Labour, Reports on the Employment of Women.

Royal Commission on Marriage and Divorce, 1956 Cmd 9678.

PART 2 THE SECOND WORLD WAR

(i) PRINTED BOOKS

Addison, P., *The Road to 1945. British Politics and the Second World War*, London, Cape, 1975.

Addison, P., *Now the War is Over. A Social History of Britain 1945–51*, London, BBC/Cape, 1985.

Allen, M., 'The Domestic Ideal and the Mobilisation of Woman Power in World War II', *Women's Studies International Forum*, vol. 6, no. 4, pp. 401–12.

Ayers, P., and Lambertz, J., 'Marriage Relations, Money and Domestic Violence in Working Class Liverpool 1919–39' in Lewis, J. (ed.), *Labour and Love, Women's Experience of Home and Family 1850–1940*, Oxford, Blackwell, 1986.

Bannister, C., *A Wartime Childhood*, Fleetwood, Celia Bannister, 1984.

Benney, M., *Over to Bombers, An account of work in an aircraft factory*, London, Allen & Unwin, 1943.

Benson, T., *Sweethearts and Wives. Their Part in the War*, London, Faber, 1942.

Brittain, V., *Women's Work in Modern England*, London, Noel Douglas, 1928.

Brittain, V., *England's Hour*, London, Futura, 1981.

Broad, R., and Fleming, S. (eds), *Nella Last's War, a mother's diary 1939–45*, Bristol, Falling Wall Press, 1981.

Brookes, P., *Women at Westminster*, London, Peter Davies, 1967.

Burnett, J., *A Social History of Housing 1815–1970*, London, Methuen, 1978.

Burton, E., *What of the Women? A Study of Women in Wartime*, London, Frederick Muller, 1941.

Calder, A., *The People's War, Britain 1939–45*, London, Panther, 1971.

Calder, A., and Sheridan, D., *Speak for Yourself. A Mass-Observation Anthology 1937–49*, London, Cape, 1984.

Central Statistical Office, *Statistical Digest of the War*, London, HMSO, 1951.

Chorley, K., *Manchester Made Them*, London, Faber, 1950.

Douie, V., *The Lesser Half: A Survey of the Laws, Regulations and Practices Introduced during the present war which embody discrimination against women*, London, Women's Publicity Planning Association, 1943.

The Engineer, 1939–1945.

Ferguson, N.A., 'Women's Work: Employment Opportunities and Economic Roles, 1918–1939', *Albion*, 1963.

Ferguson, S.M., and Fitzgerald, H., *Studies in the Social Services*, London, HMSO, 1954.

Forrester, H., *Liverpool Miss*, Glasgow, Fontana, 1982.

Gittins, D., *Fair Sex. Family Size and Structure 1900–1939*, London, Hutchinson, 1982.

Haldane, C., *Motherhood and Its Enemies*, New York, Doubleday, 1928.

Hall, E., *Canary Girls and Stockpots*, Luton, WEA, 1977.

Hall, R., *Marie Stopes*, London, Virago, 1978.

Hamilton, C., *The Englishwoman*, London, Longmans Green, 1940.

Harding, K., and Gibbs, C., *Tough Annie: from Suffragette to Stepney Councillor*, London, Stepney Books, 1980.

Harrisson, T., *Living Through the Blitz*, London, Collins, 1976.

Holden, B.I.L., *Night Shift*, London, Bodley Head, 1941.

Holtby, W., *Women and a Changing Civilisation*, London, Lane, 1934.

Hooks, J.M., *British Policies and Methods of Employing Women in Wartime*, U.S. Government, Washington, 1944.

Howard, K., *Sex Problems of the Returning Soldier*, Manchester, Sydney Pemberton, n.d. [1945].

Hughes, G., *Millstone Grit*, London, Gollancz, 1975.

Inman, P., *Labour in the Munitions Industries*, London, HMSO, 1957.

Joseph, S., *If Their Mothers Only Knew, an unofficial account of life in the Women's Land Army*, London, Faber, 1946.

Katin, Z., *Clippie. The autobiography of a war-time conductress*, London, John Gifford, 1944.

Klein, V., *Britain's Married Women Workers*, London, Routledge & Kegan Paul, London, 1965.

Leitch, M. (ed.), *Great Songs of World War II*, London, Wise, 1975.

Liddington, J., *The Life and Times of a Respectable Rebel: Selina Cooper 1864–1942*, London, Virago, 1985.

Little, A., and Westergaard, J., 'The Trend of Class Differentials in Educational Opportunity in England and Wales', *British Journal of Sociology*, vol. 15, no. 4, 1964.

Long, P., 'Speaking Out on Age', *Spare Rib*, no. 82, May 1979.

Longmate, N., *How We Lived Then: a history of everyday life during the Second World War*, London, Arrow, 1973.

MacNalty, Sir A. (ed.), *The Civilian Health and Medical Services, Medical History of the Second World War*, London, HMSO, 1953.

Madge, C., *War-time Patterns of Saving and Spending*, Cambridge, Cambridge University Press, 1943.

Marwick, A., *British Society Since 1945*, Harmondsworth, Penguin, 1982.

Mass-Observation, *People in Production, An Enquiry into British War Production*, London, John Murray, 1942.

Mass-Observation, *The Journey Home*, London, John Murray, 1944.

Mass-Observation, *War Factory*, London, Gollancz, 1943.

Mellor, Franklin W. (ed.), *History of the Second World War, UK Medical Series, Casualties and Medical Statistics*, London, HMSO, 1972.

Minns, R., *Bombers and Mash. The Domestic Front 1939–45*, London, Virago, 1979.

Mitchell, G. (ed.), *The Hard Way Up: the autobiography of Hannah Mitchell, Suffragette and Rebel*, London, Virago, 1977.

Murphy, J.T., *Victory Production!*, London, John Lane, 1942.

Newsome, J. and E., *Patterns of Infant Care in an Urban Community*, London, Allen & Unwin, 1963.

Parker, H.M.D., *Manpower: a study of wartime policy and administration*, London, HMSO, 1957.

Partridge, F., *A Pacifist's War*, London, Robin Clark, 1983.

Patterson, S., *Dark Strangers*, Harmondsworth, Penguin, 1965.

Pelling, H., *Britain in the Second World War*, London, Collins, 1970.

Pilgrim Trust, *Men Without Work*, Cambridge, Cambridge University Press, 1938.

Riley, D., *War in the Nursery, Theories of the Child and Mother*, London, Virago, 1983.

Roberts, E., 'Working Class Women in the North West', *Oral History*, vol. 5, Autumn 1977, pp. 7–30.

Roberts, E., *A Woman's Place*, Oxford, Blackwell, 1984.

Russell, D., *The Tamarisk Tree*, vol. 2, London, Virago, 1981.

Sackville-West, V., *The Women's Land Army*, London, Michael Joseph, 1944.

Scott, P., *British Women in War*, London, Hutchinson, 1940.

Schweitzer, P., Hilton, L., Moss, J. (eds), *What Did You Do in the War, Mum?*, London, Age Exchange, 1985.

Settle, M.L., *All the Brave Promises. Memories of Aircraft Woman 2nd Class 2146391*, London, Pandora, 1984.

Short, J.R., *Housing in Britain, the Post-War Experience*, London, Methuen, 1982.

Smith, H., 'The Problems of "Equal Pay for Equal Work" in Great Britain during World War II', *Journal of Modern History*, vol. 53, no. 4, December 1981.

Spring Rice, M., *Working Class Wives*, London, Penguin, 1939.

Summerfield, P., *Women Workers in the Second World War. Production and Patriarchy in Conflict*, London, Croom Helm, 1984.

Taylor, P., 'Daughters and mothers – maids and mistresses: domestic service between the wars', in Clarke, J., Critcher, C., and Johnson, R. (eds), *Working Class Culture, Studies in History and Theory*, London, Hutchinson, 1979.

Titmuss, R.M., *Parents' Revolt, A study of the declining birth-rate in acquisitive societies*, London, 1942.

Vernon, B.D., *Ellen Wilkinson 1891–1947*, London, Croom Helm, 1982.

White, D., *D for Doris, V for Victory*, Milton Keynes, Oakleaf Books, 1981.

Williams, G., *Women and Work*, London, Nicholson & Watson, 1945.

Williams-Ellis, A., *Women in War Factories*, London, Gollancz, 1943.

(ii) UNPUBLISHED SOURCES: PAPERS AND COLLECTIONS

Papers

Briar, C., 'Policies towards Women's Employment in the Second World War', unpublished paper, Lancaster, 1985.

Lewenhak, S., 'Trade Union Membership among Women and girls in the United Kingdom, 1920–65', unpublished Ph.D. thesis, University of London, 1971.

Windle, R., 'War and Social Change', unpublished paper compiled from material collected by the Durham University Extra Mural Department Class on Social Change in the North-East, 1975.

Interviews and correspondence

Personal collection (Penny Summerfield)
Kay Jenner, October 1977.
Sadie MacDougal, July 1977.
Mrs Shipley, November 1977.
Marjorie Wardle (interview with Mark Easterby-Smith), April 1986.
Aline Whalley, March 1986.

BBC Radio
Mary Sweeney, Radio 4, 2 April 1986.

Thames Television/Channel 4 'A People's War' Interview
Transcripts:
Barbara Davies; Hetty Fowler; Agnes McLean; Mona Marshall; Vi Maxwell; Clara Moore; Kitty Murphy; Miriam Power; Therese Roberts; Mickie Hutton Storie.

Mass-Observation Archive

File Report (F.R.) 15b, December 1939, Working Women in this War.
F.R. 757, June 1941, General Picture of WAAF Life.
F.R. 952, November 1941, ATS Campaign.
F.R. 1620, March 1943, 'After the War' Feelings in the WAAF.
F.R. 1631, March 1943, Absenteeism and Industrial Morale.

F.R. 1970, January 1944, Women in Pubs.

F.R. 2205, January 1945, Sex, Morality and the Birthrate.

F.R. 2315, January 1946, Survey of Laundry Usage 1945.

F.R. 2495, June 1947, The State of Matrimony.

Topic Collection (T.C.) Industry, 1941–7, Box 120.

T.C. v/6/3, Industry, 1941–7, Box 140.

T.C. 19, Day Nurseries 1941–2, Box 276.

T.C. 32, Women in Wartime, Box 1, File A; Box 3, File E; Box 3, File F.

T.C. 66/4/C-H, Town and District Survey.

Public Record Office (PRO)

Cab 65/20, War Cabinet Conclusions, 1941.

Cab 67/9, War Cabinet memoranda, 1941

Lab 26/57, Provision for the Care of Married Women in Industry; Wartime Nurseries, general policy, 1940.

Lab 26/58, Provision for the Care of Children of Married Women in Industry; Wartime Nurseries, general policy, 1940–42.

Lab 26/61, Shopping Difficulties, 1941–43.

Lab 26/63, Women's Services, (Welfare and Amenities), Committee, Recruiting of Womanpower.

Lab 26/130, Meetings of the Women's Consultative Committee, 1941.

Lab 26/131, Industrial efficiency and absenteeism, Enquiry into absence from work, 1942–3.

(iii) GOVERNMENT PAPERS

Board of Education, *Report of the Consultative Committee on Secondary Education with special reference to grammar schools and technical high schools*, London, HMSO, 1938.

Census of England and Wales, *Occupational tables*, 1911, 1921, 1931.

Central Office of Information, *Wartime Social Survey*:

An investigation of the attitudes of women, the general public and ATS personnel to the Auxiliary Territorial Service, October, 1941.

Food. An inquiry into a typical day's meals and attitudes to wartime food in selected groups of the English working population, April-July 1942.

Food. An inquiry into (i) a day's meals and (ii) attitudes to wartime food in selected groups of British workers, Jne 1943.

Women at Work, by Geoffrey Thomas. The attitudes of working women towards post-war employment and some related problems, June 1944.

Parliamentary Papers

Cmd 3508, A study of the factors which have operated in the past and those which are operating now to determine the distribution of women in industry, December 1929.

Cmd 5556, Twenty-second annual abstract of labour statistics of the UK for 1922 to 1936.

Cmd 6937, Royal Commission on Equal Pay, *Report*, 1946, and *Minutes of Evidence*, 1945–6.

Cmd 7225, Ministry of Labour and National Service, 'Report for the Years 1939–45', 1947.

Cmd 7695, Royal Commission on Population, *Report*, 1949.

Cmd 9678, Royal Commission on Marriage and Divorce, *Report*, 1956.

Select Committee on National Expenditure

Eleventh Report 1941–2, Royal Ordnance Factories, July 1942.

Third Report 1942–3, Health and Welfare of Women in War Factories, December 1942.

INDEX

Note: Abbreviations 'WW I' and 'WW II' are used for the
First and Second World Wars, respectively. Page
references in *italics* are to illustrations.

All the Brave Promises

Memories of Aircraftwoman 2nd Class 2146391

Mary Lee Settle was a young American woman living a comfortable life in Washington D.C. when the Second World War broke out. In 1942 she boarded a train, carrying 'a last bottle of champagne and an armful of roses,' and left for England to join the WAAF. She witnessed the horror of war – the bombing raids, the planes lost in fog, the children evacuated, a blacked-out Britain of austerity and strain. She also witnessed the women, her fellow recruits, as they struggled to adapt to their new identities and new lives at the bottom of the uniformed pile.

Dedicated 'to the wartime other ranks of the Women's Auxiliary Air Force – below the rank of Sergeant,' this rare book captures women's wartime experience; a remarkable and important story by one of America's prizewinning novelists.

'One of the most moving accounts of war experience ever encountered'   *Library Journal*

£3.95
0 86358 033 5

Most Dangerous Women

Feminist Peace Campaigners of the Great War

Anne Wiltsher

'All Tilbury is laughing at the Peacettes, the misguided English-women who, baggage in hand, are waiting at Tilbury for a boat to take them to Holland, where they are anxious to talk peace with German fraus over the teapot'.
Daily Express, 1915

'When I hear that women are unfit to be diplomats, I wonder by what standards of duplicity and frivolity they could possibly prove themselves inferior to the men who represented the victors at Versailles'.   *Helena Swanwick*

It is perhaps surprising to learn that the women of Greenham are not the first women to have dedicated their lives to peace. Half the leading women of the British suffrage movement opposed the First World War. Working through the international women's suffrage movement, they linked up with other feminists in Europe and America and tried to push the men in power towards a negotiated peace. In April 1915, 2,000 women met in Holland, conceived an original plan to end the war and sent envoys to lobby governments accordingly. The rest of the delegates went home and by the end of that year there were active women's peace groups in eleven European countries as well as America.

Anne Wiltsher describes the extraordinary exploits of these women in *Most Dangerous Women*, which unravels their fascinating story. She describes their determination to cross international borders despite wartime travel restrictions, their encounters with leading statesmen, their vilification by the Press and the general public, their philosophies and friendships.

£5.95 net
0 86358 010 6

The Spinster and Her Enemies

Feminism and Sexuality 1890 to 1930

Sheila Jeffreys

The Spinster and Her Enemies is an important book on a watershed period in the history of sexuality which challenges the reputations of established sexologists and sex reformers.

It is generally accepted by traditional historical interpreters, that the sexual puritanism of Victorian England gave way to the first 'sexual revolution' of the Twentieth Century. Sheila Jeffreys presents a different thesis which she supports with a wealth of evidence.

She examines the activities of feminist campaigners around such issues as child abuse and prostitution and assesses how these campaigns shaped social purity in the 1880s and 1890s. She demonstrates how the work of sexologists such as Carpenter and Havelock Ellis undermined and attacked the thriving, militant feminism of the late Nineteenth and early Twentieth centuries and asserts that the decline of this feminism was due largely to the promotion of a sexual ideology which was hostile to women's independence.

£5.95
0 86358 050 5

Women's Silence, Men's Violence

Sexual Assault in England 1770–1845

Anna Clark

Women's Silence, Men's violence tells the stories of women whose voices have long been suppressed: the victims of sexual violence in late eighteenth-century and early nineteenth-century England.

Women's experience of sexual violence in the past sometimes strikingly resembled that of today. From the Yorkshire farm labourer who fought off her attacker for three hours, to the London servant 'forcibly seduced' by her sweetheart, women faced the danger of rape at home and work, from strangers and friends.

This book is unique in providing the vivid testimony of the victims themselves. It contrasts the words and experiences of these women with the patriarchal practices and prejudices of the law courts, doctors and charity officials, which masked the reality of male violence.

'A moving account of the history of sexual assaults against women, that resurrects women's anger and sense of sexual vulnerability, and examines the cultural resources at their disposal to articulate their feelings. *Women's Silence, Men's Violence* demonstrates the crucial link between freedom from sexual violence and freedom to speak out on sexuality.'

Judith Walkowitz

£5.95
0 86358 103 X

Working Your Way to the Bottom

The Feminization of Poverty

Hilda Scott

The 'new poor' of today are invisible.
They are also women.

It is a special kind of poverty, the causes of which are not fully understood by most men working in official and unofficial poverty research. Hilda Scott argues that they are blinded by assumptions about 'women's place' to the work that women actually do and the incomes they actually receive. For example, is a secretary considered working class if married to an assembly line worker but middle class if married to an accountant? And what happens if she is divorced from the accountant?

Hilda Scott produces startling evidence to prove that women the world over are rapidly becoming the 'new poor'. She argues that unless there is a radical re-think of economic policy women will keep on 'working their way to the bottom'.

£5.25
0 86358 011 4

Discovering Women's History

A Practical Manual

Deirdre Beddoe

Rainy Sunday afternoons, long winter evenings: why not set yourself a research project, either on your own or in a group or classroom? This is the message from Deirdre Beddoe, an historian who tears away the mystique of her own profession in this step-by-step guide to researching the lives of ordinary women in Britain from 1800 to 1945. *Discovering Women's History* tells you how to get started on the detective trail of history and how to stalk your quarry through attics and art galleries, museums and old newspapers, church archives and the Public Records Office – and how to publish your findings once you have completed your project.

'an invaluable and fascinating guide to the raw material for anyone approaching this unexplored territory'   *The Sunday Times*

'Thrilling and rewarding and jolly good fun'   *South Wales Argus*

£4.95
0 86358 008 4

The Dora Russell Reader

57 Years of Writing and Journalism 1925–1982

Dora Russell was one of the most remarkable women of this century. Her extraordinary life and work can now be appreciated in this, the first collection of her writings and journalism.

Dora Russell campaigned tirelessly for peace since the First World War until her death in 1986. In the 1950s she took the women's Caravan of Peace into Eastern Europe. In the 1980s she was as active as ever, as her passionate 1982 article on *The Challenge of Humanism in the Nuclear Age* demonstrates.

This book introduces a new generation to the powerful mix of intellect and compassion in the work of this courageous woman.

£4.50
0 86358 020 3

Olive Schreiner Reader

Writings on Women and South Africa

Edited by Carol Barash
With an afterword by Nadine Gordimer

This is the first collection to bring together Olive Schreiner's shorter writings on women and South Africa. It covers the full range of her political and imaginative works, and is arranged chronologically to trace her shifting alliances with both the feminist movement in England and the South African struggle for independence. Olive Schreiner's writing will not give us politically correct heroines; instead it raises central questions about the interdependence of our attitudes towards gender and race.

Cloth: 0 86358 180 3 £12.95
Paperback: 0 86358 118 8 £5.95

Letters for my Children: One Mother's Quest for Answers about the Nuclear Threat

Deirdre Rhys-Thomas

'Mummy, will there be a nuclear war?'

In order to answer her 12-year old son's question, Deirdre Rhys-Thomas began an extraordinary and courageous correspondence with world leaders and public figures. She wanted the facts – not only about the risk of a holocaust, but also about the dangers of radiation and the nuclear power industry. She wrote to politicians, performers and the Pope, to the Ministry of Defence, the Pentagon and the U.S. Embassy, and to British Nuclear Fuels, building societies and Buckingham Palace. She sought the opinions of such diverse people as Indira Gandhi, David Puttnam, Dr Spock, Senator John Glenn and Lynn Redgrave. Their replies are fascinating: sincere, saddening, and occasionally, grimly amusing.

This unique collection of letters, spanning four years from the first Greenham Common demonstrations to the Chernobyl nuclear accident in 1986, makes remarkable and moving reading. Deirdre Rhys-Thomas has no party political axe to grind: she is an ordinary mother, living in Wales with her husband and two sons, who is, like many of us, worried about what the future might hold, baffled by bureaucracy and weary of official statements. Letters For My Children is an enthralling and enlightening book which provides a social record of the times we live in and a picture of the future we might all have to face.

'This book is both heartbreaking and heartwarming. Heartbreaking because it is dreadful that a child should have to be as afraid as Deirdre Rhys-Thomas's son was. But heartwarming because she didn't just flinch and weep at his question – she set out to find and answer.'

Claire Rayner

Cloth: 0 86358 181 1 £9.95
Paperback: 0 86358 055 6 £3.95